The Nebraska Symposium on Motivation: 1956 is Volume IV of
the series in CURRENT THEORY AND RESEARCH IN MOTIVATION

nebraska symposium on motivation
1956

MARSHALL R. JONES, Editor

Frank A. Beach

Professor of Psychology
Yale University

Sigmund Koch

Professor of Psychology
Duke University

Melvin H. Marx

Professor of Psychology
University of Missouri

Daniel R. Miller
and
Guy E. Swanson

Professors of Psychology
University of Michigan

John P. Seward

Professor of Psychology
*University of California
at Los Angeles*

Richard L. Solomon
with
Elinor S. Brush

Professor of Psychology
Harvard University
McGill University

university of nebraska press
lincoln
1956

Publishers on the Plains

UNP

Copyright, 1956, University of Nebraska Press
Library of Congress Catalog Card Number 56-11655
Manufactured in the United States of America

TABLE OF CONTENTS

Introduction
by
Professor Marshall R. Jones

V

INTRODUCTION

The papers in this volume were presented originally at the fourth annual symposium on Current Theory and Research in Motivation sponsored by the Psychology Department of the University of Nebraska and financed through a training grant from the U. S. Public Health Service.

The serious reading of the papers in this volume, as well as those in the previous volumes in this series, will lead one to some inescapable conclusions about the status of the psychology of motivation. In the first place, it is abundantly apparent that motivation is a problem, and even a central problem, in practically every area of modern psychology. It also is a persistent problem with many facets and complexities which demands the attention of psychologists of every stripe, creed, or persuasion.

The scope and range of problems in the psychology of motivation seem to me remarkable. The papers in the present volume raise issues, and sometimes suggest solutions, for problems ranging all the way from specific details of research methodology to the attitudinal "climate" necessary to the nurturance of a systematic theory of motivation. Even though there is no narrowing of the range of problems raised and struggled with in the papers presented in this series, there is very little overlap or repetition. The papers in this volume obviously are related to the same general topic, and related to the previous papers in this series, yet duplication is almost nonexistent, and each paper raises new problems, reports new research, or presents a fresh point of view. Even a cursory glance at the Table of Contents will indicate the variety available in the scholarly efforts of these outstanding psychologists.

In behalf of the Department of Psychology, I should like to express appreciation to each of the participants for his cooperation in making the symposium a stimulating intellectual experience for our colleagues and ourselves. Our gratitude goes also to the U. S. Public Health Service for the grants which have made this series of symposia possible. For myself I should like to express my gratitude to each of the participants, not only for participating in the symposium, but also for the care and promptness with which they prepared their manuscripts and made them available. I also am most grateful to my colleagues in the Department of Psychology for their assistance in arranging the symposia, and to Miss Emily Schossberger, editor of the University of Nebraska Press, and her staff for their splendid cooperation in getting this volume published promptly.

Marshall R. Jones

Lincoln, Nebraska
July 11, 1956

CHARACTERISTICS OF MASCULINE "SEX DRIVE"

Frank A. Beach

Department of Psychology, Yale University

From the earliest days of scientific psychology, sex has been described as a powerful drive affecting many aspects of behavior. In the realms of abnormal, developmental, social, and clinical psychology a good deal of attention has been paid to the ways in which sexual motives directly or indirectly shape and guide various activities of the individual. Sexual factors have been accorded less emphasis in strictly experimental psychology, presumably because of the manifold difficulties involved in the quantitative analysis of sexuality.

Nonetheless, some experimental work in this area has been done, and a start has been made toward understanding some of the variables which control the arousal and expression of sexual impulses. The following discussion deals with the experimental findings and their interpretation.

The aim of the discussion is threefold: (1) to consider some conceptual problems involved in the definition and classification of sex as a drive, (2) to examine the most recent experimental findings relevant to sexual behavior in animals, and (3) to propose a working hypothesis which may account for certain aspects of the evidence.

Problems of Definition and Classification

Definitions

The term "sexual drive" is widely and loosely used by psychologists, and by specialists in many other disciplines as well. More often than not, it is employed without any accompanying definition. Most writers are satisfied to begin with the uncritical assumption of a mutual understanding between their readers and themselves. A brief scanning of the literature will show that such an assumption has little to share with Caesar's wife.

In Freudian psychology, the individual's sexual needs and tendencies are so inextricably embedded in the more broadly conceived libido that an unambiguous definition of "sexual drive" is difficult to formulate. Some modern psychologists use the term to describe almost any form of heterosexual attraction, whereas others restrict its reference to frankly erotic or even genital activities.

Many behavior theorists define sex as one of the "primary," "unlearned," or "innate" drives that energize human and animal conduct (14). It is often contrasted with the "secondary" or "learned" drives which are conceived of as products of the life experiences of the individual (26). The primacy or innateness of sexual motivation is open to serious dispute, especially with respect to human psychology, but this point is not essential to the argument I wish to develop. Leaving aside all questions of the "innateness" of sexual tendencies and their expression, let us consider the problems of drive classification.

Classification

The prevalent tendency to place sex in the same category with hunger, thirst, and other "primary" drives implies, it seems to me, that these drives share certain fundamental characteristics and probably obey the same basic laws. Let us examine the facts and see if these implications are born out.

Biological function. To describe a drive as "primary" suggests that it serves some widespread, elementary function, and this surely is true of hunger, thirst, and sex. But the functions are obviously different. Sensations of hunger and thirst are biological indicators that the organism needs food or liquid. Failure to heed these indications can result in death. These, then, should be classified with pain and all other drives which function to protect and preserve the individual.

Sexual activity is not, in the biological sense, essential to the well-being of the individual. Despite the fact that arguments to the contrary often provide a convenient rationalization during certain stages of life, no one ever died for the lack of sex. Sexual activity, of course, has an indispensable function, but it is indispensable to the species rather than to the individual. Other drives essential to the preservation of the species are involved in parental care of the young and, for some animals, in those seasonal migrations which occur with such astonishing regularity and exquisite precision.[1]

Inasmuch as drives essential to preservation of the individual serve a somewhat different function than that served by sexual drive, it is quite conceivable that the two categories of drives have different evolutionary histories and will be found to obey different kinds of laws.

Meaning of deprivation or state of need. We are accustomed to think of drives as being called into play when the organism is in a state of need, frequently as the result of some preceding deprivation. What does this mean as applied to the drives I have been discussing?

When an individual is deprived of food, the result is, in a sense, catabolic. The body's stores of energy-producing substances, such as sugars and fats, are gradually depleted to maintain normal metabolism. Even-

[1]Space does not permit expansion of the idea, but it seems likely that "individual drives" usually take precedence over "species drives" whenever the two come into conflict.

tually a serious state of need is reached, and if the body tissues do not receive nourishment derived from the breakdown of newly ingested foodstuff, their efficiency is impaired. Indefinite prolongation of the period of deprivation is fatal.

Water deprivation has comparable effects, but they are exerted over a much briefer time-span.

The individual deprived of sexual outlet does not perish, regardless of the length of time involved. No genuine tissue or biological needs are generated by sexual abstinence. It used to be believed that prolonged sexual inactivity in adulthood resulted in the progressive accumulation of secretions within the accessory sex glands, and that nerve impulses from these distended receptacles gave rise to sexual urges. Modern evidence negates this hypothesis. Work in my own laboratory has shown that male animals which have been surgically deprived of the glands in question continue to display unmistakable signs of sexual arousal and potency. Furthermore, homologous structures in the female are undeveloped, and yet, if we are to believe Professor Kinsey and other experts, sexual motivation is not exclusively a masculine prerogative.

What is commonly confused with a primary drive associated with sexual deprivation is in actuality sexual appetite, and this has little or no relation to biological or physiological needs. The individual who is surfeited with food may crave a sweet dessert. This is a product of his previous experience and does not involve a low-ered level of blood-sugar or a series of stomach contrac-tions. In fact, for most of us in middle age, yielding to the demands of a sweet tooth is an act contrary to physical well-being.

Sexual appetite is likewise a product of experience, actual or vicarious. The adolescent boy's periodic pre-occupation with sexual matters is traceable to psycho-logical stimuli, external or phantasied, and is not de-

pendent upon his recently matured reproductive glands.
His erotic urges stem more from socio-cultural factors
than from those of a strictly physiological nature.

To a much greater extent than is true of hunger or
thirst, the sexual tendencies depend for their arousal
upon external stimuli. The quasi-romantic concept of
the rutting stag actively seeking a mate is quite misleading. When he encounters a receptive female, the
male animal may or may not become sexually excited,
but it is most unlikely that in the absence of erotic
stimuli he exists in a constant state of undischarged
sexual tensions. This would be equally true for the
human male, were it not for the potent effects of symbolic stimuli which he tends to carry with him wherever
he goes.

Meaning of satiation and recovery. The food-de-
prived organism reverses its depleted condition and
achieves satiation by the ingestion of those substances
which relieve the state of tissue need. This is, crudely
speaking, an anabolic process which returns the individual to an optimal, physiological condition. In contrast, the sexually deprived male who engages in unlimited sexual activity experiences a depletion of energy which continues in catabolic fashion until the endpoint
of exhaustion is reached.

The sequel to food satiation is gradual reinstatement
of the condition of tissue need. The sequel to sexual
satiation--or better, "sexual exhaustion"--is gradual
return to a rested condition, or recovery from fatigue.

This "arm-chair analysis" of what appear to be
different types of drives may or may not be valid. We
cannot judge on the basis of present evidence because
sex has not been subjected to the careful and detailed
scrutiny to which hunger, thirst, and a few other drives
have been exposed. However, until the necessary studies
have been executed, it is advisable to refrain from pre-
mature categorization of drives.

In the sections which follow, an attempt will be made to summarize the more important methods of studying sexual motivation and the results that these techniques have yielded.

Methods of Studying Sexual Motivation

Descriptive Analyses of Sexual Behavior

The character and intensity of sexual motivation have often been inferred from descriptions of courtship and mating. This is, in essence, Kinsey's approach, for, at least by implication, he equates sexual drive with frequency of orgasm. The same reasoning has been applied to animals, but here direct observation makes the technique more reliable, though not necessarily more valid.

Studies of the reproductive behavior of fishes show that many species come into breeding condition and exhibit sexual drive for a limited part of each year. Analysis of courtship and mating in the three-spined stickleback reveals that the male's reactions to the gravid female constitute a stereotyped sequence of movements beginning with "threat" and changing to a "zig-zag" swimming pattern in which the male alternately approaches the female and then darts away from her, moving in the direction of the nest which he has previously constructed (39). After a period of such courtship, the female follows the male to the nest and deposits her eggs therein. Van Iersel (20) infers the intensity of the male's sexual motivation on the basis of the relative distance traveled each time that he moves toward the nest or toward the female.

Baerends (1) has shown that the color pattern of the male guppy undergoes a series of regular changes while courtship is in progress and as copulation becomes imminent. Baerends suggests that color patterns may therefore serve as one indicator of the level of sexual moti-

-6-

vation in this species.

Observations of seagulls (30), ducks and geese (25), and various passerines (19) plainly indicate that different intensities of sexual arousal are consistently associated with different types or frequencies of "display movements," so that the pattern of overt response correlates with the level of excitement in each member of a pair.

Darling (13) has described the seasonal eruption of sexual activity in male and female red deer. His account creates the impression that, in this species, sexual drive is present only during the period of rut and can be detected by the appearance of new behavior patterns in both sexes. Descriptions of reproduction in the Alaskan fur seal (3) likewise indicate a situation in which sexual motivation is confined to a limited number of weeks in each year and is signalled in the male by the onset of territoriality, fighting, and other activities which are not seen at any other time.

The most complete field studies of primates are those of Carpenter (10, 11), who observed the mating of various species of monkeys. The adult male macaque appears to be erotically responsive at all times of the year, and exhibits lowered sexual drive only after periods of prolonged copulatory activity. Females of this species come into heat once every twenty-eight days, approximately, and remain receptive for about nine days. This cycle is repeated with regularity, unless pregnancy intervenes. Sexual responsiveness or readiness in both males and females can be detected by the experienced observer on the basis of characteristic postural and vocal reactions.

Under controlled conditions in the laboratory, observations can be repeated, and simple description can be supplemented by experimental techniques. For example, Ball (2) devised a ten-point scale on which the receptivity of female rats could be scored. The validity of the scoring technique was established by demonstrating that females ranked highly receptive (i. e., sexually motivated) elicited

-7-

more sexual advances on the part of males than did low-ranking females.

Young and his co-workers have described a heirarchy of responses shown by male guinea pigs in the presence of estrous females (43). At one end of the scale are those reactions indicative of only mild interest on the part of the male, and at the opposite extreme belongs the indicator of maximal sexual response, namely, the occurrence of ejaculation. Utilizing the maximal scores achieved by a male during successive subdivisions of a ten-minute test, one can arrive at a composite value which is interpreted as a measure of sex drive.

By means of this scoring system, Young and his collaborators were able to measure the relative intensity of male sexual drive in three strains of guinea pigs and to demonstrate genetic differences (40). They showed further that comparable differences in drive are eliminated by castration and restored by administration of exogenous androgen, even though all groups received identical amounts of hormone (18). With the same technique, the relation of sexual drive to several other variables, ranging from basal metabolism to infantile experience, has been measured quantitatively (33, 41).

Several experimenters (6, 32, 38) have arrived at estimates of the strength of sexual motivation in male rats by quantifying and measuring various items in the total pattern of mating behavior. For instance, it is a simple matter to time the delay between introduction of the female in the observation cage and the male's first mating response The duration of this "latency" has been shown under some conditions to vary inversely with the amount of androgen administered to castrated male rats (7), and it could be hypothesized that high levels of sexual responsiveness would be associated with attenuated latencies.

In this same species, the male's ejaculation follows a series of mounting reactions, during most of which insertion is effected. A second potential measure of sexual

drive might be the number of intromissions necessary
to produce ejaculation. Other indications of the level
of sexual motivation might be the number of ejaculations
achieved in a time-limited test, or the length of time
needed to recover sexual responsiveness following an
ejaculation.

All of these measures have been employed by different experimenters at different times, and their significance will be discussed at a later point. It will be
noted that they are applicable primarily to the male,
rather than to the female. As a matter of fact, there
have been very few attempts to measure the feminine
sex drive. As noted earlier, Ball used a rating scale
in her study of female rats, and recently Young and his
associates (17) have described several measures of
receptivity in the female guinea pig. These consist of
(1) the length of time after hormone treatment when heat
responses first appear, (2) the maximal duration of the
lordosis reflex at the peak of heat, and (3) the total time
over which the mating reaction can be elicited. These
items were found to vary from one genetic strain to another but to be relatively independent of the concentration
of ovarian hormones, provided the supply was adequate
to support any receptivity at all.

One more technique for estimating the strength of
sexual motivation by studying mating behavior is to observe the degree to which these responses can be evoked
by suboptimal stimulation. This method has been most
effectively employed by European and British experimenters working with submammalian vertebrates. Although their primary goal has been identification of the
stimulus components responsible for the evocation of
courtship and mating, these studies have at the same time
revealed that differences in sexual readiness may be reflected in the degree to which suboptimal stimuli are capable of eliciting sexual responses.

For example, the normal stimulus for courtship in
the male three-spined stickleback is a gravid female

whose physiological condition, and hence readiness to mate, is signalled, among other things, by her swollen abdomen (10). Most males will display courtship toward dummy females, provided the abdominal swelling is accurately imitated. Highly aroused males may court inanimate models which do not perfectly copy the body shape of the normal mate.

Similarly, male robins attack a stuffed skin which has a red breast and is mounted in an erect position; but they court and attempt to copulate with a taxidermic preparation that lacks the red breast and is placed in the stooping position which characterizes the receptive female (24). It is obvious that the degree to which a male will tolerate deviations from the optimal pattern and still attempt to mate might be taken as a measure of his sexual motivation.

In somewhat comparable experiments with mammals, I have studied the reactions of sexually inexperienced male rats to a variety of stimulus objects, including receptive and nonreceptive females, immobilized estrous females, males, small guinea pigs, and infant rabbits (4). It was found that the initial mating reactions of most males can be elicited only by the receptive female rat. However, an occasional male may respond sexually to one of the biologically inadequate stimulus partners.

When these results were obtained, it was hypothesized that a tendency to attempt coitus with partners other than the estrous female was indicative of a high level of sexual motivation. This interpretation was strengthened by the results of a subsequent experiment (4) in which inexperienced male rats were exposed successively to most of the stimulus partners used in the preceding study but were injected with large amounts of testosterone propionate before the sex tests. Under these conditions, there was a marked increase in the proportion of the group directing their initial mating reactions to animals other than the receptive female rat.

Learning for a Sexual Reward

According to some theories, the efficiency of learning depends in part upon the intensity of motivation or
strength of drive. Learning for a sexual reward has
been studied.

Kagan found that male rats would learn to make the
correct turn in a single T-maze when the reward was opportunity to mate with a receptive female and achieve
an ejaculation. A second study was designed to isolate
the reinforcing element or elements in the total mating
pattern. It was found that opportunity to mount the female with or without vaginal penetration has a definite
reward value, but maximal reinforcement depends on
the occurrence of an ejaculation. The data gave some
indication that repeated intromissions which never cul-
minate in orgasm tend to become punishing and may lead
to an avoidance reaction on the part of the male (22).

Performance on Interpolated Tasks

It has been shown that the speed or frequency with
which animals will perform a previously learned response can be varied by varying the strength of drive.
For example, the rate at which rats press a bar to obtain a food reward increases within limits as the period
of food deprivation is increased (36).

Schwartz (34) investigated the rate of bar-pressing
in male rats when execution of the interpolated task was
rewarded by opportunity to mate with a receptive female.
He found that the bar-pressing habit could be established
under these conditions, and although maximal rates were
appreciably lower than those obtained with hunger or
thirst, there appeared to be some relationship between
bar-pressing and the presumed level of sexual motivation. For example, during tests in which males failed
to copulate with the female, the average rate of pressing
was lower than it was in tests where primary sexual
activity occurred.

Another common measure of drive strength is the
speed with which an animal will traverse a straight
runway at the end of which reinforcement is provided.
When food is available in the goal box, the running speed
of rats varies as a function of the length of the preceding deprivation period (12).

Recent experiments have revealed that alley speeds
can be employed as a measure of sexual motivation in
male rats (8). Males were trained to traverse a straight
runway and enter a goal box containing a receptive female.
After one copulation, the male was returned to the starting point and given another trial in the alley. The day's
testing concluded with the trial on which ejaculation occurred.

There was a positive relationship between the male
rat's running speed and the intensity of his sexual reactions to the receptive female in the goal box. Males
that had been running rapidly and mating promptly were
castrated. The operation produced a gradual loss of
sexual ability, as shown by a progressive decrease in
the intensity, completeness, and frequency of mating
responses shown in the goal box. When the consummatory responses began to weaken and disappear, the time
spent traversing the alley increased. When copulatory
responses were abolished, many males remained in the
start box and failed to enter the alley.

Male rats that had become sexually inactive subsequent to castration were sexually reactivated by the administration of testicular hormone. The castrates reacted to daily injections of testosterone propionate with a
progressive decrease in time to reach the goal box and
a concomitant increase in sexual reactions to the estrous
female.

Seward and Seward (35) measured the speed with
which male guinea pigs crossed a hurdle to get to a receptive female. They found that males would cross
more readily if they had been sexually deprived for sev-

eral days than if they had recently copulated with the female.

An as yet unpublished study from my own laboratory revealed that male dogs will learn to run down an alley to get to a receptive bitch. Running speeds were positively related to sexual performance.

Resistance to Punishment

John J. B. Morgan was one of the first psychologists to propose that the intensity of a drive might be expressed in terms of the strength of aversive stimulation necessary to prevent the behavior normally associated with it.

> The amount of inhibition necessary to overcome any tendency may be used as a measure of the strength of that tendency (28, p. 94).

An early investigator who applied this principle to the study of sexual motivation was F. A. Moss (29). He interposed an electrically charged floor plate between male and female rats and recorded the number of males that endured the shock and joined the female. Moss's technique was primitive by modern standards, and his understanding of the rat's sexual habits was so limited that his experiment is of no more than historical interest.

Several more sophisticated studies were carried out at Columbia University during the 1920's. The familiar Columbia Obstruction Apparatus was used by Warner, Nissen, Jenkins, and others to measure the strength of sexual motivation under a variety of conditions. Warner (42) concluded that male rats which have had opportunity for unlimited mating activity for two hours recover full sexual responsiveness after a 24-hour rest.

Nissen (31) found that castration decreased the male rat's tendency to cross the electrified grid and reach a female, but that this deficiency could be at least partly corrected by the injection of crude extracts containing testis secretions. Jenkins (21) compared the grid-crossing tendency of male rats that had been reared with other males and that of other males reared in heterosexual groups. She found that the sexually segregated animals showed a reduction in readiness to cross to a female and, under some conditions, an increased tendency to cross to a second male.

One obstacle to interpretation of the results of these three investigations is posed by the fact that a high percentage of those males which endured the shock and approached the female failed to exhibit any mating reactions. This raises a question concerning the motivation involved.

This question does not arise in connection with a more recent experiment conducted at Yale (5). Sexually experienced male rats were accustomed to mate while wearing a light harness which held a metal electrode firmly against a shaved area of skin just between the shoulder blades. A flexible wire lead passed vertically from the harness through an overhead pulley and thence to the current source. A wire mesh floor served as the second electrode.

After males had become thoroughly adapted and would mate freely while wearing the harness with the lead attached, they were punished each time they mounted the receptive female. Members of a "low shock" group received a momentary shock of 100 volts, A. C. Males in the "high shock" group were subjected to 380 volts each time they attempted to mate with the stimulus female.

The effects of low shock were quite interesting. None of the males ceased copulating or ejaculating, although some of them received as many as 20 to 25 shocks per test. The only perceptible change in behavior consisted of a steady, test-to-test increase in the number of incomplete attempts at copulation. The number of intromissions (successful copulations) per test did not change, but prior to the introduction of low shock, 21 per cent of all mounts were incomplete, and this value had risen to

44 per cent by the time of the final punishment test. The overall result was a significant increase in the total number of mounts per time-limited test.

High shock promptly eliminated the ejaculatory response in all subjects. It also built up inhibition at a fairly rapid rate. Premonitory signs of complete inhibition included a rise in average latencies in successive punishment tests. Eventually the inhibition became so strong that males failed to mount the receptive female in two successive tests. After this criterion of inhibition had been met, testing was continued at four-day intervals, using the harness and attached wire, but without delivering an electric shock. Two-thirds of the rats recovered from the experimentally induced sexual inhibition within two to four weeks after the last test with high shock. The remaining one-third of the group did not recover spontaneously although some of them were tested for as long as 100 days after the last shock. These animals were then subjected to a series of electroconvulsions and all resumed mating.

Measurement of Sexual Exhaustion and Recovery

Insight into the nature of sexual motivation may be provided by systematic studies of the course of sexual exhaustion and subsequent recovery. As noted earlier, Warner made a partial attempt to achieve this objective. He left male rats for two hours with females which were supposedly receptive. (The only criterion was the vaginal smear, which is not an entirely reliable behavior indicator.) Subsequent measurements on the Columbia Obstruction Apparatus lead to the conclusion that the males' sex drive, as measured by grid-crossings, had "reached its high point" after a 24-hour rest.

There are two sources of ambiguity in Warner's experiment. In the first place, the condition of males after two hours with females was unknown, since sexual behavior was not observed. In the second place, grid-crossing scores are so poorly correlated with performance

-15-

in mating tests that their validity as a measure of sex drive is doubtful (37).

The use of barriers or interpolated tasks to estimate recovery of sexual responsiveness after a period of unlimited copulation probably should be preceded by some sort of normative study that will tell us what changes occur in the consummatory response itself during the onset of sexual exhaustion and after varying periods of sexual rest.

In a recent experiment, Jordan and I (9) placed male rats with receptive females and left the pair together until the male met the criterion of "exhaustion" by allowing 30 minutes to elapse without mounting the female. Males were then retested after one, three, six or 15 days of rest. Results of tests occurring after a 15-day rest were analyzed in an attempt to describe the course of sexual exhaustion.

Individual differences were evident. Some animals reached the criterion of exhaustion after five ejaculations, whereas others ejaculated ten times before becoming inactive. Some rats began to copulate within two seconds, and other animals delayed for nearly ten minutes before initiating sexual relations.

Once mating had begun, copulatory responses occurred at regular intervals until the first ejaculation. Approximately ten intromissions preceded the first ejaculation, but for each succeeding ejaculation, the number of intromissions decreased, with the result that the sixth ejaculation occurred after an average of 4.1 insertions.

In the male rat, as in males of many mammalian species, an ejaculation is followed by a period of sexual unresponsiveness. The duration of this "postejaculatory refractory period" varies from species to species and from individual to individual. When several successive ejaculations occur, the refractory period may serve as a sensitive indicator of the course of sexual exhaustion.

In the experiment I have been discussing, the average refractory period following the first ejaculation was 324 seconds. This measure increased with successive ejaculations, and recovery from the sixth ejaculation took an average of 818 seconds. These findings appear somewhat paradoxical. Successive ejaculations were achieved with fewer and fewer intromissions, which might suggest that sexual motivation or responsiveness was steadily increasing as the test progressed. But at the same time, the number of seconds needed for recovery from each succeeding ejaculation progressively increased, and this might indicate a gradual reduction in the motivational level. Rationalization of this difference will be considered at a later point.

Mating tests conducted after various periods of rest gave a reasonably clear picture of the course of recovery from sexual exhaustion. The number of ejaculations of which males were capable increased with longer periods of rest. Only one animal ejaculated in a test given after 24 hours of rest, and this male could ejaculate only once. Rats that ejaculated after a three-day rest showed an average of three ejaculations before they ceased to mate. After six days of inactivity, the average number of ejaculations was 5.0, and in 15-day tests, this value rose to 6.0. According to this particular measure, the curve of recovery from sexual exhaustion is negatively accelerated, and tends to become asymptotic at some point between the tenth and fifteenth day of rest.

Another measure of the extent to which full sexual motivation has been restored is the initial latency. Other things being equal, it might be predicted that highly motivated animals would initiate sexual contact after shorter delays than would less strongly motivated individuals. In tests conducted after a one-day rest, the median number of seconds preceding the first intromission was 3600 seconds. Comparable scores were 623 seconds for three-day tests, 135 seconds for six-day

tests, and 18 seconds for tests following a 15-day rest.
It is apparent that latency is a very sensitive index to
recovery from sexual exhaustion.

It has been shown that males with less than the
optimal amount of rest tended to reach exhaustion after
fewer ejaculations than were achieved by fully rested
animals. There were other indications that the onset
of exhaustion or the lowering of motivation is more
rapid in individuals that have not fully recovered from
a test in which they were given opportunity for unlimited
sexual activity. This is most clearly shown by changes
in postejaculatory refractory periods. In the first place,
recovery from the first ejaculation took longer in three-
day tests than in six-day tests, and longer in six-day
tests than in 15-day tests. In the second place, although
there was a progressive increase in the length of successive refractory periods for tests conducted after three,
six and 15 days, the rate of such increase tended to differ according to the duration of the rest period preceding
the test. In general, the shorter the rest, the more rapid
the lengthening of the refractory period; the longer the
rest, the more gradual was the increase in refractory
periods following successive ejaculations.

Mechanisms Involved in Sexual Behavior

The evidence is fragmentary and occasionally con-
tradictory. It does not justify an attempt to formulate
a comprehensive theory of sexual arousal and mating
behavior. Interspecific differences in the normal pattern are so pronounced that it is difficult to imagine a
theoretical interpretation which would apply with equal
validity to rodents, carnivores, ungulates, primates,
and other mammals, to say nothing of lower vertebrates.

Nevertheless, a start must be made somewhere, and
the most reasonable approach is to formulate a set of
hypotheses which appear applicable to a single species.
If we can frame a theory that deals satisfactorily with

-18-

one species, then it will prove profitable to examine
the generality of that theory. To attempt a multispe-
cific explanation from the beginning would be fruitless
and ultimately frustrating.

The choice of a species is not difficult, because
there are only two for which the evidence is sufficient
to justify even preliminary theorizing. These are the
domestic guinea pig and rat. I have selected the rat
because it is the more widely studied and because I am
more familiar with the behavior of this species.

A further restriction should be made explicit. The
following interpretation deals exclusively with the male.
There have been very few systematic experiments on the
sexual behavior of female rats, and much more work
will have to be done before any useful theory of feminine
arousal and performance can be formulated.

I do not pretend to have thought out an all-inclusive
theory of sexual behavior--not even for the male rat.
Instead, I have drawn up a list of the principal facts
with which such a theory must deal; and at some points,
I have suggested what should be regarded as "working
hypotheses" that constitute potential explanations of
some of these facts.

The Dual Nature of Sexual Arousal and Performances

Several writers have pointed out the possibility of
subdividing human sexual behavior into two phases.
Moll (27) described a "contrectation drive" which leads
to the establishment of bodily contact and more or less
generalized physical stimulation, and he contrasted this
with the "detumescence drive" which leads to sexual
orgasm. Havelock Ellis and others have put forth more
or less similar proposals (15).

Experimental studies of male animals suggest similar
conclusions. It is as though execution of the complete,
masculine copulatory pattern involved the attainment of

-19-

two successive levels of excitement, or the crossing of
two thresholds. It is convenient, though entirely spec-
ulative, to think in terms of an internal state or process
which must be evoked and maintained until a critical
level of excitement is reached. This appears to be a
two-step phenomenon and to rest upon the activity of
two at least partially independent mechanisms.

If mating responses are to occur, it is essential
that the male become sufficiently aroused to make contact with the female and to achieve intromission. Occurrence of this initial part of the total pattern will be
provisionally referred to the mediation of a hypothetical
sexual arousal mechanism (SAM). The main function of
the SAM is to increase the male's sexual excitement to
such a pitch that the copulatory threshold is attained.

Crossing the copulatory threshold results in mounting and intromission. In normal mating, erection and
insertion must occur, for mounting alone is not enough
to activate the second mechanism or mechanisms which
now assume at least partial control of the male's behavior.
Considered collectively, these may be designated as the
intromission and ejaculatory mechanism (IEM). The
initial intromission and those that follow provide a new
source of sensory impulses which serve to modify further the internal state of the animal and eventually to
bring the male to the ejaculatory threshold.

Behavioral Characteristics of the SAM

The functioning of the SAM is most clearly reflected
in the response of sexually inexperienced rats to the
receptive female. The male's initial reaction usually
consists of a thorough investigation of the female, particular attention being paid to the anogenital region. A
secondary focus of interest is the female's head and ears.

The female's response to the male's investigations
consists principally of three kinds of behavior. The most
common reaction to genital stimulation is a "courting run"

in which the female darts swiftly away from the male
for a relatively short distance and then comes to an
abrupt halt, posing with the head pointed slightly up-
ward and the hind feet planted somewhat farther apart
than usual. This pseudo-retreat usually elicits prompt
pursuit and renewed investigation on the male's part.

When a male fails to follow her, or is slow to initiate contact, the estrous female displays a different
kind of behavior. Under these circumstances, she assumes the initiative and approaches the male, often investigating his genitalia. As soon as he evinces interest
in her, the female shifts to the pattern of pseudo-retreat
and posing.

The final element in the female's sexual pattern
consists of the lordosis response in which the back is
arched concavely, the pudendal area is elevated, and
the tail is moved to one side, exposing the vaginal opening. This response may occur if the male places one
paw on the female's back, but it is more likely to be
evoked if he mounts from the rear, clasping her flanks
between his forelegs. The mounting reaction is usually
accompanied by rapid movements of the male's fore-
limbs which "palpate" the female and intensify her lordosis response. At the same time, the male's hindquarters
move in and out in a series of extremely rapid pelvic
thrusts. If erection occurs and the male's orientation
is appropriate, a final pelvic thrust results in insertion
of the penis into the vagina. Penetration lasts but a
fraction of a second and is terminated as the male "bounces
off" the female and throws himself vigorously to the rear
in a clearly recognizable "backward lunge."

In some individuals, activation of the SAM and achievement of the copulatory threshold is a very rapid process.
Males that have never before been exposed to receptive
females may mount and effect intromission within ten
seconds after the female becomes accessible. In other
individuals, the first intromission is preceded by signs
of intense excitement associated with investigation of

the female and a tendency to crawl over her back without getting into the copulatory position. This behavior either leads to the achievement of intromission within a few minutes or grows less frequent and vigorous until the male's interest abates and he breaks off contact with the female.

A very important characteristic of the SAM is its susceptibility to habituation. The process of sexual arousal tends to decay unless the copulatory threshold is attained within a fairly short time. Every experimenter who has studied mating in rats has found that a male who fails to copulate within the first five or ten minutes after the female is introduced is unlikely to do so on that test, even if left with the female for an hour or more.

It is as though two opposing processes were occurring simultaneously. On the one hand, the male is reacting positively to the stimuli associated with the receptive female. Continuous exposure to these stimuli tends to produce increasing excitement until the copulatory threshold is reached, at which time new types of stimulation come into play. At the same time, there is a tendency for the male to become habituated or adapted to the visual, olfactory, and tactile cues provided by the female, and therefore they gradually lose their power to evoke excitement.

If mating is to occur, the trend toward increasing arousal must reach the copulatory threshold before the habituation process produces too great a reduction in reactivity to erotic stimuli. Otherwise the male evinces gradual loss of interest in the female and cannot be rearoused during that period. This model of sexual arousal and habituation was suggested by Fuller and Williams' theory of the physiological processes underlying the occurence of sound-induced seizures in mice (16). In this case, as in sexual behavior, animals either react to the inciting stimulus within a short time or they become less and less attentive to it.

As noted above, some sexually naive males exhibit generalized excitement and abortive or incomplete responses when they are first confronted with a receptive female. They may temporarily leave the female and dash erratically about the observation cage. Or they may seize the female's skin in their teeth and drag her about the floor. Crawling over the female is common. This behavior usually disappears with dramatic suddeness as soon as one or two successful copulations have occurred. Now the male proceeds rather calmly and methodically to mount and penetrate the female at regular intervals until ejaculation occurs. It looks very much as though the behavior had come under the control of a new mechanism which is here designated the IEM.

Once the IEM has been called into play, most males maintain sufficient excitement to copulate until ejaculation occurs. Ejaculation is followed by an abrupt loss of sexual responsiveness which lasts for several minutes. When this postejaculatory refractory period has elapsed, the SAM is reactivated and mating is resumed.

Studies in sexual exhaustion have shown that the refractory periods following successive ejaculations grow progressively longer (9). One group of males tested after 15 days of sexual inactivity ejaculated from five to ten times before ceasing to copulate. Refractory periods following the first six ejaculations were respectively 324, 395, 468, 495, 597, and 818 seconds in length.

This could be taken to indicate a decreasing responsiveness of the SAM, but alternative interpretations are conceivable, and it is impossible to make a choice on the basis of present evidence.

Behavioral Characteristics of the IEM

Whereas the functions of the SAM may be discharged in a few seconds, the role of the IEM is such that it remains in operation for longer periods of time. Under normal conditions, the majority of male rats must achieve

-23-

intromission from eight to 15 times before ejaculation occurs. One possible explanation is that the state of sexual excitement is progressively increased by the occurrence of successive intromissions until the ejaculatory threshold is reached. Alternatively, it might be supposed that time is the important variable, and repeated intromissions simply maintain the necessary level of excitement until ejaculation occurs.

Regulation of copulation. Once the copulatory threshold has been reached, the male mounts the female and effects intromission. He then dismounts and engages in autogenital cleaning. When this is completed, the male may approach the female and copulate again, or he may wait for a brief period before renewing contact. The interval between copulations varies from approximately 30 to 60 seconds for different individuals but is exceedingly consistent for the same male. In my laboratory, 101 rats were observed in four tests, and the odd-even reliability of the average intercopulatory delay was found to be +.94.

The fact that intromissions are spaced rather than massed can be explained by two assumptions. First, one copulation cannot be followed immediately by another because an incompatible response takes precedence, namely the reaction of autogenital cleaning. This behavior is almost invariable after the male has penetrated the female, but does not occur as frequently following an unsuccessful attempt to copulate. Second, each intromission can be thought of as temporarily reducing sexual excitement, so that the copulatory threshold has to be regained before another sexual act can occur.

Regulation of ejaculation. Ejaculation during sexual intercourse is controlled by a mechanism which is influenced by stimulation derived from a series of intromissions. Males have been tested with females whose vaginas were surgically closed, and although attempts at copulation were frequent, ejaculation did not occur (23). Adult males with underdeveloped copulatory organs

mount the female repeatedly but cannot penetrate her
and therefore do not ejaculate (6). Experienced copu-
lators continue to mount the female after removal of
the os penis but never ejaculate due to inability to achieve
intromission (6).

How does a sequence of intromissions produce the
ejaculatory reflex? As noted above, each copulation
may exert an additive effect upon the ejaculatory mechanism, producing an increasing level of excitement until an
explosive discharge finally occurs. At present, the evidence favors an alternative hypothesis. This is that the
initial insertion excites the ejaculatory mechanism to
its fullest extent and that subsequent copulations serve
a maintenance function, sustaining the level of excitement
in the ejaculatory mechanism.

According to this point of view, the crucial factor in
eliciting ejaculation is not the amount of genital stimulation or the number óf intromissions but rather the
persistance of excitation in the ejaculatory mechanism
for some critical period. The duration of this critical
period is highly consistent for different individuals. We
have measured the length of time from the first insertion
to the occurrence of ejaculation in 101 rats during four
mating tests. The reliability of this measure proved to
be +.82. For the same tests, the reliability of number
of copulations preceding ejaculation was +.58.

Another line of evidence against a simple "additive"
theory comes from studies which show that the number
of copulations necessary to produce an ejaculation varies
under different conditions. Schwartz (34) and Beach and
Jordan (8) noted incidentally that when mating was interrupted after each intromission, males tended to ejaculate
after fewer copulations than they normally showed in the
free-mating situation. Rasmussen (32) studied this phenomenon systematically.

It is apparent that one insertion every 300 seconds
is at least as effective in inducing ejaculation as one

every 66 seconds. This may mean that the ejaculatory
mechanism retains the excitatory effect of an intromission for at least five minutes. In contrast, much of
this effect is dissipated by the end of ten minutes. Of
12 rats tested with the 600-second intercopulatory delay, only ten attained the ejaculatory threshold. The
eleventh animal executed 44 copulations over a seven-
hour period, and the twelfth case copulated 56 times in
nine hours without ejaculating.

   Regulation of recovery after ejaculation. Immediately
after ejaculating, the male rat becomes sexually unre-
sponsive to the receptive female. The length of this "refractory period" after the first ejaculation averages approximately five minutes but varies considerably among
individuals. In four tests of 99 males, we found the mean
duration of the postejaculatory refractory period to have
a reliability of +.82. The reduction in responsiveness
following an ejaculation is a major version of the low-
ered excitability which succeeds each intromission, and
similar if not identical factors may be at work in both
instances. At any rate, tests conducted at Yale showed
a significant correlation between mean intercopulatory
delay and average length of the postejaculatory interval
$(r = +.50)$.

   The effects of an ejaculation are twofold. As just
noted, they include a temporary loss of sexual responsiveness, but at the same time, they appear to involve
some kind of sensitization of the ejaculatory mechanism.
The latter conclusion is inferred from reports of several
investigators to the effect that when mating is resumed,
the second ejaculation is produced in less time and with
fewer copulations than the first (9, 32, 38). Jordan and
I (9) found that in one group of male rats, the first ejaculation occurred after an average of 10.64 intromissions,
whereas the succeeding five ejaculations were preceded
by 6.00, 5.73, 5.09, and 4.10 copulations.

   The length of time needed to recover from successive
ejaculations takes the opposite course, growing more

-26-

and more protracted as the test progresses. For the time being, it seems most parsimonious to refer this change to decreasing capacity for recovery in the SAM.

Concluding Statement

It will be evident that we are not yet ready to answer the question as to the place of sex as a "drive" in general psychological theory. Much systematic research remains to be done before this objective is accomplished. In particular, we need to know whether the model suggested here can be applied to other species, and we need a comparable model for the female. It is reasonably certain that the feminine arousal and sexual satiation involve quite different sorts of events than those described in the case of the male.

On the basis of the incomplete evidence presently available, it is not unreasonable to assume as a working hypothesis that the mechanisms described above can be employed in the analysis of sexual behavior of the human male. The principal difference between man and the lower mammals lies in the extent to which the SAM is affected by symbolic factors. There appears to have been no saltatory evolutionary change in the IEM, but the unique features of human sexuality revolve about the extreme lability of the SAM.

Human sexual arousal is subject to extensive modification as a result of experience. Sexual values may become attached to a wide variety of biologically inappropriate stimulus objects or partners. Conversely, responsiveness in the usual heterosexual situation may be partly or completely blocked.

Analysis of the clinical evidence in terms of the multiple-mechanism theory will have to be carried out before the fact can be established, but it is entirely conceivable that considering the functions of the SAM and the IEM separately will prove helpful in increasing our understanding of human sexual life.

References

1. Baerends, G. P., Brouwer, R., and Waterbolk, H. Tj. Ethólogical studies on Lebistes reticulatus (Peters). I: An analysis of the male courtship pattern. Behaviour, 1955, 8, 249 - 334.

2. Ball, J. A test for measuring sexual excitability in the female rat. Comp. psychol. Monog., 1937, 14, 1 - 37.

3. Bartholomew, G. Reproductive behavior of the Alaska fur seal. J. Mammal., 1953, 34, 417 - 436.

4. Beach, F. A. Analysis of the stimuli adequate to elicit mating behavior in the sexually-inexperienced male rat. J. comp. Psychol., 1942, 33, 163 - 207.

5. Beach, F. A., Conovitz, M. W., Steinberg, F., and Goldstein, A. C. Experimental inhibition and restoration of mating behavior in male rats. J. genet. Psychol., in press.

6. Beach, F. A., and Holz, M. Mating behavior in male rats castrated at various ages and injected with androgen. J. exp. Zool., 1946, 101, 91 - 142.

7. Beach, F. A., and Holz-Tucker, A. M. Effects of different concentrations of androgen upon sexual behavior in castrated male rats. J. comp. physiol. Psychol., 1949, 42, 433 - 453.

8. Beach, F. A., and Jordan, L. Effects of sexual reinforcement upon the performance of male rats in a straight runway. J. comp. physiol. Psychol., 1956, 49, 105 - 110.

9. Beach, F. A., and Jordan, L. Sexual exhaustion and recovery in the male rat. Quart. j. exp. Psychol., in press.

10. Carpenter, C. R. Sexual behavior of free-ranging rhesus monkeys (Macaca mulatta). I. Specimens, procedures and behavioral characteristics of estrus. J. comp. Psychol., 1942, 33, 113 - 138.

11. Carpenter, C. R. Sexual behavior of free-ranging rhesus monkeys (Macaca mulatta). II. Periodicity of estrus, homosexual, autoerotic and nonconformist behavior. J. comp. Psychol., 1942, 33, 143 - 160.

12. Cotton, J. W. Running time as a function of amount of food deprivation. J. exp. Psychol., 1953, 46, 188 - 198.

13. Darling, F. F. A Herd of Red Deer. London: Oxford Press, 1937.

14. Dollard, J., and Miller, N. E. Personality and Psychotherapy: An Analysis in Terms of Learning, Thinking and Culture. New York: McGraw-Hill, 1950.

15. Ellis, H. Studies in the Psychology of Sex. New York: Random House, 1936.

16. Fuller, J. L., and Williams, E. Gene-controlled time constants in convulsive behavior. Proc. nat. acad. Sci., 1951, 37, 349 - 356.

17. Goy, R. W., and Young, W. C. Strain differences in the behavioral responses of spayed female guinea pigs to alpha-estradiol benzoate and progesterone. Behaviour, in press.

18. Grunt, J. A., and Young, W. C. Consistency of sexual behavior patterns in individual male guinea pigs following castration and androgen therapy. J. comp. physiol. Psychol., 1953, 46, 138 - 144.

19. Hinde, R. A. The behavior of the Great Tit (Parus major) and some other related species. Behaviour, Suppl. 2, 1952.

20. Iersel, J. J. A. van. An analysis of the parental behaviour of the male three-spined stickleback (Gasterostens aculeatus, L.). Behaviour, Suppl. 3, 1953.

21. Jenkins, M. The effect of segregation on the sex behavior of the white rat as measured by the obstruction method. Genet. psychol. Monog., 1928, 3, 455 - 571.

22. Kagan, J. Comparison of incomplete and complete sexual behavior as rewards for maze learning in rats. J. comp. physiol. Psychol., in press.

23. Kaufman, R. S. Effects of preventing intromission upon sexual behavior of rats. J. comp. physiol. Psychol., 1953, 46, 209 - 211.

24. Lack, D. The Life of the Robin. London, 1943.

25. Lorenz, K. Der Kumpan in der Umvelt des Vogels. J. f. Ornithol., 1935, 83, 137 - 213, 289 - 413.

26. Miller, N. E., and Dollard, J. Social Learning and Imitation. New Haven: Yale Press, 1941.

27. Moll, A. Untersuchungen über die Libido Sexualis. Berlin: Fischer, 1897.

28. Morgan, J. J. B. The measurements of instincts. Proc. 31st Ann. Meet. A. P. A., Cambridge, Mass., 1922, 94 - 96.

29. Moss, F. A. A study of animal drives. J. exp. Psychol., 1924, 7, 165 - 185.

30. Moynihan, M. Some aspects of reproductive be-

haviour in the Black-Hooded Gull (Larus ridibundus ridibundus L.) and related species. Behaviour, Suppl. 4, 1955.

31. Nissen, H. W. The effects of gonadectomy, vasotomy, and injections of placental and orchic extracts on the sex behavior of the white rat. Genet. psychol. Monog., 1929, 5, 451 - 547.

32. Rasmussen, E. W. The effect of an enforced pause between each coitus on the number of copulations necessary to achieve ejaculation in the albino rat. Unpubl. mss.

33. Riss, W. Sex drive, oxygen consumption and heart rate in genetically different strains of male guinea pigs. Am. j. Physiol., 1955, 180, 530 - 534.

34. Schwartz, M. Instrumental and consummatory measures of sexual capacity in the male rat. J. comp. physiol. Psychol., in press.

35. Seward, J. P., and Seward, G. H. Studies on reproductive activities of the guinea pig. IV: A comparison of sex drive in males and females. J. genet. Psychol., 1940, 57, 429 - 440.

36. Skinner, B. F. The Behavior of Organisms: An Experimental Analysis. New York: Appleton, 1938.

37. Stone, C. P., Barker, R. G., and Tomlin, M. I. Sexual drive in potent and impotent male rats as measured by the Columbia obstruction apparatus. J. genet. Psychol., 1935, 47, 33 - 48.

38. Stone, C. P., Ferguson, L. W., and Wright, C. Consistency in lengths of postejaculatory quiescent periods in adult male rats. Proc. soc. exp. biol. & Med., 1940, 45, 120 - 121.

39. Tinbergen, N. The Study of Instinct. Oxford:

Clarendon Press, 1951.

40. Valenstein, E. S., Riss, R. W., and Young, W. C.
Sex drive in genetically heterogeneous and highly
inbred strains of male guinea pigs. J. comp.
physiol. Psychol., 1954, 47, 162 - 165.

41. Valenstein, E. S., Riss, W., and Young, W. C.
Experiential and genetic factors in the organization
of sexual behavior in male guinea pigs. J. comp.
physiol. Psychol., 1955, 48, 397 - 403.

42. Warner, L. H. A study of sex drive in the white
rat by means of the obstruction method. Comp.
psychol. Monog., 1927, 4, 1 - 67.

43. Young, W. C., and Grunt, J. A. The pattern and
measurement of sexual behavior in the male guinea
pig. J. comp. physiol. Psychol., 1951, 44, 492 -
500.

COMMENTS ON PROFESSOR BEACH'S PAPER

by
John P. Seward

In his stimulating paper Dr. Beach has given only
a small sample of his own and others' extensive research on sex behavior, rightly subordinating data to
theory. In this area, as compared with that of learning,
theories are more likely to be physiological, probably
because neural and hormonal factors can be more directly manipulated. This is as it should be, and whatever
Dr. Beach may think of neurological theory in other
fields, he is actively pursuing it in his own. As a result, his paper is full of provocative suggestions and
problems, of which I should like to discuss three: (a)
classification of sex behavior; (b) the two proposed
mechanisms; (c) theory of sexual exhaustion and re-

-32-

covery. I should also like to add one empirical observation of my own.

(a) Beach classes sexual motivation as an appetite rather than a "primary" drive. I believe the distinction has important implications. He bases it largely on negative grounds: sexual deprivation poses no threat to the life or health of the individual, nor does it produce any internal stimulus necessary to instigate sex activity. But what are the positive criteria of appetites, that sex presumably shares? An appetite is always identified by some typical goal object or consummatory response; it is _for_ eating candy or smoking a cigarette. Somehow this final act seems to direct and maintain the behavior that leads up to it. The question is: What mechanism performs this integrating function? If sex is an appetite, it should help us to find an answer.

Analysis of sex behavior suggests two tentative hypotheses. One is that erotic stimuli arouse visceral responses, such as engorgement of erectile tissue, that in turn produce powerful stimuli to action and persist until terminated by orgasm. The mechanism is closely analogous to the one proposed by Mowrer (6) and Miller (5) for fear, implying a remarkable similarity between at least one appetite and one aversion. But this is probably not the whole story. Root and Bard (7) denervated the entire genital region in male cats without diminishing sexual aggressiveness. And Beach reports a transitory increase in number of copulatory attempts by castrated male rats, which he attributes to _failure_ of erection.

A second approach is to apply to sex behavior the hypothesis I have elsewhere proposed for appetites in general (9). Briefly, I suggested that a partly aroused consummatory response functions as a motive through the summating effect of impulses circulating in closed neural chains. Applied to the male rat, the theory would specify that stimuli from the receptive female would stir up incipient activity in some subcortical center (perhaps for what Beach calls the _ejaculatory mechanism_) and

that this would add _positive_ _feedback_ to the afferent discharge.

It seems plausible that two such mechanisms may
both contribute to sexual motivation under normal conditions.

(b) Beach describes two stages in normal sex behavior and proposes that each is controlled by a different mechanism until it reaches a critical threshold. I
accept his distinction, since it is borne out by evidence
of differential effects of surgery, previous experience,
and preceding ejaculations. I have one suggestion concerning terminology. If an _arousal_ _mechanism_ culmi-
nates in achieving a _copulatory_ _threshold,_ it would seem
more consistent to characterize the succeeding stage by
a _copulatory_ _mechanism_ and an _ejaculatory_ _threshold._
This revision has the added, and more important, advantage of leaving room for a third possible mechanism,
that of ejaculation itself. Beach leaves undecided the
question of whether copulation and ejaculation have
separate neural correlates, but, as we shall see, some
of his evidence implies indirectly that they do.

My main point is that in recognizing two such stages,
or three, we should not lose sight of their interdependence.
To what extent this integration depends on experience is
not known, but Beach shows clearly that experience plays
a part. The practiced rat that copulates immediately
gives much less evidence of separate mechanisms than
the novice. Before practice it is true that the copulatory
mechanism depends on arousal; but after practice, at
least, it is fair to say that arousal depends on the copulatory and even the ejaculatory mechanism, if we assume
both. I should go further and say that the second statement is true on the first occasion.

In terms of the theory of appetites discussed above,
the arousal mechanism includes fragments of the complete
copulatory act long before its threshold is reached. These
fragments are assumed to generate recurrent impulses

-34-

and thereby heighten the excitatory state. The role of the ascending reticular system, for which Beach argues cogently, may well be to provide the network necessary for this type of summation.

Two pieces of evidence cited by Beach suggest, if they do not establish, that later mechanisms are involved in the initial stages of sex behavior.

(i) After ejaculation the male rat shows no interest in the female for some minutes, indicating that the arousal mechanism is refractory. Repeated ejaculations increase the refractory period. Intromission alone does not have this effect but seems to excite rather than inhibit. We may infer a specific ejaculatory mechanism, the state of which exerts a decisive influence on sexual arousal.

(ii) Kagan (3) found that when male rats in a T-maze were rewarded for a correct choice by a chance to copulate but with ejaculation prevented, they showed some learning, but they also showed a progressive decrease in number of copulatory attempts. In one experiment they even deteriorated in maze performance. This finding is open to various interpretations, but it suggests the possibility that a partly aroused ejaculatory mechanism may exert a differential effect on behavior in advance of sexual contact.

(c) Beach has assembled the main facts to be explained by a theory of sexual exhaustion and recovery in the male rat. They are as follows:

(i) After "exhaustion," males gradually recovered libido over 15 days, as measured by decrease of initial latency, increase in number of ejaculations, decrease in number of intromissions to ejaculation, and other criteria.

(ii) In the course of free mating, length of refractory period increased from one ejaculation to the next.

-35-

(iii) Paradoxically, in the same situation the number of intromissions preceding each ejaculation decreased progressively.

Beach resolves the paradox by suggesting that ejaculation depresses the arousal mechanism at the same time that it lowers the ejaculatory threshold. He reports another finding that may be pertinent here: The number of intromissions required to reach ejaculation decreases with time between them to an optimal interval, after which it increases. If it were found that exhaustion went with longer intervals between successive intromissions, this might account for the observed changes in their number both within a single session and during recovery. Beach probably has data available for checking this possibility.

Without asking Dr. Beach's permission, I should like to incorporate some of his ideas in my theory--which is really Hebb's (2)--and try it out on his facts. In the fully potent male, I assume that through the arousal mechanism stimuli from the receptive female activate some part of the copulatory, and, to a less extent, the ejaculatory mechanism. These centers, together with the smooth and striped muscles they innervate, send back impulses to excite the arousal mechanism further. As the excitatory level rises, first the copulatory and finally the ejaculatory threshold is passed. Once the ejaculatory center fires, however, and becomes temporarily inactive, it is no longer a source of sustaining impulses. Meanwhile activity of the arousal mechanism has increased synaptic conductance so that incoming impulses quickly extinguish themselves by way of short closed chains. This process, corresponding to what Hebb calls "short-circuiting of the phase sequence" (2, p. 228), is proposed as a neural mechanism of adaptation or refractoriness. Only when the shorter chains again become less excitable can circular impulses summate until they involve the consummatory reflexes.

So much for the refractory period following a single

ejaculation. If these effects are cumulative, they will also account for the increasing length of successive refractory periods and for the prolonged sluggishness after repeated cycles. But what of the diminishing number of intromissions between successive ejaculations in a single session? Here I subscribe to Beach's notion of a lowered threshold; along with the increased conductance of the exciting circuits, I attribute it provisionally to Eccles's presynaptic potentiation (1). One fact the theory does not explain is that the same measure--number of intromissions before ejaculation--that decreases during a mating period does not increase progressively in the course of recovery, as we might expect. But if the theory explained everything, you would probably suspect it even more than you do.

In answer to Dr. Beach's unspoken challenge, I propose one experimental test of the hypothesis. Sexual "exhaustion," you will note, is attributed, not to fatigue, but to adaptation caused by increased transmission through short-circuiting devices in the arousal mechanism, a condition supposedly produced by excessive activity. It follows that if, after exhaustion, a male were given repeated opportunities to copulate without reaching the ejaculatory threshold, his recovery should be delayed. If, on the other hand, ejaculation could be artificially induced, it should have no effect on rate of recovery.

The empirical observation I promised to add was called to mind by Beach's comparison between orgasm and audiogenic seizure. I was reminded of the rage reactions that frequently occurred in male rats during my observations of fighting behavior (8). These, too, consisted of diffuse, stereotyped, convulsive movements. Especially noteworthy was the long refractory period after a battle. When an aggressive rat saw action once a day, even though he always won, he became less and less willing to attack. Psychoanalysts have taken account of the seizure-like character of the orgasm and the temper tantrum in interpreting epileptic reactions (see 4). Whether

the relationship is more than an interesting parallel is
a question deserving careful investigation.

References

1. Eccles, J. C. The Neurophysiological Basis of
    Mind. London: Oxford Univ. Press, 1953.

2. Hebb, D. O. The Organization of Behavior: A
    Neuropsychological Theory. New York: Wiley,
    1949.

3. Kagan, J. Differential reward value of incomplete
    and complete sexual behavior. J. comp. physiol.
    Psychol., 1955, 48, 59-64.

4. Kessler, C. R. A comparison of hostile verbal
    expression and incidence of convulsive seizures
    in a group of epileptic patients. Unpublished doc-
    tor's dissertation, Univ. S. Calif., 1951.

5. Miller, N. E. Learnable drives and rewards. In
    Stevens, S. S. (Ed.), Handbook of Experimental
    Psychology. New York: Wiley, 1951. Pp. 435-472.

6. Mowrer, O. H. Learning Theory and Personality
    Dynamics. New York: Ronald, 1950.

7. Root, W. S., and Bard, P. Erection in the cat
    following removal of lumbo-sacral segments. Amer.
    J. Physiol., 1937, 119, 392-393.

8. Seward, J. P. Aggressive behavior in the rat. J.
    comp. Psychol., 1945, 38, 175-197, 213-224, 225-
    238; 1946, 39, 51-76.

9. Seward, J. P. A neurological approach to motiva-
    tion. In Jones, Marshall R. (Ed.), Nebraska Sym-
    posium on Motivation 1956. Lincoln: Univ. Nebr.
    Press, 1956. P. 180.

COMMENTS ON PROFESSOR BEACH'S PAPER

by
Melvin Marx

Professor Beach has presented a most interesting
and impressive array of coordinated researches. It is
particularly instructive to learn of the complexity that
inheres even within the biologically based sex drive.
If this is a valid picture of what will develop as behavioral
analysis proceeds in what appear to be even more complex
drive functions, then it is difficult to see how the relatively simplified and unitary types of constructs that we have
been working with in learning and behavior theory will
be able to handle even the most rudimentary of analytic
data. The failure of neurophysiological analyses to
develop simple interpretations of such functions as sleep
and fatigue may also be noted in this respect. All of the
signs point to the necessity for behavior scientists to
recognize the need for opening up their vistas to include
more complex approaches to even the simplest of phenomena. This should not be taken to mean that they will
need to leave the theoretical-experimental attacks that
they have been pursuing. Rather they will need, I think,
to supplement their thinking with respect to the complexity
inherent in their presumably unitary constructs and to
express a greater willingness to leave some of the old
theoretical grooves. There has been, fortunately, considerable evidence of these changes within the past few
years.

To turn now to Beach's data, certain salient points
should be noted. His suggestion of two separate mechanisms in sexual behavior is especially promising. With
regard to this problem, several interesting questions
arise.

First, the data on exhaustion and recovery offer a
considerable stimulus to theoretical interpretations.
Within an experimental session, the number of intromissions to ejaculation becomes progressively less for suc-

cessive ejaculations, but the time necessary for recovery progressively increases. This contrast in results is suggestive of two interacting thresholds: an ejaculatory threshold, which shows a regular decrement (with regard to the number of intromissions measure, at least), and a copulatory threshold, which shows a regular increment. There seems to be a cumulative habituation or satiation effect on the arousal side--which fits in well with the evidence for the importance of learning in this respect-- and a cumulative sensitization on the consummatory side. One problem here concerns the intensity of the successive ejaculatory responses; as Beach noted, this has not been determined, but it seems rather unlikely that it would remain constant.

Second, there is a surprising contrast between the extensive sexual activity that occurs within a session and the long recovery period necessary (at least seven to ten days for the male rat) for maximal sexual arousal. This contrast is strongly suggestive of the great importance of proprioceptive cues ("warm-up"?) once aroused. Why recovery should require so long is a challenging question. The role of central brain-state functions and of hormonal factors requires experimental attack.

Third, there is an interesting suggestion of the phylogenetic encroachment of learning and external stimulus control on the ejaculatory mechanism itself, as one surveys the evidence from rat to cat. In the rat, the influence of learning seems to be restricted to the arousal mechanism. Male rats which run to receptive females but do not copulate are presumably in a state of emotionality comparable to that evident in animals which run to food but do not eat.

It is quite apparent that we need an experimental analysis of the underlying relationships between the two postulated mechanisms, or among the variety of measures that seem to represent two such mechanisms. What kind of commonality is there between the arousal and the consummatory parts of the male rat's sexual behavior?

Specifically, for example, do the hormones facilitate both phases of behavior? And what about the role of "drive" or motivational factors? Questions such as these are immediately suggested by Beach's presentation and require experimental answers.

One last comment might be made in relation to some of the interesting work that was mentioned in the discussion period with regard to the greater resistance to extinction produced by an empty goal box as compared to a male rat. One suggestion that might be made regards an analysis of the results in terms of associative factors. In a sexually experienced and sexually motivated male $\underline{S}$, responses to male and female rats have probably become clearly differentiated. That is, such an $\underline{S}$ has learned to ignore other male rats. Being placed in an empty box, however, has frequently been followed by the appearance of a receptive female. Thus it is not surprising that greater resistance to extinction should occur with the empty box.

I would like to see this experiment run with degree of learning in the male $\underline{S}$ as a variable. The prediction here is clearly that the obtained result would occur more readily as a function of greater sexual experience in the male $\underline{S}$.

BEHAVIOR AS "INTRINSICALLY" REGULATED: WORK NOTES TOWARDS A PRE-THEORY OF PHENOMENA CALLED "MOTIVATIONAL"

Sigmund Koch

Duke University

I.

As a student of what is called "theoretical methodology," I have for the past decade or so been progressively forced into the position of creating the grounds for my own technological unemployment. As a perfectionist, though, I find compromise values like partial retirement uncongenial. I am therefore delighted to report that I am beginning to find substantial grounds militating towards my unemployment as a student of what is <u>currently</u> called "motivation." My situation is not entirely without precedent. A long time ago, the philosopher Wittgenstein was forced to conclude, by virtue of relentless epistemological analysis, that the only proper course of philosophic action is silence. My own conception of retirement, however, is less astringent. Unfortunately, I will continue to talk.

In 1951, I violated the Wittgensteinian golden rule by publishing an article called "The Current Status of Motivational Psychology" (18). The thesis took more or less this form:

It was contended that the "chief pre-war theoretical programs were over-ambitious in scope, prematurely timed in relation to extant expirical knowledge ..." (p. 147). Psychology was seen to be undergoing a crisis of re-evaluation, prompted by recognition of such characteristics of the pre-war theoretical orthodoxies, and by other factors. It was felt that though such recognition of inadequacy was <u>in principle</u> salutary, the unhappy fact was that the <u>new</u> theoretical messages (resulting

from the post-war spasm of restlessness) in most cases
repeated, or even compounded, the inadequacies of the
synoptic pre-war theories.

The moral of such considerations did not sound
nearly so commonplace then, as it perhaps does now.
To wit:

> Psychology is not ready for high-order theory of any
> great range or predictive power. We lack basic areas
> of empirical knowledge of the sort necessary for ade-
> quate theory. We are even a long way from the reso-
> lution of many methodological problems, answers to
> which are crucial to adequate construction of theory.
> Contrary to certain of the stereotypes of the thirties
> and forties, we are not in a "Galilean era" of theoret-
> ical construction; we are closer to Thales than we
> are to Galileo. We are a science still groping for
> the identification of our own basic variables (18, p.148).

I proceeded to apply such considerations to the special
case of "motivational" theory by pointing to the very lush
profusion of conflicting motivational concepts and principles
characteristic of recent formulations, and dourly apposing
this bounty of words to the slim distribution and fragile
character of the experimental and observational "facts."

From all this, I concluded that psychology must face
the alternative -- drab to many -- "of working modestly
towards theory, " and that "in the area of motivation the
most important need is for a sharp acceleration of prog-
ess in the accumulation of 'theoretically neutral' empirical knowledge" (p. 149). The expression "theoretically
neutral" was explained as follows:

> There is good evidence to suggest that, at those points
> where the major theoretical programs have been in
> contact with empirical materials, there has been a
> growing convergence towards the identification, manip-
> ulation, and recording of common experimental vari-
> ables, both independent and dependent. Such common-

ly acknowledged experimental variables may be regarded as "theoretically neutral" and experiments designed to explore relations among such variables may be said to give "theoretically neutral" knowledge (18, p. 149).

As an initial gesture towards facilitating work in this direction, I then proceeded to construct a "'theoretically neutral' map" of empirical knowledge relevant to motivation which ordered extant work into five "problem clusters," in the way dear to the hearts of graduate students in search of relief from qualifying examination anxiety.

I have gone into this 1950 set of attitudes in such shameless detail only because I now want to cut back from what must have been a major implication of that position. The position suggests -- and I think I <u>believed</u> at that time -- that <u>somehow matters would improve as some kind of function of further work calculated to fill in the details of the map</u>. I stressed, of course, that such work was only "one of the preconditions to sound progress in a field like motivation," and I emphasized that such a map could be no more stable or determinate than was the terrain to which it was ordered. I now feel that I was still, five years ago, a residual victim of the period of heroic autism in theoretical psychology. I did <u>not</u> sufficiently call into question the possibility that no amount of research conducted within the terms of certain of the variables which have dominated "motivational" thinking, even so-called "theoretically neutral" ones, could carry us much closer to the solution of central problems relevant to the aims of psychology. In short, I was inconsistent with my contention that "we are a science still groping for the identification of our basic variables."

Most of the research of the past five years which, at least to me, provides insight into motivational phenomena, falls outside of my map, i.e., is concerned with identifying, or studying the effects of, empirical variables on which major theoretical programs of the recent past have by no means "converged." Furthermore, the very great increment of research which, in fact, has fallen <u>within</u> the terms of the map (and which, I am glad to say, would surely have taken place without any invitation from me) seems progressively to provide better grounds against any heuristic use of the map.

These are strong statements, and I shall not be the slightest bit disappointed if we ultimately find them to be overstatements. But there are times in science when strong talk provides the only wedge that can separate thinking from its cake of custom.

But let me -- at the risk of losing friends -- be honest from the start. When I question the adequacy of conventionally manipulated motivational variables to "central problems of our science," it is, in the first instance, scientific insight into <u>human</u> behavior that I have in mind. I regret having to confess this crass, middleaged foible, but it seems to me that questions concerning the actual and potential adequacy of research concepts to human phenomena are legitimate, even if entertaining them is contingent on the climacteric. My temerity is nourished by the fact that even certain fundamental psychologists have recently begun to dig into such murky human matters as the need for money, while current concern with the behavioral repercussions of <u>human</u> anxiety suggests that the rat's privacy has been vulgarly violated by many of his presumptive friends.

I am becoming increasingly impressed with the damage that has been wrought by the stereotype of science as some kind of inexorable bulldozer which carves out great, linear, ever-lengthening highways of truth. Science, like any other human activity product, is some function of a complex of rational and extra-rational factors. The kind of methodological and comparative theoretical analysis that has been fashionable for the past few decades -- painstaking or illuminating as it has occasionally been -- has often been rendered sterile or worse by its failure to challenge this stereotype with sufficient clarity. As a result, the

so-called "theories" or systematic formulations under
analysis have been given an importance -- a flavor of
historic grandeur -- which no set of ideas, no matter
how brilliant, can deserve in the present phase of our
science.

For such reasons, I would like to practice a different type of analysis in this paper -- a type of analysis
which I feel is badly needed. I would like to raise questions about the nature of the pretheoretical attitudinal
climate -- the orienting attitudes shared by human beings
towards the tasks and strategies of the science -- that
in some not too indirect way resulted in the selection
and concentration upon those variables which set the problems of motivational research today. I shall then attempt
to assess some of the requirements for a more adequate
treatment of certain of the problems and phenomena called
"motivational."

II.

I shall concentrate on some rather <u>general</u> aspects
of the attitudinal climate which has set the terms of
motivational research. The issues involved are terribly
obvious and are related to rather hoary contexts of discussion of the sort that carry a stale and corny flavor to
the modern streamlined sensibility. Nevertheless, it is
often such stale and corny issues which most require honest
re-examination when we face a scientific impasse. I refer
to attitudes having to do with <u>the significance of animal
research, and in general, the generalization range of molar
behavioral laws.</u>

Most of the independent variables which dominate recent motivational research were, in the first instance,
systematically explored, or even discriminated, within
the context of animal studies. I refer to such variables
as:

   1. "Primary drive strength" as varied by maintenance

schedule operations, by direct modification of internal "state" (e.g., hormones, drugs), or by direct presentation of drive-producing stimulation (e.g., shock).

2. Independently variable properties of "rewards" or goals as, e.g., amount, quality (on various unclassified dimensions such as preference value and appearance), and so on.

3. Variables defined in terms of a relation between drive and reward conditions, e.g., "appropriateness" of goal, "relevance" of goal to the prevailing drive conditions.

4. Variables defined in terms of a relation between the reward and coincident stimulus conditions (e.g., secondary reinforcers).

5. Variables which are some function of conditions which are believed to produce "acquired" or derived drives (e.g., pairing of a "neutral" stimulus with a pain-producing UC).

6. Variables which specify manipulable dimensions of variation in the <u>relations</u> between certain of the above <u>and</u> empirical conditions that are believed to govern non-motivational determinants of behavior (e.g., temporal and spatial relations between occurrence of S-R coincidences, or sign-significate, etc., sequences and <u>reward</u>; combinations and permutations of given numbers of repetitions of such behavior sequences, or varieties of such sequence, with various conditions of drive).

To some extent such variables are suggested by certain agreements -- common to major psychological theories of the modern period -- as to descriptive characteristics of all behavior, including human behavior. Thus there is widespread agreement that human behavior is ubiquitously -- or more or less so -- "purposive" or "goal-directed."

There is much evidence to suggest that organisms, including humans, "search" for various goal commodities; that organisms show restless and varied, often directed, behavior in their absence, and relative quiescence after some kind of functional interaction with such objects. Biological knowledge (and doctrine) and informal observation make it clear that many such "sought-after" objects are necessary conditions to survival, or have some other place in the adaptive economy. It becomes possible to discriminate such goal-directed sequences of behavior into orderly classes and to make guesses as to the kinds of causal system to which they conform. Let us not waste time on the details of the story: ultimately almost every major theorist of the modern period agrees that the facts of "goal-directedness" (and of behavior in general) must be handled in terms of postulating at least two major classes of internal behavior determinants -- a set of "structural," "habit," or "cognitive" arrangements, and a class of "dynamic," "motivational," or "driving" conditions.

For a time it was felt possible to make modest progress towards the immensely complex problem of sub-specifying each of these classes of determinants and working out their causal relations to various contexts of antecedent and consequent conditions, by observation and experimentation on human activity, and by comparative work at varied phyletic levels. Let us not forget, as the ethologists do, that during the first few decades of the present century we did have a "genuine" comparative psychology in America. (It is pleasant and reassuring to acknowledge that one of my colleagues in the present symposium has done much to encourage the revival of this tradition.)

Towards the end of the 'twenties, however, a great change was shaping up in the presystematic ideology of psychology. I have elsewhere (19) presented a clinical profile of this ideology. The keynote was that we were going to have "theory" in some strict, self-respecting, natural-science sense of the term, and we were going

-48-

to have it rapidly.   The only preconditions were:

1. to master some canonical technique of theory construction that philosophers of science had generously made avilable, and

2. to work intensively and carefully, in accordance with this canonical method, on populations of organisms having the following properties:

   a) The populations should derive from a pre-linguistic species.

   b) All populations should derive from the <u>same species</u>.

   c) The species should be "high" in the phyletic scale, preferably mammalian, but

   d) It must be readily available, fecund, have a short gestation cycle, be portable, disease-resistant, not too excitable, not unattractive, and easy to represent diagrammatically.

   Both proposals, as history developed, were fruitful in certain ways. Psychologists were no longer content with general and rather vague formulations concerning the functional determinants of behavior, couched in allusive language and tied down only casually to data.   Instead, by a combination of clever <u>a priori</u> guesses, and intensive systematic variations of the conditions of various rat behavior situations, they were able to differentiate and subspecify variables with a degree of specificity and detail that had not before been achieved. From the early 'thirties on, the Hulls, Tolmans, Skinners, and their followers, together with many other individuals working in the intellectual climate of the day, were able to reduce rat behavior <u>in a number of standard learning and performance situations</u> to remarkable predictability and even control.

   But such workers had another aim in mind.   They

-49-

were formulating <u>comprehensive theories of all behavior</u>.
In the words of Hull, they were forging formulations
which would ultimately be relevant to:

> the theory of skills and their acquisition; of com-
> municational symbolism or language (semantics);
> of the use of symbolism in individual problem solu-
> tion involving thought and reasoning; of social or
> ritualistic symbolism; of economic values and valu-
> ation; of moral values and valuation; of aesthetic
> values and valuation; of familial behavior; of indi-
> vidual adaptive efficiency (intelligence); of the formal
> educative processes; of psychogenic disorders; of
> social control and delinquency; of character and
> personality; of culture and acculturation; of magic
> and religious practices; of custom, law, and juris-
> prudence; of politics and government; and of many
> other specialized behavior fields (15, p. 399).

Now it is important to be fair. Every major theorist
owned a bilaterally symmetrical mouth, the two sides of
which could function independently. There were frequent
protestations of tentativeness and modesty in the theorists
of this day -- but the object of such tentativeness was more
often the concrete <u>results</u> of the theoretical programs in
question than the <u>methods and metatheory</u> which generated
the results.

In this atmosphere, there flourished a certain curious
attitude about the significance of animal (and, in particular,
rat) results for the understanding of human behavior. Let
us examine this attitude in various of its forms.

Here is the Tolman version:

> Let me close, now, with a final confession of faith.
> I believe that everything important in psychology
> (except perhaps such matters as the building up of
> a superego, that is everything save such matters
> as involve society and words) can be investigated
> in essence through the continued experimental and

theoretical analysis of the determiners of rat behavior at a choice point in a maze. Herein I believe I agree with Professor Hull and also with
Professor Thorndike (32, p. 34).

Let me note, not with malice, but in order to convey
the flavor of the period, that there is some indication of
the independent variability of the two sides of the author's
mouth in the parenthetical expression about the "superego"
and "society," and in the use of such qualifiers as "everything important" and "can be investigated in essence."
The Tolman of this period, however, did not show a comparable ambivalence in his theoretical behavior; nor was
it likely that many of the properly tough-minded fundamental psychologists of the time even noted the above
parenthetical asides and qualifications.

No comparably pithy statement of the position is to
be found in Hull -- largely, I suspect, because he was
reluctant to consider questions having to do with the
generality of the "constants" in his equations until relatively late in his career. However, at the end of a book
presenting a set of molar behavioral principles which
are based in the most painstaking way on the ordinal and
quantitative details of rat experimentation, Hull finds it
possible to say:

> The main concern of this work has been to isolate
> and present the primary or basic principles or laws
> of behavior as they appear in the current state of
> behavioral knowledge; at present there have been
> isolated sixteen such principles. In so far as these
> principles or postulates are sound and sufficient, it
> should be possible to deduce from them an extensive
> logical hierarchy of secondary principles which will
> exactly parallel all of the objectively observable
> phenomena of the behavior of higher organisms; such
> a hierarchy would constitute a systematic theory of
> all the social sciences (15, p. 398).

Three years later, in the article, "The Place of Innate

Individual and Species Differences in a Natural Science Theory of Behavior" (16), Hull <u>did</u> make it clear that he intended to handle such differences in terms of differing values of the constants in his equations. As we shall see in a moment, at a still later phase of his career, he made further concessions to the possible quiddities of behavioral data.

In general terms, the Hull-Tolman (etc.) Golden Age attitude towards the significance of rat research for psychological theory can be roughly rendered in some such terms as these:

Lawful relations between selected aspects of rat behavior and selected antecedent conditions, constructed on the basis of rat data competently developed in a limited variety of experimental behavior situations deemed fundamental, can be expected to hold ----- over a wide but unspecified segment of the phylogenetic scale sometimes referred to as "higher mammals" or "higher organisms," but more frequently referred unqualifiedly to "all . . . behavior." Depending upon such factors as phase of career, momentary mood, etc., different "clauses" indicative of differing confidence levels might be substituted for the dashes in the above expression. The "strong clause" version would maintain that such rat laws could be transposed in full quantitative detail. The "weak clause" version would maintain that the <u>general form</u> of the function was transposable, while leaving open the possibility that certain constant parameters might vary. Note further that the general position also maintained that not only were such laws transposable in the above senses but that it was possible in principle, with a sufficient number of theoretical statements derived from such sources, to account for <u>all</u> (Hull) or at least the <u>important</u> (Tolman) characteristics of the behavior of a species like man.

Now if there is anyone in this audience who was sceptical when I alluded to the possibility of extra-rational elements in science, I wonder if he can continue to nourish his doubt in the face of this. At the present late date in history, it is hardly necessary to evaluate the rationality of the above attitudes. Those who have followed the course of rat research for the past decade know that there are very few contexts in which we can be confident of the generality of behavioral relationships of reasonable specificity, even in two different populations of academic rats, particularly if they are matriculating at different universities. If this seems too cynical, collect the poignant (frequently unpublished) experiences of those who at some time have conducted "replication" experiments.

I need not add, among this group of sophisticates, that often such failure of intra-species generality, even in the case of "low-order" empirical relationships, occurs in the context of highly standardized, intensively used experimental techniques -- not only the maze and discrimination box, but even the Skinner box and the straight runway. We are all sensitized to the circumstance that "results" are contingent on "the operations" and "the conditions," but are we uniformly prepared to anticipate that many of the relevant "operations" and "conditions" have not been discriminated even in frequently used standard situations?

Nor can we console ourselves by assuming that such non-discriminated variables will usually affect "absolute values" only, leaving our pure Platonic "function forms" unimpaired; they can just as easily alter obtained functional relationships. For instance, several years ago, one of my students (26) discovered that the functional relation between so simple a dependent variable as "operant level" and "hunger" varies in the Yale form of the Skinner box for two different lever sizes. Nothing astounding about this, except that any "fundamental law" of hunger drive as an "energizer" of operant level would be badly embarrassed by one or the other of these levers.

May I add that I do not wish to be merely maudlin about all this, but as well to be constructive. It is a crying shame that no one has directly confronted either the logic or the empirical questions concerning the gen-

-53-

eralization ranges over which behavioral relationships, having given specificity levels (and other formal features), can be rationally expected to hold. We will not have escaped from the age of autism until such questions are squarely faced.

Be all the above as it may, it is past history. Few believe any longer that _all,_ or even the _essential_ laws of human behavior are going to get generated, even in qualitative form, from rat data or even infra-human data in general. What _are_ the beliefs, insofar as they materially differ from the attitudes discussed above? I would say that they fall into two main classes, as entertained respectively by people who might be designated "formalists" and "gradualists."

The Hull of the _1951_ theory (17) was veering toward formalism. As I have tried to show in a recent analysis (20), there were in 1951 widespread alterations in the "tone" of Hull's theory language in the direction of "increased localism." This is represented by the frequent occurrence of highly specific expressions and "situational" references in presumably general behavioral postulates. The postulates of the 1951 theory (Essentials of Behavior), for instance, no longer relate variables of complete and hygienic universality as did the postulates of _Principles of Behavior._ They talk about the "weight of food given as reinforcement," rather than "magnitude of need reduction," and "at least some drive conditions," or sometimes just plain "hunger," rather than "drive" in general. They talk also about "the work (W) . . . involved in operating the manipulandum" (of a modified Skinner box) instead of "work" in general; indeed, what used to be the "amplitude (A) of response mediated by the autonomic nervous system" or even ordinary, unqualified "amplitude of reaction" is now "the Tarchanoff galvanic skin reaction amplitude." As an example of some kind of extreme in localism for this or any other theory, we cite Hull's "preliminary suggestion" for the definition of the basic quantitative unit of the system, the wat:

The wat is the mean standard deviation of the momentary reaction potential ($_s\overline{E}_R$) of standard albino
rats, 90 days of age, learning a simple manipulative
act requiring a 10 gram pressure by 24-hour distrib-
uted trials under 23 hours' hunger, water available,
with reward in the form of a 2.5-gram pellet of the
usual dry dog food, the mean being taken from all
the reinforcement trials producing the habit strength
from .75 to .85 habs inclusive (17, p. 100).

In other words, Hull seems to be saying at this time
that (a) his theory was limited in scope, that (b) it was
restricted to certain aspects of the behavior of the white
rat, and even possibly (or at least sometimes) (c) that
these aspects were so limited as to be coextensive with
the details of the single calibration experiment utilized
for the quantification of $_sE_R$ in the new formulation. But
even at this time, Hull was an inconsistent formalist,
because the localism of the 1951 theory language, while
conspicuous, is uneven; certain of the variables are represented with the same unbridled generality as before.

Perhaps the elder statesman, part-time formalist
in the Hullian camp had been Spence, who frequently in
the late 'thirties and the 'forties had referred the range
of application of his version of reinforcement theory to
rat data, but did not consistently make such a referral.

Pure formalism, of course, is currently represented
by certain of the explicity limited-scope "modelists" of
rat behavior who regard any question about the inter-species
transposability of their principles as vulgar. As compared
with the excesses of the past, this is an entirely impeccable
attitude, even when refreshingly violated by a statement
such as the following, which I find in Estes's Annual Review
survey of learning:

A very recent development is the vigorous extension
of these concepts (S-R reinforcement concepts) to
human learning. Doubtless no one expects all phenomena of human learning to yield to this type of analysis:

but surprising success has attended efforts to re-
produce the better established laws of animal learning with human S's, both child and adult, under suit-
ably simplified conditions (7, p. 33).

The above slight deviation from Estes's ordinarily
sober wont shades over into the attitude of gradualism --
in essence, the program of exploiting the well known
superior controllability, operability, portability, etc.,
of our intrepid "high-order mammal" as a source for the
identification of behavioral variables and functions, in the
hope that certain of the variables or certain of the functions, or both, will prove extensible to human behavior,
but with full anticipation of the possibility that such variables and functions will require supplementation, modification, realignment, possibly in fundamental ways. It
is possible that people like Miller and Dollard could be
edged into this category, since they have long toyed with
human behavior only in terms of the most abstract and
"deparametricized" rat reinforcement principles and, I
suspect, have often worked out the rat details of mechanisms suggested by human behavior only, as it were, to
reassure themselves. Unquestionably, those of the current cognitive theorists who prefer the rat (from Tolman
on down) fall into this group. Certainly people like Lashley
Hebb, Harlow, Beach, Nissen, and all workers who pride
themselves on being "genuinely" comparative fall into this
category, if we may depart for a moment from exclusive
fanciers of the rat.

There is another rationale for intensive concentration
on the rat, or on a few infra-human species, which makes
very sound sense -- at least up to a point. A cultural
historian, looking over the work of the past several decades
would be likely to render its spirit in some such terms as
the following:

Were the behavior theorists of the 'thirties and 'forties
in any definite sense of the term, actualizing their grandios
programs for a comprehensive theory of behavior? The
answer is clearly "no." The frequent explicit statements

-56-

of such aims were largely an affective superstructure
which reflected and bred enthusiasm -- but, unfortunately,
conviction, too. These men, in reality, were feeling
out the prospects for arriving at systematic formulations
of behavior in perhaps more concrete and sharper terms
than had hitherto been attempted. The major recent behavior "theories" may best be regarded as explorations --
mislabeled but honest -- of the preliminary issues which must
precede the preliminary assessment of a class of moot
hypotheses to the effect that it may be possible to make
systematic statements about behavior which are similar
to "successful" systematic statements about non-behavioral
natural events, in such-and-such specified respects. In
line with this (as is now well known), alternate types of
variables -- both empirical and explanatory -- were tried
out; various experimental arrangements were tried out as
induction bases for guesses after construct relations; various techniques for the construction and quantitative specification of function forms were assayed, as were techniques for the measurement of independent and dependent
variables. In brief, then, these "theorists" were trying
to grope their way towards an answer to the complex
methodological and strategic question: how to construct
stable, predictive laws of behavior.

For purposes of this sort, it is clearly rational to
believe that the intensive, systematic study of the behavior -- or even selected aspects of the behavior -- of
one or a few species is adequate as a start. If we regard the rat, then, as a possibly useful source of information about the potentialities of various pre-systematic
guesses concerning the strategy and tactics for the analysis of behavior, the use to which he has been put by behavior theorists becomes eminently reasonable. I suspect that the formalists have some such rationale in mind,
even if they would regard it as a bit "Girl-Guidish" to
verbalize such things. And, of course, the gradualists --
even those who have a number of other things in mind as
well -- would certainly assent to such a position.

Now, a few years ago, I would have been perfectly

happy to refer my hours in the rat laboratory to some
such rationale. I can still see the justification of such
hours on this and other bases -- but not with the same
equanimity. For the possibility must be faced that the
putting of questions in the strategy and logic of general
behavior analysis to rats can settle few such questions
except for rats. Certainly, the recent development of
systematic psychology does not provide much evidence
to the contrary. Furthermore, as comparative psychologists have long emphasized, it is even possible that
staying on the rat level in and for the solution of such
questions with respect to rats can mislead us -- even
with respect to rats.

Now our entire discussion of attitudes towards the
significance of animal research has been a series of
caricatures. People are obviously more complex than
their occasional statements, or even than the complexity
of my two-sentence characterizations of them. And I
have not essayed even an exhaustive assemblage of caricatures -- I have omitted, for instance, the thoroughly
meaningful and satisfactory rationale of the physiological
psychologists and zoologists in their use of animal subjects.

Further, each link in my chain of caricatures has
been thoroughly obvious and perhaps not worthy of reconstruction. Yet it is the present and recent temper of
fundamental psychology which must take part of the blame
for all this triviality and dullness. For it has been necessary for me to establish something that you might not have
initially granted -- namely, that neither in underlying
logic nor in actual accomplishment has the animal research
per se provided very much insight into problems of human
behavior in general, and human motivation in particular.
No one can deny that the animal research has set the terms
of the problems and determined many of the variables.
But the status of rat laws of motivation and the character
of the empirical variables on which they are based are not,
with respect to such criteria as trans-situational generality
(and others), such as to hold out much hope, even for the

rat. And, more particularly, the gap between the rat variables and human behavior is bridged only by the thinnest of autisms.

I am therefore going to commit a final and incorrigible lewdness. I am going to assess certain of the broad requirements for analyses of human motivation by examining human motivational phenomena. Insofar as may be possible, I am going to try, at least initially, to forget the rat variables.

Furthermore, I will not be ashamed to consult the phenomena of human experience as well as human behavior. To those who would not agree that a re-analysis of behaviorist epistemology is badly needed, I would indicate that I will be describing phenomena which create explanatory problems for theory, not formulating theory. To those who still insist that I cannot use experiential or phenomenal language of the sort which constitutes the coin of ordinary human communication even as data language, I need only reply that such language is, according to the best empiricist scripture, reducible in principle to an objectivistic definition base.

III.

We have argued that the detailed and sub-specified variables that have functioned in recent speculation about motivation have derived from the animal research; as we already implied, this is not the case with regard to certain general properties and functions assigned to "motivational" variables in many of the "theories" of the modern period. Such general acknowledgments as, e.g., the ubiquitous "goal-directedness" of molar behavior, the guess that there must be special systems of intraorganismic events which are responsible for certain observable characteristics of various classes of goal-directedness, the guess that given instances of goal-directedness may be analyzable into underlying "knowledge" or steering variables and "goal-setting" or driving variables -- such guesses have historically derived from the survey of a very wide range of evidence, including, and in the first instance, human evidence. The history of motivational theory, in some sense of the term, is very old indeed.

Now, this is not the place for a long-range excursion into the history of ideas, but it will be useful to make some rash generalizations as to the derivation of certain of our general motivational notions.

It is often not sufficiently held in mind that psychology does not start with neutral and unmanipulated data, but that the conditions of human life are such as to force us to entertain theories of ourselves. These "theories of ourselves" -- the syntax of which we seldom explore -- are often, to the extent that they are acknowledged, allocated to "common sense" or "practical life" or some such limbo and then forgotten. What is not acknowledged is that such theory itself constitutes a most abstract and epistemologically complex ordering of the data of experience and behavior. What is truly remarkable is the degree of success that has attended such naive theoretical effort, despite evident imperfections. Nevertheless, one aim of psychological science must, by definition, be at least ultimately to supplant such "theory" with better theory. In the light of this, it seems surprising that much psychological theory -- unwittingly, as it were -- seems to carry over certain of the postulates of our "theories of ourselves" without even subjecting them to rational question. Once carried over, of course, the possibility that such "postulates" will ever be subjected to rational question diminishes as a function of the walls which are erected between "scientific" knowledge and its human origin -- particularly such walls as result from concentration on non-human problems. I should like as my central theme to consider the possibility that some such thing has taken place in our "scientific" phrasing of motivational phenomena.

I would like to suggest, in other words, the possibility that at some point in our scientific thinking about motivational phenomena -- perhaps an early and fundamental point -- we have been markedly misled by certain ancient and deeply rigidified common characteristics of "our theories of ourselves." At least in Western culture, the dominant theme in such common-sense theorizing has for a long time been a <u>certain kind of rough-and-ready instrumentalism, such that we believe ourselves to be "doing things" for certain specifiable ends.</u> <u>These ends are phrased as extrinsic to the given context of "doing," and in practical life are specified variably and usually grossly in terms that suggest the ends to be pleasure-producing, "goods"- or "advantages"-increasing, irritant-removing, pain-decreasing, comfort-increasing, rest-producing, or whatnot.</u>

The central predictive and "explanatory" relation in this common-sense theory is "in order to," and the uniform presumption is that behavior is made predictable and intelligible when the form "X does Y in order to ---" is completed. In a very large number of instances in practical life it is possible to fill in this form in a predictively useful way. Often, however, a readily identifiable referent for the end-term is not available. In such cases we assume that the form must hold, and so we hypothesize or invent an end-term which may or may not turn out to be predictively trivial and empty. For instance, X does Y in order to be happy, punish himself, be peaceful, potent, respected, titillated, excited, to be mischievious, playful, or wise.

Now I submit that, in the long historical view, "technical" speculation about motivation, whether in ethics, philosophy, or psychology, has been intimately bound up with this "common-sense" extrinsic theory. In the broadest sense, the history of motivational "theory" has involved such procedures as the following:

1. The classification of such extrinsic ends into orderly classes, which are then taken as evidence for the assumption of corresponding "end-determining" systems called desires, motives,

-61-

urges, wishes, wants, needs, instincts, demands, drives, or whatnot.

2. The specification, usually in terms of a loose metaphor, of some canonical type of causal system (or model) to which the "functional properties" of all motives must conform (e.g., deficit-replacement, tension-reduction, equilibrium-restoral, homeostasis, quiescence-restoral, drive-reduction). I might add that usually the terminology and mystique built up around such a metaphor is far more impressive than are its rather primitive logical and substantive properties.

3. (Closely interrelated with 2.) The attempt to find some common, highly abstract property (or properties) of such extrinsic ends, which can serve as "criterial" conditions or "end-state" characteristics of the proposed causal system. The preference is for achieving generality by discriminating the smallest possible number of such properties: e.g., pleasure, pain, satisfaction-annoyance, tension release, quiescence, or drive-stimulus diminution. The selection of such properties usually depends on a loose analogy which involves reading the requirements of the proposed causal model into the array of given "extrinsic ends."

4. In many cases, the attempt to discriminate the end-classes (or motives), as described in 1. above, into groups such that a given group can be regarded as fundamental in some sense (usually genetically given or primary), while others are regarded as derivative. The attempt, further, to "recompose" the characteristics of the derivative class from the properties of the causal model discriminated in 2. above, together with assumptions about the conditions of learning.

The dependence of the ultimate theoretical superstructures which result from such procedures on the "common-sense" theory is revealed by the fact that all such scientific formulations ultimately agree or imply that the "unit" of molar behavior is defined in terms of "in-order-to" relations: the "mark" of molar behavior is its "goal-directedness" or, what amounts to the same thing, all behavior is extrinsically <u>motivated</u>.

Now it has occasionally come to the notice of scientific thinkers that there are cases in which X does Y, but no readily identifiable "extrinsic end" may be found. We already saw that this difficulty confronts the common-sense theory, and thus there is no reason to expect that motivational scientists will be exempt from it. The scientists tend to handle such "apparent" exceptions with comparable fluency. Here are some of the possibilities:

1. The behavior Y tends to be energized by some motive other than the one it usually accompanies. On the occasion in question, the extrinsic end of behavior Y is the extrinsic end of this other motive. One theory would call this "irrelevant drive." Others would postulate more specific substitutional relations among motives.

2. The behavior Y belongs to a larger context of behavior which is relevantly motivated. When that context is identified, the relevant motive and "extrinsic end" will be revealed.

3. A motive corresponding to the specific descriptive properties of the behavior Y is postulated; and an appropriate "extrinsic end-state" is likewise postulated -- e.g., "exploratory drive" and its satiation, "curiosity drive" and its satisfaction.

4. The behavior Y is said to lead to an extrinsic end-state of the sort discriminated by the theory, but that end-state is not, for various reasons, readily observable, and is mediated by an object with extrinsic-end properties derivative from historically prior, unambiguously observable extrinsic ends.

Some mechanism of learning is usually specified
to account for such "derivative" extrinsic ends,
as e. g., the principle of secondary reinforcement,
sub-goal learning, equivalence beliefs, secondary
cathexis.

5. The behavior Y is said to lead to an extrinsic end-
    state which is not observable but which is postu-
    lated as appropriate to a motive that is genetically
    related to other motives assigned to behaviors whose
    extrinsic ends are identificable. Again a suitable
    learning mechanism is specified, and we are in
    possession of a "theory" of "acquired" or "learned"
    or "second-order" motivation.

6. The behavior Y is said to lead to no extrinsic end
    of any sort. It is a genuine, rather than an ap-
    parent, exception to the assumption that all be-
    havior is related to extrinsic ends, or is motivat-
    ed. Such cases are sometimes made to appear
    as lawful exceptions by a principle of "the trans-
    formation of mechanisms into drives" or "func-
    tional autonomy. "

Observe what has happened. These scientific theories
began with the common-sense assumption of universal
"extrinsic" motivation. But, curiously enough, one gets
the impression that most of the energy of the theorists
has gone into devising clever accounts for the exceptions
to this assumption. No matter how specific the analysis
of these exceptions becomes, no matter how ingenious,
no matter how firmly pinned to the details of animal data,
the feeling is inescapable that this line of development can
only make the theories in question more arbitrary and forced.
Could it perhaps make sense to return to the world of human
phenomena and ask a few terribly elementary questions?

IV.

When fundamental psychologists do make excursions

into the human motivational world, they tend to concern
themselves with such mammoth generalizations as the
need for money, the achievement need, prestige, affection. Or they may note -- with some awe -- that human
beings crave knowledge, stimulation, excitement, roller-
coaster rides. It is rare that they survey the requirements for theory or pre-theory by intensive descriptive
analysis of behavior related to such motives as produced
by concrete human beings. More remote still is the chance
that anyone will select for illustration, let alone analysis,
behavior or experience relevant to man in his most characteristically human performances: man as he creates or
loves or plays or responds to the aesthetic surfaces of the
human and natural environment. Such matters are threat-
eningly complex, and besides -- as a predecessor at a former Nebraska Symposium has phrased it -- "Part of the
motivation behind this attitude may stem from a desire to
elevate man to a unique, emergent position on the phylogenetic scale. Biological drives are regarded as too crass
for an organism as noble as man" (2, p. 1).

Despite this portentious warning, let me present a
few observations about a type of "motivation" that is of
some importance to a person I know well. These observations concern "creative" behavior, insofar as this ad-
jective is applicable to such frantic performances as may
occasionally result in a pedestrian professional article.

With respect to creative work or intellectual work of
any degree of complexity, I cannot distinguish any continuum
of differential motivational "strength." All I can succeed
in doing is roughly to distinguish two qualitatively different
"states." This distinction may be "all or none," or it could
conceivably be argued that there are two qualitatively different intensity continua, each of rather small compass. Call
these states "A" and "B." Specific dated occurrences of
these states may, of course, vary in activity content and
in temporal spread. The temporal unit may be a matter of
a few hours to a few weeks. In making the following observations, I have in mind selected characteristics of relatively
long-range A and B states.

State A

I am distractable, flighty, self-prepossessed, rueful
over the course of my life and the value choices it has
entailed. I feel depressed, continually drowsy, guilty
about my purposelessness and general ineffectiveness.
The world is a flaccid structure of neutral tone and value.
My responses towards people are bumbling, inert, ineffective, rejective. There is evidence to suggest that I
am unpleasant to live with. My self-image constricts into
a small, desiccated thing: I am physically unattractive,
devoid of color, wit, or style. An enormous distance seems
to supervene between myself and my most prized values.
I am aesthetically desensitized (relative to my image of
myself); my system of tastes becomes cheapened and more
tolerant.

State A, though partially and casually described here,
is a system predicated of and involving the entire person.
And the "consequent" of the state which is now the object
of interest -- performance, with reference to a specified
context of creative and intellectual work -- is but another
part of the same "system."

Under conditions of State A, creative or complex intellectual activity is first of all unlikely. Unfortunately,
the conditions of life are such as frequently to demand that
it occur. These "conditions" may be endogenously defined
as, e.g., guilt, anxiety, or they may be pressures deriving
from external agencies, e.g., deadlines, teaching obligations.
Either of these classes of conditions can be characterized,
if we follow conventional motivational logic, as defining
extrinsic contexts for the performances that are called for.
In other words, if such conditions are effective, then I will
be working in order to relieve guilt, meet a deadline, get
a promotion, please a friend. What is the performance like
under these circumstances?

I rapidly pass over the fact that under such pressures
one passes through innumerable resistances, escape detours,
rationalizations, before getting into the problem situation.

-66-

One may finally "get" or be impelled into the problem situation, but one never, as it were, "gets committed." Thinking is slow, rigid, disorganized, formless, and inelegant. Memory tends towards the "rote" and is saturated with spotty amnesia. Verbalization and writing is unfluent, stilted, imprecise, turgid -- either overliteral or overallusive -- devoid of wit or flavor. Reading is slow, with much backtracking. The absolute ceiling with respect to the apprehension of complex relationships, the perception of subtle similarities and differences and of meaning nuances, the ability to filter the thought sequence through a complex assemblage of constraints -- becomes suffocatingly low.

The unhappy fact about State A, at least for me, is that no manipulation of "extrinsic" conditions, or augmentation in the strength thereof, seems to improve matters much. One remains a prisoner to State A until it runs its course.

State B

Like State A, State B also constitutes a quite specific syndrome. It can be partly characterized as exhibiting the opposite (in some sense) of many of the properties that we attributed to State A. To the extent that this is true, I shall spare you the details.

The central and decisive "mark" of State B is domination of the person by the problem context, or, better, by a certain direction defined by the problem context -- a "diffuse" but absolutely compelling direction. All systems of personality seem "polarized" into the behavior; thus the personality is either integrated or, in a special sense, simplified, as you will. In State B, you do not merely "work at" or "on" the task; you have committed yourself to the task, and in some sense you are the task, or vice versa.

Perhaps one of the most remarkable properties of B is that thoughts relevant to the problem context seem to well up with no apparent effort. They merely present themselves. The spontaneity and fluency of ideation and the freedom from customary blockages seem similar to certain characteristics of the dream or certain states of near dissociation. As in these latter conditions, it is often difficult to "fix," hold in mind, the thoughts which occur. In fact, in State B, most of the "effortfulness" or "strain" encountered has to do not with the generation of ideas relevant to the problem context but with their decoding, fixing, or verbalization, and their selection and assemblage with respect to socially standardized requirements of communication. Effortful as such operations may be, verbalization, writing, reading, and all functionally significant breakdowns thereof are at a qualitatively different level from the A state of affairs.

Subtle and organized descriptive phenomenologies of B states are badly needed by science -- but not from individuals whose B-state products are "creative" only by extravagant metaphor. I wish merely to list a few additional properties of B states, and in some cases contrast them with the dismal state of affairs in A.

1. The B state carries with it tremendous tolerance for fatigue. One can work eight, ten, fourteen hours continuously with no marked subjective fatigue and no evidence of impairment of performance. (In A, two or three hours can be unbearably tiring.) Curiously enough, there seem to be two occasions in the B sequence of a given day when the spontaneous emergence of ideas (the "it thinks" phenomenon) is at a maximum. One is shortly after awakening -- even from a sleep produced by strong sedation. (In A, on the other hand, not an engram begins to twitch until late in the afternoon.) The other occasion is towards the very end of the work sequence, either during its terminal phase, or while preparing for, or falling, asleep. I might add that the ideas which present themselves on these occasions tend to be, in some sense, the most organized, the most relevant to the problem context,

of any in the entire pedestrian array of a given day.

2. It may be of some relevance to note that, in addition to suppression of fatigue, there is marked suppression of hunger and certain other so-called primary drive conditions. The need for alcohol also decreases markedly.

3. The primary affect-tone of State B is that of mild to strong euphoria. One feels energized but peaceful. Anxiety, in any reportable sense of the term, is minimal or non-existent. In fact, in my experience, one of the essential pre-conditions (onset conditions) of B is that anxiety be at a minimal level. Should some external or internal factor produce anxiety during B, then most characteristics of the state of the sort specified above become disrupted to an extent commensurable with the amount of anxiety.

4. During State B, any conditions, whether they arise from the environment or from the self, which define an extrinsic context to which the performance is seen as related, tend to produce disruption of B -- a deviation of B towards the A state of affairs. Any factor, that is, that leads to an "in-order-to" consideration, that brackets the work on the task as instrumental to success or accomplishment or a raise or relaxation, will tend to throw the B state, in specifiable respects, towards A and will disrupt or impair the performance. Any anticipation of, or speculation about, the consequences to which the finished work might lead -- praise, reproof, understanding, misunderstanding, acceptance, rejection -- will also vitiate the performance. I am sorry if the entelechy that organizes my B states seems like a Boy Scout, but I suspect that there are such Boy Scouts in us all.

Now I am not asking of any current theory -- or scientific mode of phrasing motivational relationships -- that it in some sense "explain" A and B states. If that is a reasonable request, even in principle, it is a request for the very distant future. I am merely indicating that such things as B or B-ish states occur, that they are important to the life of man, that they are instances of behavior in its most organized, "energized," "motivated" form. It is not too much to demand that psychological theories do not talk a language the grammar of which is incompatible with the recognition, or even acknowledgment, of B states. Are the foundation assumptions of most "theories" of motivation such that they will at least allow "B-ish" phenomena to take place?

I do not see how we can escape a negative verdict with respect to this question. One cannot say very much at present that reduces B phenomena to scientific order, but the one thing clearly definitive of B is that the attendant problem-solving behavior is intrinsically regulated and maintained, i.e., maintained by the intrinsic "laws" of its own context. We can only set the B performance into an "in-order-to" context by violating the descriptive characteristics of the phenomena -- by converting it essentially into a case of State A behavior.

To the extent that State B performance is regarded as instrumental to a context defined by some other need or manifold of such (e.g., approval, prestige, dominance, achievement), this not only is to run a danger of introducing empty verbalisms, but is also to distort violently the character of the phenomena. To maintain that B performance is motivated by "curiosity" or "need to know" or "exploration" or "creativity" is merely to assert that B occurs, and then to provide an artificial extrinsic context for the assertion. To assert that B behavior is a superstructure motivated and triggered by anxiety is to assert that a central condition for the non-occurrence of B is a condition for its occurrence. To assert that B behavior is a multiplicative function of $_sH_R$ and a pooled D value, representing the contributions of all contemporaneously active primary and/or acquired drives, is to assert nothing.

The conclusion seems inescapable that B performance is in fundamental respects intrinsically determined within the conditions of its own context, that it is self-regulated, self-determining, self-motivated, self-energizing, and, unfortunately, self-liquidating.

V.

Creative or pseudo-creative behavior, of course, may represent a very special case. Views which stress the discontinuity of "creative" and ordinary behavior may, after all, be correct. Perhaps they are discontinuous in most respects, but it may at least be legitimate to question this in certain respects. Let us ask this question: During our purposive, goal-directed, adaptive, drive-reducing, striving day, what is the frequency of behavior instances which do not, in any clear-cut and obvious way, fall into an "in-order-to" context of the sort demanded by conventional motivational "logic"? I shall proceed to return this question in slightly expanded form.

How much of our day do we find ourselves "doodling," tapping out rhythms, being the owners of perseverating melodies, nonsense rhymes, "irrelevant" memory episodes? How much of our day do we spend noting the attractiveness of a woman, the fetching quality of a small child, the charm of a shadow pattern on the wall, the loveliness of a familiar object in a particular distribution of light; looking at the picture over our desk, or out of the window; feeling disturbed at someone's tie, repelled by a face, entranced by a voice? How much of our day is given to wondering why a friend looks sad, to the telling of jokes, to idle conversation? How much of the day do we spend reading novels, poetry, comic strips; listening to hi-fi, going to concerts, theatres, movies? How much of the day do we spend taking photographs, riding in fast open cars, sketching, playing the piano, adjusting the wrong position of a picture or a vase, gardening, doing woodwork, playing chess, charades, tennis, bridge, fishing, luxuriating near a fireplace?

A great deal of what we do falls into no obvious "in-order-to" context, unless, in some variable degree, we force matters by exploiting the ever-available flexibility of everyday or theoretical language. It may give us some degree of comfort to complete "in-order-to" forms for such behaviors with constructions like "have fun," "get stimulated," "derive pleasure," "relax," "satisfy play or aesthetic needs" -- but such constructions can give us little _more_ than comfort.

It cannot be denied, of course, that conventional motivational grammar can make sense in certain of these cases, depending on the concrete circumstances in which specific instances of such behaviors occur. For instance: I _can_ be fishing "in order to" carry out the doctor's orders, i.e.; in order to get well. I can be "suffering" the memorial re-enactment of some idiotic movie "in order to" crowd out, i.e., reduce, anxiety or "in order to" fall asleep. I _can_ be riding in a fast open car "in order to" get to the grocer's "in order to" satisfy hunger. I _can_ be in State B "in order to" advance my career, "in order to" reduce "tension" associated with long-term bafflement, "in order to" subserve self-actualizing or perhaps self-destructive needs. As we made plain early in the discussion, the motivational grammar of "common sense" has been very successful in its long history of mediating practical predictions. To the _extent_ that it has, it must reflect _something_ within the structure of experience and behavior. Because of this, sophisticated _technical_ elaborations of the "common-sense" grammar can seem even more compelling.

Now the relation between "extrinsic" and "intrinsic" determinants of behavior -- or, rather, these two modes of talk about the causal conditions of behavior -- constitute perhaps the most difficult problem in a metatheory of motivation. We are very far from a solution to such matters for a very simple reason. Science has so far given only the most casual attention to problems connected with "intrinsic" regulation. If there has not been an actual conspiracy of silence about such matters, it is at least the case that the trend of motivational theory has been dominated by the common-sense "in-order-to" model. There is as yet only the most halting kind of "grammar" for dealing with the conditions of behavior of the "in and for itself" variety. For this reason let us -- just as a kind of intellectual game -- see where it might lead if we assume that intrinsic determination is the primary and typical case, rather than the derivative and exceptional one.

Let us start with a simple example. X looks at a painting for five minutes, and we ask, "Why?" The grammar of extrinsic determination will generate a lush supply of answers. X looks in order to satisfy a need for aesthetic experience. X looks in order to derive pleasure. X looks because the picture happens to contain Napoleon and because he has a strong drive to dominate. X looks because "paintings" are learned reducers of anxiety. X looks in order to satisfy a need based on the association of the color of his mother's dress with the ground-color of the painting. Answers of this order have only two common properties: They all refer the behavior to an extrinsic, end-determining system, and they contain very little, if any, information. Anyone who has looked at paintings knows that if X is really responding to the painting, then any of the above statements, which may happen to be true, are trivial.

A psychologically naive person who can respond to paintings would say that an important part of the story -- the essential part -- has been omitted. There is a sense in which X could be looking at the painting only because of something intrinsic in the act of looking at this particular painting. Such a person would say that if the conditions of our example presuppose that X is really looking at the painting as a painting, the painting will produce a differentiated process in X which is correlated with the act of viewing. The fact that X continues to view the painting or shows "adience" towards it in other ways is equivalent to the fact that this process occurs. X may report on this process only in very general terms ("interesting," "lovely," "pleasurable"), or he may be able to specify certain qualities of the experience by virtue of which he

-73-

is "held" by the painting.

Let us remember that we are under the difficult discipline of holding "short" of hypothesis or "theory"; we
are assessing requirements. Suppose we assume that
there are certain immanent qualities and relations within the process which are specifically responsible for any
evidence of "adience" which X displays. Call these "value-
determining properties." We can then, with full tautological sanction, say that X looks at the painting for five
minutes because it produces a process characterized by
certain value-determining properties. This statement,
of course, is an empty form -- but note immediately that
it is not necessarily more empty than calling behavior,
say, "drive-reducing." It now becomes an empirical question as to what such value-determining properties, intrinsic
to the viewing of paintings, may be, either for X or for
populations of viewers.

Though it is extraordinarily difficult to answer such
questions, it is by no means impossible. The degree of
agreement in aesthetic responsiveness and valuation among
individuals of widely varied environmental background but
of comparable sensitivity and intelligence is very remarkable indeed. Articulate and perceptive art historians,
practicing artists, critics, and teachers have also proved
it possible to develop a sufficiently differentiated vocabulary
about painting-produced intradermal processes to communicate, at least within limits, intersubjectively. I say this
with full appreciation of the high incidence of gibberish
generated by many such individuals all of the time, and by
some of them part of the time. Perhaps the incidence of
such gibberish would decrease if fewer scientists legislated
painting-produced processes out of existence.

Looking at a painting can, of course, be the terminal
segment of a sequence of "directed" activity. If I take a
cab in order to go to the museum to see a Klee exhibit,
there is a valid sense in which I can say that the behavior
is directed towards an anticipated process having "positive"
value-determining properties. I can build up expectation

-74-

chains which terminate in anticipated processes with value properties. The occurrence of a process with "positive" value-determining property may be functionally related to behavior modification in many of the ways currently attributed to the reduction or satisfaction of extrinsic motives, except that for the occurrence of processes having positive value, the postulation of no extrinsic motive is required.

Before going further, it will be helpful to discriminate some of the things that we do not imply when we phrase directed behavior in terms of intrinsic-value properties. We are not, for instance, suggesting something tantamount to a "hedonism." I must flatly say that "positive value properties," as immanent within the processes that determine behavior, are not "pleasure," and "negative value properties" (as the basis of "abience") are not "pain." There are circumstances under which feedback from the act of tearing off one's ear might be characterized as engendering positive value properties. More importantly, it must be stressed that, to the extent that hedonistic language is not formulated in the extrinsic mode (i. e. , to the extent that hedonism acknowledges intrinsic regulation), it makes a very general and homogeneous identification of the nature and range of intrinsic value properties (viz. , "pleasure and pain"). It introduces, as it were, an enormous pre-judgment, or simplification of, the nature and range of possible value-determining properties, and thus of the conditions by virtue of which the "adience" (or abience) of behavior may be governed. It gives up the ghost before the scientific task is started.

Now impugning hedonism is a respectable pursuit, but I should like to point out that much of the "sophisticated" motivational theory of the modern period leads to the same constriction of the scientific enterprise. The only sense in which these theories, written as they are in extrinsic grammar, direct attention to intrinsic value-determining properties (and intrinsic determination in general) is in the identification of the "end-state" criterion of their favored causal model for a "motive." Thus, the intrinsic character of the process towards which (or away from which) behavior tends is identified as one global, serve-all grab-bag, variable like tension-release or drive-reduction or equilibrium-restoral or strong-stimulus removal.

This, to be sure, provides the setting for endless dispute and interminable experiment on, say, whether "drive-reduction theory" is violated by evidence which purports to show that "increased stimulation" can "reinforce" (3); that, at least in rats, coitus-interruptus is its own reward (29); that monkeys strive and learn for visual access to the world (4). But these global, single (or double or triple) "mechanism" theories of motivation have grooved thinking and research in such a way as to minimize the likelihood of investigating more detailed and differentiated properties of the processes which regulate behavior and its changes over time. More particularly, these theories, like hedonism, make an a priori and very limiting prejudgment of the range of value-determining properties that science can fruitfully isolate or lawfully relate to behavior.

So far, in talking about intrinsic behavior determination, we have placed primary emphasis on aesthetic, creative, and other contexts of behavior which are often regarded as too complex, or perhaps too ephemeral, to merit attention. Does this mean that an "intrinsic grammar" is to be restricted to such rarified contexts of activity, while exclusively extrinsic grammar is to hold sway in the realm of the reassuringly "crass" biogenic drives?

Let us take hunger as our example. The fact that men eat and show adience towards and within "eating behavior" has been interpreted both by common sense and by science as evidence for the postulation of the "intervening variable," hunger. Ordinary people and scientists (physiologists, nutritionists, psychologists) have raised many questions about the properties of this end-determining state in the extrinsic mode, and have accumulated a large and, within limits, solid body of facts about the relation of this state to antecedent environmental conditions, to physiological and biochemical processes, and to consequent behavior. Such information mediates many practically useful predictions and is certainly scientifically meaningful. If X is observed eating, one possible answer to the question, "Why does X eat?" is clearly that he is _hungry_ in the sense specified by all this knowledge.

However, most men know that there are conditions under which the above explanation is false (X eats but is not hungry) and conditions under which it is trivial (X eats and is hungry but will drop an insufficiently rare steak on the floor). Most of us know, that is, that there is a sense in which eating behavior takes place in and for itself, a sense in which it must be some function of an immediate, specific, ongoing, internal process having other and more differentiated properties than those assigned to hunger as a _general_ variable of the sort defined by "extrinsic" analysis. And, if X is adient towards this plate of food, it is entirely legitimate to apply our tautological rule and say that the behavior persists and varies through time in a certain way by virtue of certain value-determining properties intrinsic to the eating process.

Is there any evidence that our blank form may be filled in -- evidence that such value properties are isolable? I need only remind you that, in civilized cultures, cooking is an art form, and that the discriminating ingestion of food is a form of connoisseurship. There is no reason in principle why value properties (or classes of such) of the sort intrinsic to eating processes may not yield to increasingly accurate identification. Indeed, it is already possible for some individuals to praise their hostess's cooking in more differentiated terms than that "it was enjoyable." Further, though there is no reason to prejudge such matters, it is entirely possible that certain of the value properties intrinsic to eating processes may be of the same order as, or in some way analogous to, value properties involved, say, in visual, art-produced processes.

Now, facts of the eating _qua_ eating variety have not escaped the attention of scientists. However, when such phenomena are approached (e.g., individual variance in food preferences, eating behavior when non-hungry), the tendency is to deal with them in the extrinsic mode -- i.e., by various extensions, sub-specifications, or elaborations of the same type of causal model presupposed by concepts like hunger. In this way, we come by a new set of extrinsic systems -- specific and partial hungers, learned appetites and aversions -- and the intrinsic properties of eating behavior, insofar as they are dealt with, are referred to the joint interplay of a multitude of dated instances of such extrinsic systems. The empirical knowledge on the basis of which such systems are postulated may be very sound indeed. Nevertheless, in the light of the arbitrariness and complexity of the resulting theoretical picture and the increasingly tenuous character of the relation between general hunger and such special hungers, one can begin to doubt the fruitfulness of the causal (i.e., formal) model in terms of which such phenomena are organized.

The fact that neither I nor anyone else can specify the details of a more adequate causal model, at present, for eating behavior or any other "biogenic drive-behavior" does not one whit diminish the arbitrariness of the present model nor its inadequacy for large "ranges" of eating behavior. The scientific dangers inherent in such an "extrinsic" model, however, are far more conspicuous when it is extended to other areas of behavior. To take the most obvious possible example, there was a time not too many years ago when a direct pipeline extended between Cannon's stomach balloon and the entire domain of "motivational" psychology. Hooking in a few extra pipes to the hypothalamus or squirting some blood-sugar into the system does not necessarily help matters in the sense I have in mind.

The immanent value properties (or classes of such), in terms of which the regulation of adient and abient behavior may be phrased, need not be unlimited, or even very great in number. Relational or formal similarities in the "phenomenal grain," so to speak, of activities varying widely in content, environmental, and adaptive context suggests the possibility of modeling such value properties on a few fundamental, if systematically complex, dimensions. There is much reason to believe, from the protocols of

experientially sensitive and articulate people, as well as
from the observation of behavior, that certain of the value
properties intrinsic to such varied contexts of events as
the "perception" of (and directed behavior towards) a
picture, of a poem, of a "problem," whether scientific,
mathematical, or personal, of a "puzzle" in and for itself,
are of an analogous order and in some sense overlap. Indeed, as has already been suggested, it is not unreasonable
to believe that the so-called consummatory aspects of hunger or of sex "contain" relational qualities not unrelated
to some of the value properties immanent in "complex"
activities of the sort just mentioned. Though it would involve a most vicious kind of prejudgmentalism to estimate
the number of fruitfully isolable value properties, there
is no reason to believe that an "intrinsic grammar" forces
science into some impotent communion with the non-nom-
othetic and the unique.

Theoretical neutrality is not bought cheaply, and there
will be some who will insist on reading non-naturalist over-
tones into terms like "value property" and "value-determining
property." To such individuals, I will say that a "value-
determining property" is a predicate of a behavior-determining process. The "behavior-determining process"
is "inside" a natural organism and "takes place," most
immediately, in natural neural tissue. Twist my arm further, and I might say (against my better judgment) that the
"value-defining property" is some complex (2nd, 3rd, or
n-order) relational function of part-systems of the process,
and one which in turn may influence the further direction
of the process. If you care for such talk, well and good.
I for one do not believe the time is ripe even for <u>serious</u>
patter in this idiom.

In the recent history of psychology, the importance of
intrinsic regulation has been most forcefully urged by
Wertheimer (35) and, in particular, Köhler (21, 22). It is
regrettable that in both cases no clear distinction was maintained between the importance of an intrinsic grammar,
<u>per se</u>, and certain theoretical hypotheses offered in solu-
tion of the requirements of such a grammar. Further,

insofar as an intrinsic grammar was suggested as a fruitful direction for extension of the concerns of psychology,
no detailed apposition of such a grammar with the extrinsic molds of thought in psychological theory generally
was attempted. Finally, very little concern has been given
by these men to the context in which extrinsic grammar is
perhaps most deeply embedded -- motivational theory and
research.

Several other theorists have allowed their theoretical
behavior to be determined in some degree by the recognition of intrinsically maintained phenomena but almost
uniformly have ended by slipping into the extrinsic mode.
For instance, in Lewin's emphasis on the determination
of behavior by momentary concurrent field-structures,
there is such recognition, as there is in the imagery associated with concepts like "demand-character" or "valence."
But, in his functional breakdown of field structure and the
conditions of valence, Lewin introduces the thoroughly
extrinsic mechanism of "tension-systems," and in his
theory of personality, the postulation of extrinsic "needs"
and "quasi-needs" proceeds with an abandon unmatched
perhaps by any other theorist. Tolman, too, has at times
generated a construct-language imagery richly suggestive
of the "facts" of intrinsic determination, and such imagery
has been given force by the consistent tendency, throughout his career (e.g., 30, 33), to stress principles which
phrase performance as relatively independent of its historical conditions. Nevertheless, his doctrine of "appetites"
and "aversions" and of "demands" (30, 31), and more recently of "needs" and the "need-system" (33), are uniformly
cast in conventional extrinsic grammar. Allport's "motives"
acknowledge intrinsic determination insofar as they are
"functionally autonomous," but they become functionally
autonomous "in the service of" extrinsic needs.

A grammar of "intrinsic determination" tends, of
course, to work against the convention of dealing with behavior in terms of independently variable "steering" and
"energizing" systems. A "value-determining property"
is a predicate of a complex process, and there are no laws

of value-determining properties independently of the laws of the process. In this sense, the earlier form of Hebb's theory (13) observed good hygiene in not giving motivation constructs a systematic niche, but the theory has more recently (14) contracted a generalized D and other complications via the "arousal system." Among S-R theorists, perhaps Guthrie has been most sensitive to the phenomena of intrinsic determination. He has steadfastly refused to acknowledge "motivation" as a causal condition of behavior, and, if he has violated this refusal in his concept of the "maintaining stimulus," he has softened the sin by using this notion only rarely.

At the beginning of this paper, I indicated that much of the research which seems to me to provide insight into motivational phenomena is concerned with variables which fall outside my 1950 map (18). Perhaps the most exciting strand in this research is the growing concern with the phenomena of the more patently "in and for itself" or intrinsically maintained variety, phenomena which strain the resources of an extrinsic grammar and which give promise of human relevance even when studied in animals. I have in mind, of course, the work related to "exploratory" and "manipulation drives," on so-called "exteroceptive drives," on "perceptual drives," and "need to know" (e.g., 1, 4, 5, 6, 8, 9, 10, 11, 14, 23, 24, 25, 27, 28, 34). Such research, in my terms, has accomplished two important things:

(1) It makes more patent the vacuity of a universal "extrinsic" grammar. It must seem the thinnest kind of talk, even to the talkers, to talk of "satiation of the exploratory drive" or "satisfaction" of manipulative or perceptual drives.

(2) Such research, liberated as it is from a prejudgment as to the range and nature of goal-setting systems (and consequently of "reinforcing" events), can begin to isolate the conditions of directed behavior and its modification in a more detailed and differentiated fashion. Such research, in other words, can be interpreted as a small step in the necessarily slow movement towards the isolation

of the value-determining properties governing the adience
and abience of organisms. If less time were spent postulating new drive systems and more time devoted, say, to
narrowing down the range of characters which cause monkeys
to "solve" some manipulative problems and not others, this
would truly put us on the track of facts required by an "intrinsic grammar." If more effort, say, were devoted, not
to whether increased stimulation can "reinforce," but to
what the detailed properties might be of those "stimulus"
increases which do reinforce, psychology might find itself
at a new threshold.

In the present paper, I have sought to define a direction for thinking -- one that seems to me desperately required if psychology is ever to rise to the challenge defined by important ranges of phenomena within its province.
The difficulties of working our way out of the predominantly
extrinsic molds of psychological thought, together with the
difficulties, say, even in the initial mapping of what we
have called "value-properties," are such as to require the
efforts of the most imaginative investigators our field can
produce for many years. There are obvious possibilities
of experimental implementation -- e.g., in the use of
phenomenological reports from "gifted," creative, and in
other ways relevantly sensitive subjects, in the performance
of certain types of "stimulus equivalance" experiments with
child and animal subjects. But these possibilities, like the
development of intrinsic grammar in general, must also
be regarded as directions of work, not programs of the
sort that can be wired into some electronic control system.

The facts pointing to "intrinsic determination" are
available to all of us. Any line of criticism that discounts
these facts and the pre-theoretical requirements which they
define because of the circumstance that theoretical requirements are not theory or that these requirements are not
immediately and easily translated into a sure-fire experimental program -- any such line of criticism is merely
to substitute defensive complacency for scientific curiosity
and courage. The time is past due for psychology to cease
devoting most of its efforts to reassurance rituals and un-

-82-

ashamedly to face real problems, even if exacting adherence to some professionally standardized cookbook cannot lead to their solution next week. The mark of scientific maturity may not be the number of contexts in which apparent quantification can be pointed to, or apparent hypothetico-deductive rigor, or even the number of experimental "facts," solidly established or otherwise. Even solidly established facts can be artifacts, or they may be trivial or in some sense off-center with respect to the problems at issue. It is barely possible that the mark of maturity of a science is the maturity to face its own problems.

In closing, may I say that I am truly sorry that I have not been able to launch in your midst a new chain of intervening variables. Further, I apologize most humbly for an absence of postulates, coordinating definitions, operational definitions, reduction chains, mathematical models, and a properly specified syntax and object language, respectively. My regret is profound at not being in a position to hand out refrigerated thesis problems or bottled topics for entire research careers. Nor have I given you an organizing principle for scholarly debate, not even a filing system for sorting out "the literature." Nor have I asked crisp questions or blocked out crisp, quick methods for their solution. I have merely invited you to think.

References

1. Berlyne, D. E. The arousal and satiation of perceptual curiosity in the rat. J. comp. physiol. Psychol., 1955, 48, 238-246.

2. Brown, J. S. Problems presented by the concept of acquired drives. In Current Theory and Research in Motivation: A Symposium. Lincoln: Univ. Nebr. Press, 1953, 1-21.

3. Brown, J. S. Pleasure-seeking behavior and the

drive-reduction hypothesis. <u>Psychol. Rev., 1955,</u>
<u>62,</u> 169-179.

4. Butler, R. A. Discrimination learning by rhesus
    monkeys to visual-exploration motivation. <u>J. comp.</u>
    <u>physiol. Psychol.</u>, 1953, <u>46,</u> 95-98.

5. Cole, M. B., and Caldwell, W. E. The utilization
    of light as exteroceptive motivation in the comet
    goldfish (<u>Carassius Auratus</u>). <u>J. comp. physiol.</u>
    <u>Psychol.</u>, 1956, <u>49,</u> 71-76.

6. Dember, W. N. Response by the rat to environmental
    change. <u>J. comp. physiol. Psychol.</u>, 1956, <u>49,</u> 93-95.

7. Estes, W. K. Learning. In Farnsworth, P. R.,
    (Ed.), <u>Annual Review of Psychology</u>. Vol. 7.
    Stanford: Annual Reviews, Inc., 1956.

8. Harlow, H. F. Learning and satiation of response in
    intrinsically motivated complex puzzle performance
    by monkeys. <u>J. comp. physiol. Psychol.</u>, 1950, <u>43,</u>
    289-294.

9. Harlow, H. F. Motivation as a factor in the acquisi-
    tion of new responses. In <u>Current Theory and Re-</u>
    <u>search in Motivation: A Symposium</u>. Lincoln: Univ.
    Nebr. Press, 1953, 24-49.

10. Harlow, H. F., Harlow, M. K., and Meyer, D. R.
    Learning motivated by a manipulation drive. <u>J. exp.</u>
    <u>Psychol.</u>, 1950, <u>40,</u> 228-234.

11. Harlow, H. F., and McClearn, G. E. Object dis-
    crimination learned by monkeys on the basis of manip-
    ulation motives. <u>J. Comp. physiol. Psychol.</u>, 1954,
    <u>47,</u> 73-76.

12. Hebb, D. O. <u>The Organization of Behavior.</u> New
    York: Wiley, 1949.

13. Hebb, D. O. Drives and the CNS (conceptual nervous

system). Psychol. Rev., 1955, 62, 243-254.

14. Hill, W. F. Activity as an autonomous drive. J. comp. physiol. Psychol., 1956, 49, 15-19.

15. Hull, C. L. Principles of Behavior: An Introduction to Behavior Theory. New York: Appleton-Century-Crofts, 1943.

16. Hull, C. L. The place of innate individual and species differences in a natural-science theory of behavior. Psychol. Rev., 1945, 52, 55-60.

17. Hull, C. L. Essentials of Behavior. New Haven: Yale Univ. Press, 1951.

18. Koch, S. The current status of motivational psychology. Psychol. Rev., 1951, 58, 147-154.

19. Koch, S. Theoretical psychology, 1950: an overview. Psychol. Rev., 1951, 58, 295-301.

20. Koch, S. Clark L. Hull. Section 1 in Estes, W. K., et al., Modern Learning Theory. New York: Appleton-Century-Crofts, 1954.

21. Köhler, W. The Place of Value in a World of Facts. New York: Liveright, 1938.

22. Köhler, W. Dynamics in Psychology. New York: Liveright, 1940.

23. Montgomery, K. C. The effect of activity deprivation upon exploratory behavior. J. comp. physiol. Psychol., 1953, 46, 438-441.

24. Montgomery, K. C. The role of the exploratory drive in learning. J. comp. physiol. Psychol., 1954, 47, 60-64.

25. Montgomery, K. C., and Segall, M. Discrimination

learning based upon the exploratory drive. J. comp. physiol. Psychol., 1955, 48, 225-228.

26. Murray, E. J. The effects of hunger and type of manipulandum on spontaneous instrumental responding. J. comp. physiol. Psychol., 1953, 46, 182-183.

27. Nissen, H. W. Instinct as seen by a psychologist. (In Allee, W. C., Nissen, H. W., and Nimkoff, M. F.: A re-examination of the concept of instinct.) Psychol. Rev., 1953, 60, 291-294.

28. Nissen, H. W. The nature of the drive as innate determinant of behavioral organization. In Jones, Marshall R. (Ed.) Nebraska Symposium on Motivation, 1954. Lincoln: Univ. Nebr. Press, 1954, 281-321.

29. Sheffield, F. D., Wulff, J. J., and Backer, R. Reward value of copulation without sex drive reduction. J. comp. physiol. Psychol., 1951, 44, 3-8.

30. Tolman, E. C. Purposive Behavior in Animals and Men. New York: Century Company, 1932.

31. Tolman, E. C. Operational behaviorism and current trends in psychology. In Proc. 25th Anniv. Celebration Inaug. Grad. Studies. Los Angeles: Univ. of Southern California, 1936, 89-103.

32. Tolman, E. C. The determiners of behavior at a choice point. Psychol. Rev., 1938, 45, 1-41.

33. Tolman, E. C. A psychological model. In Parsons, T., and Shils, E. A., (Eds.), Towards a General Theory of Action. Cambridge: Harvard Univ. Press, 1951.

34. Welker, W. I. Variability of play and exploratory behavior in chimpanzees. J. comp. physiol. Psychol., 1956, 49, 181-185.

35. Wertheimer, M. Productive Thinking. New York:
     Harper, 1945.

COMMENTS ON PAPERS BY
DRS. KOCH, SOLOMON AND BRUSH

by
Daniel R. Miller

The specialized problems of a discipline often claim
the researcher's attention to such an extent that he for-
gets about the significance of his more general, fundamental assumptions. Dr. Koch has focused a glaring and
much needed light on the sacred idols of the psychologist.
The objects of Dr. Koch's iconoclasm are the ordinarily
unquestioned assumptions implicit in such practices as
interpreting all motivated behavior in terms of end-states,
creating parsimonious systems, seeking genotypic variables, and devising certain mathematical models. Too
often we ignore the fact that such goals are the products
of a specific epistemology and reflect the special values
of a given society. Few psychologists have seriously
concerned themselves with other philosophic positions,
with the sociology of our profession, or with the degree
to which our insecurities motivate us to exaggerate the
generalizability of our findings. It is very necessary,
therefore, for one of us to step outside the group, so to
speak, and to examine our work with the relatively dispassionate eye of a member of another culture. In part,
Dr. Koch has performed this task very effectively. I hope
his is the first of a number of papers devoted to the objective examination of current biases.

There are, however, some pitfalls in this type of
evaluation. Anthropologists have become very sensitive
to the ethnocentric distortions of the ethnologist who views
his own culture. I feel that an analogous distortion may
underlie some of Dr. Koch's jeremiads. While he claims
he speaks in caricature, he paints a bleak and hopeless

picture when he says that "neither in underlying logic, nor actual accomplishment, has the animal research, per se, provided very much insight into problems of human behavior in general, and human motivation in particular." Surely this is an overreaction to the unjustified optimism of the animal psychologists of a generation ago. As Dr. Koch admits in his next sentence, "No one can deny that animal research has set the terms of the problems and determined many of the variables." I find it difficult to dismiss the many valuable studies of such topics as the law of effect, the distinction between acquisition and performance, and the components of conflict.

The experiments cited by Drs. Solomon and Brush illustrate some of the important contributions of research with animals. Aversion has been sufficiently studied to permit a summary of basic problems, a description of a large number of methods, and the suggestion of important, unexplored areas. Solomon and Brush have performed these tasks very capably. That the issues which they raise may apply to emotional disturbances or purposive behavior in humans, as Solomon and Brush claim, is yet to be demonstrated. But the fact that this has not yet been done is hardly cause to "view with alarm."

Dr. Koch's paper raises the hoary but still moot problem of the conditions under which animal experiments can help us to understand human behavior. The paper of Solomon and Brush answers this question implicitly. To use animals, we must have a faith that the principle under investigation is basic enough to apply to all mammals. Avoidance seems to meet this criterion. Animals also permit experiments which are not feasible with humans. In animal investigations, certain controls may be introduced which are difficult to match in the observation of humans. Had experimenters restricted themselves to college sophomores, it is unlikely that Dr. Solomon would have been able to make his important distinction between the rules which apply to the learning and extinction of anxiety and those which apply to instrumental avoidance responses.

While I am optimistic about the potential contribution to theory of experiments with animals, I do share Dr. Koch's concern with the tendency of certain "fundamental psychologists" to ignore "behavior or experience relevant to man in his most characteristically human performances." They have tended to neglect not only motivated behavior without apparent end-states but also a variety of processes such as affective states, symbolic thinking, and unconscious reactions. Occasionally the tentative first steps required to explore such topics are compared invidiously with the rigorous, tough-minded methods of the animal psychologist. But such attitudes are much less fashionable than they used to be in the days when the answers to most problems of human learning and motivation were sought by studies of the rat's quest for food in the maze. Researchers have begun to show an increasing appreciation of the cultural relativism of an epistemology, theory, and subject matter. Those who still express a smug superiority on the grounds that theirs is the orientation most similar to the one used by classical physicists can gain a much needed lesson in humility from a careful reading of Dr. Koch's paper.

COMMENTS ON PROFESSOR KOCH'S PAPER

by
Richard L. Solomon

Dr. Koch has raised some puzzling and, indeed, disturbing questions. Many psychologists share his skepticism about the applicability of empirical generalizations from rat experiments to the prediction, control, and understanding of human behavior. His misgivings tend to emphasize the need for a healthy comparative psychology. The generalizability of behavioral laws across species is primarily an empirical rather than a theoretical question.

Dr. Koch's emphasis on intrinsically controlled motivational processes is interesting. It comes at a strategic

moment when both psychologists and physiologists are
discovering more and more about perseverating states
which, once aroused, seem to feed on themselves or run
a course which is partially free of extrinsic factors. But
how free? Koch's State "A" seems pretty bad, State "B"
seems more pleasant, and both states occur for no extrinsic reason. Yet, paradoxically, anxiety, an extrinsic
motivation concept, makes State B hard to maintain.

Koch's states, derived from his own experience, are
highly personal. Could a dirt farmer share these experiences? If not, then are intrinsic states related to past
experience? Can any behavioral sequence happen in and
of itself and be unrelated to extrinsic causal factors? It
is not easy to answer such questions, but it is interesting
to think about them.

The distinction between motivational concepts which
are "extrinsic" and those described in the "intrinsic mode"
is hard to maintain. First of all, there seems to be a
temporal distinction implicit in Dr. Koch's argument. Intrinsic motivation lasts longer? Secondly, there is the
factor of relative ignorance. When we know how to control
an item of behavior well, it tends to be described in extrinsic terms, providing there is a known reinforcing agent.
But possible exceptions would be Pavlovian conditioning
and some types of instinctive behavior, where extrinsic
motivation may be absent, yet control by E may be great.

A fictitious example may help to show the difficulty of
maintaining Koch's distinctions. A one-day-old infant is observed to make certain mouth movements (sucking). These
occur with varying frequencies in time. They increase
when the face is touched, increase most when the lips and
mouth are stimulated. They increase as the time since
the last feeding increases. Not only that, but facial stimulation becomes more effective, and can be far from the
mouth and still be effective, when the deprivation period
lengthens. Sometimes the sucking movements "spontaneously" occur in a fashion unrelated to these two classes
of conditions. Two weeks later, after many feedings,

stimulation of the face is less effective in producing the movements than it was earlier, and mouth stimulation is more effective than it was. How do we talk about this? Does the child suck in order to do anything? Koch warns us against this interpretation, but this warning is certainly not applicable to all of our observations. After two weeks of feeding experience, the fact that the eliciting conditions have changed somewhat in their effectiveness points to the importance of feeding as an event. Is it conceptually crippling to say that the child sucks in order to get food? Initially the extrinsic factors may not have been there; there may have been no goal, no incentive. And the Freudian postulation of an oral urge to fill this gap may indeed be futile and misleading. But later on a condition for the extinction of sucking behavior may be omission of food. Yet it is clear that the initial behavior may have been subject to no such limitation. Is Koch's intrinsic mode identical to instinctive, elicited reactions, to drive-related reactions, as well as to "spontaneous" reactions whose conditions are as yet unknown? Or is there something more involved?

SOME RELATIONS BETWEEN
FRUSTRATION AND DRIVE[1]

Melvin H. Marx

University of Missouri

However frustration is defined or interpreted, investigators agree that it plays a pervasive role in many phases of behavior. It is therefore surprising that so little experimental attention has been paid to it. The frustration literature review[2] which Reed Lawson and I recently completed yielded a disappointingly small amount of systematically conceived and adequately controlled research relevant to this problem.

Perhaps the most significant recent development has been the appearance of what Lawson and I have called "two-factor" theories of frustration. According to these views (e. g., 1, 6, 8), frustration as a blocking operation has one or both of two basic products: (a) an increment in drive and (b) unique stimulus-response relations, either learned or unlearned, which may or may not be related to the drive product.

As Farber (14) has recently observed, the evidence for the notion that frustration acts as a drive has been very scanty. Despite the lack of evidence, the idea is

---

[1]I wish to thank my colleagues Reed Lawson, George Collier, and D. W. Tyler and my graduate students Eugene Wist, W. A. Hillix, and Aaron J. Brownstein for their critical reading of this paper in preliminary form and their many helpful suggestions. Certain of the experimental work described herein was performed with financial support from a research grant, M-817, from the National Institute of Mental Health, National Institutes of Health, U.S. Public Health Service.

[2]Lawson, R., and Marx, M. H. Frustration: Theories and experiments. Unpublished manuscript, 1955.

widely accepted. The present paper will examine the
evidence for this notion and the related problem of
frustration-produced stimuli as cues. Emphasis will
be on recent unpublished experimentation in the Missouri
animal laboratory, with occasional illustrative references
to the publications that are covered in the literature review.

The Conceptualization of Frustration

The term "frustration" is a notoriously slippery
one, outstanding for this characteristic in an area of
many such terms and concepts. For this reason, I
would like to discuss four independent usages of the
term. I am not implying that the term is always used
consistently even within a single report.

**Frustration as an independent variable, or experi-
mental manipulation.** This usage is closest to the dic-
tionary point of view and is also the clearest and most
readily communicated. The frustration operation involves the blocking of either (a) some part of a series
of instrumental responses or (b) the consummatory responses themselves. Such blocking may be complete
or partial. This kind of interference operation can be
completely neutral with regard to the kind of responses,
or inferred states or drives, that will ensue.

Used in this way, the term "frustration" may be
distinguished, at least on a phenotypical level, from
two closely related operations: deprivation and extinction. The term "deprivation" is different operationally
because no attempt is made to produce prior instrumental or consummatory behavior in the experimental situation. The term "extinction," at the other end of the
scale, refers to the experimentally manipulated elicitation of the complete set of instrumental responses--
without presenting the usual goal object. In certain
cases, a clear distinction between extinction and frustration cannot be made. As a matter of fact, much of

the research on "frustration" has been within the operational framework of extinction.

Frustration as an intervening construct. In this
usage, frustration is considered to be some kind of
internal state or condition, or central process, which
is initiated or produced by blocking operations of the
type described above or by extinction operations and
perhaps in some cases by deprivation operations. The
production of abrupt increases in vigor or cessation of
responding along with the instrusion of irrelevant
("emotional") responses by operations such as blocking,
interruption, or failure to reward has led to the postulation of a motivational state called frustration. This
state is typically assumed to have the status of an irrelevant drive with the usual drive-stimulus properties.
The uniqueness and reproducibility of these correlations
are yet to be established. It is still a good question
whether the particular correlations cannot be subsumed
under the ordinary concepts, such as habit, in learning
theory. Used as a pure intervening variable, frustration
should involve unique S-R relations but may utilize concepts on either side that are not themselves unique.

Investigators have generally failed to specify a
predictable set of response consequences related to
particular frustration operations. This fact is probably
a function, in part at least, of the great variety of frustration operations. For this reason, some investigators
(e. g., 8) have preferred to use the term in the first
sense only.

Frustration as a dependent variable. This usage
is exclusively concerned with the problem of specification of responses. The familial characteristics of certain "emotional" responses have led to the introduction
of the concept of frustration as a dependent variable. This
approach has usually been based on the response-response
type correlations characteristic of the test-and-measure-
ment literature. Unique functional relations with antecedent conditions need to be established in order to make

this a useful definition of a response class.

Frustration as a phenomenon. The question may
arise as to how these relatively simple factors and assumed functions are related to the kind of human experience that is commonly identified as "feelings of frustration." Such experience seems to me to represent relatively complex, derived types of phenomena that are
often if not always based on fairly sophisticated symbolic
behavior. Much of this kind of experience seems to be
related to the cumulative effects of nagging and harass-
ment (as of overbusy mothers or tired and ineffective
teachers by children) or to the feelings of inadequacy
and helplessness associated not only with past failures,
real or imagined, but also with anticipations of failure
or catastrophe (as found in "neurotic" individuals).
These are certainly important problems from many
points of view, but it is very doubtful that they are at
all closely related to the kind of blocking operation
with which we have been concerned.

That is not to say that such blocking operations do
not have relevance at the human level. As a matter of
fact, it is my own private conviction that much of the
basic emotional behavior of humans, although overlaid
with a heavy loading of imaginative and symbolic activities, is nonetheless explicable in much the same way as
the more clearly revealed behavior of the rat. But this
is obviously a matter to be decided on the basis of a
great deal of research that has not yet been formulated,
much less performed.

In the present paper, I shall restrict the term
"frustration" to the simplest and clearest usage, namely,
that referring to some kind of experimental manipulation.
Even here a large number of different types of response-
blocking have been utilized and will need to be kept separate.

The Conceptualization of Drive

Many questions have recently been raised concerning

the role of the drive construct in the explanation of behavior. Clarification of the construct is needed. The
major argument against the drive construct concerns
the great burden of explanation that is customarily
placed upon it. There is no doubt that this enormous
load is inadequately supported by empirical evidence,
as MacCorquodale (21) has recently pointed out in his
excellent annual review of the learning literature. An
obvious solution is, as he implies, clearer specification
of "the general rules for the admissibility of a drive term"
(21, p. 30).

In another excellent review of the role of drive factors
in behavior, Farber (14) has pointed out that the term
"motivational" conventionally includes some kind of associative implication. He accepts the conventional distinction between drive and motive, although he indicates that
for clarity he would prefer to follow Brown (5) and Spence
(34, 35) in treating the terms as full-blooded synonyms.
He does not say why he does not follow their practice.

I can see no advantage to glossing over the conventional distinction, vague as it may sometimes be, and
combining two concepts which are already at least partially differentiated. A more desirable procedure is to
sharpen the distinction rather than obliterate it and thereby take advantage of extant linguistic habits as much as
possible. I therefore intend to maintain the distinction
between the two terms: "drive" will refer to the more
or less generalized energizing factors, "motive" to the
energizing plus the directional.

My suggestion is that such intervening variables
as these be used in a theoretically neutral sense. The
investigator specifies a class of antecedent stimulus
conditions or experimental manipulations that are consistently associated with another class of response
measurements or behavior observations, and the observed family of relationships is represented by some
verbal tag such as "drive," "percept," etc. If this construct
is used as an intervening variable in the recommended

sense, then it refers simply to <u>whatever</u> <u>intraorganismic</u> <u>processes</u> <u>are</u> <u>necessary</u> <u>to</u> <u>account</u> <u>for</u> <u>the</u> <u>observed</u> <u>re-</u> <u>lation</u>.

Now, this sounds simple enough, but it is mighty easy to misunderstand. The issue of specification, whether by physiological identification of some "actual" structures and events or by further analytic behavioral measurement, is left entirely open. This seems to be a difficult point for some persons to grasp, or perhaps to accept.

Let us apply this usage to the drive and motive constructs.. By "drive" is meant <u>whatever</u> energizing factors are operative to account for the degree of tendencies toward general activity or for the degree of activation of some particular responsé or class of responses. By "motive" is meant <u>whatever</u> processes are involved in the more clearly selective or directional behavior that characteristically occurs from the same kind of antecedent conditions. The term "motive" is thus a more inclusive one, since it consists of both a drive, or energizing factor, and a habit, or directive factor. The fact is that these two components can be independently varied, as is evidenced by the now well accepted distinction between habit and performance. If "drive" is used to represent one of the components, "motive" can then be retained as a composite dispositional concept including both drive and habit, roughly comparable to the construct $_SE_R$ in the Hullian system. Such separation of the meaning of the terms "drive" and "motive" to fit these definitional needs seems to be an advantage of maintenance of the traditional distinction. This advantage is important, regardless of whether theoretical and experimental analyses eventually question the ultimate separability of the constructs.

Certain other advantages of this conceptual scheme should be readily apparent. For example, the question of the extent to which the "drive" construct is being replaced by "external stimulus control" (21) need no longer

bother us, or, at any rate, not in a semantic sense.
The problem is rather one of specifying the nature of
"drive." Growth of our theoretical systems does not
require abandonment of such useful, operationally
oriented terms as "drive"--so long as they do not carry
vulnerable surplus theoretical connotations.

Even if all drive functions were eventually shown to
be under external stimulus control, to take an extreme
example, this would not mean that the construct would
need to be eliminated. We would still need some term
to refer to the S-R relations activated by our experimental manipulations, to identify the "energy level" component in behavior, and to distinguish between this and
other kinds of stimulus action. We might as well keep
the one we have.

Frustration-Produced Drive Increment

Early Evidence

The issue around which I wish to organize my description and analysis of experimental work concerns the
postulated drive-increment product of the frustration
operation. The early evidence on this problem, which
I shall briefly summarize here, came largely from
studies of extinction with rat Ss. For example, Virginia
Sheffield (33) found that running time was significantly
faster with massed, as against spaced, extinction trials,
after either spaced or massed training. This suggested
a drive-increment property of nonreward, since with
massed trials the frustration-produced drive would not
have as much opportunity to dissipate between trials.
Similarly, Amsel and Roussel (2) found that rats ran
faster toward the second goal box of a two-segment runway when food was not given in the first goal box than
when they had been given food there. This effect has
been produced with intermittent nonreward in the first
box (30) as well as with consistent nonreward. Also
supporting the "frustration-drive" hypothesis are the

results of Marzocco (26) and Lambert and Solomon (20).
The former reports that early in the extinction of a bar-
pressing response, rats tended to increase the force
with which they depressed the bar. The latter found
greater "excitement" in rats extinguished closer to the
goal box of a segmented runway.

Learned vs. "Drive" Determinants of "Vigor" in Bar-pressing.[3]

To turn now to some of the recent and current research in our own laboratory, I would like to outline,
first, an approach suggested by Lawson.

The main empirical support for the drive-increment hypothesis is that the amplitude of an instrumental
response followed by frustration often shows a momentary increase ("increased vigor"). None of the other
variables that are most often used to increase response
strength--such as decreased delay of reward, increased
incentive, increased numbers of reinforcements, and
the like--change in the required manner during frustration trials. It is therefore reasoned that the increase
in amplitude is most probably due to a change in drive
level.

An alternative hypothesis was described, but not
accepted, by Brown and Farber (6) in their version of
the drive-produced-vigor hypothesis. This hypothesis
is that the animal learns in previous situations to make
more vigorous responses when frustrated. When the
animal is frustrated in the experimental situation, he
transfers, via frustration-produced cues, this earlier
learning to the new situation, and we observe an increased vigor in responding. In view of the current
controversy over the observations on the response side

---

[3] These studies were initiated by Reed Lawson and carried on in collaboration with Carl L. Roberts and myself. The suggestion for apparatus design was made
by R. S. Daniel.

necessary to require the assumption of a change in drive, this hypothesis merits serious consideration. In the environments of most organisms, the response most likely to succeed in the face of momentary goal obstruction is that of "trying harder" (increased vigor). Even if giving up momentarily (descreased vigor) might in some special cases be the most effective means of eventually reaching the goal, the delay in reward involved would--in the case of nonverbal Ss, especially--be so great as to minimize the possibility of learning such a response in many situations.

The purpose of the pilot study here summarized was to provide an artificial environment in which decreased vigor in the face of frustration would for some Ss be reinforced as often and as quickly as increased vigor typically seems to be.

Half of a sample of rats were separated at two months of age and were maintained in individual cages for three months prior to the experiment. Frustration was kept at a minimum for these Ss. More important, none of their responses were consistently associated with frustration-reduction. The remaining Ss had been living in overcrowded social cages equally long. The hypothesis was that the individually raised rats, having had little opportunity to learn any particular response to frustration, could be taught with about equal ease to respond following frustration with either increased vigor (the "Strong" group) or with decreased vigor (the "Weak" group). The socially raised Ss, on the other hand, were expected to have more difficulty learning the "weak" response, since they had lived in a competitive environment where forceful responding presumably was more frequently rewarded than weak responding.

Briefly, the procedure was as follows. After magazine training, all Ss were given ten reinforcements in a Skinner-type box suitable for recording response-amplitude. Then the bar was weighted so that S had to respond with a strong push but not a push which was near the upper limit of exertion. $\underline{S}$s were given 20 reinforcements per day for four days under these conditions.

"Frustration-training" was then initiated. The first five bar-presses each day were not rewarded, regardless of their intensity.

Thereafter, for the "Weak" groups, a response was rewarded only if it was of lesser intensity than the response just preceding. This relative intensity judgment could be made easily by $\underline{E}$, since amplitude was being recorded graphically. In the "Strong" groups, only responses stronger than the just-preceding response in the nonreward series were rewarded. Reasonable lower and upper limits of response amplitude were rewarded consistently in the respective groups. Training for both groups continued until the majority of responses for all $\underline{S}$s fell within the rewarded range. Twenty rewarded responses were required of each $\underline{S}$ each day.

Analyses were made of the average rate of emission and the percentage of correct-strength bar-presses for all training periods combined and for the final period alone. These measures all indicated that individually raised $\underline{S}$s reached a higher level of performance on the weak response than did socially raised $\underline{S}$s. For the strong response, the relationship was reversed. The interaction, although not significant in this pilot experiment, was sufficiently large to be encouraging, and we feel that the lead is worth pursuing. The results are quite consistent with the notion that increased vigor is, at least partially, a result of transfer from earlier situations in which stronger responses were learned.

There was also an overall superiority of learning in "Strong" over "Weak" $\underline{S}$s. This is inferential evidence for a nonassociative drive component in frustration. However, a plausible alternative hypothesis is that the strong bar-press involved more of the same muscles used in learning the original response than did the weak response; if this is true, the superiority of strong animals would again be the result of transfer of training. The original response required the use of both forepaws, as did the strong responses. Ss in the "Weak" group had to dispense with the "two-paw response" in order to respond consistently at the minimal level.

Furthermore, even our individually raised Ss lived with cagemates until the age of eight weeks. Thus they had some opportunity to learn "increased vigor" responses. Individual feeding from weaning, if not birth, would be necessary to control this possiblity.

Discrimination Training: Nonreward Following Introduction of a Stimulus Rat

A series of experiments performed as a doctoral dissertation by Elaine Holder (15) offers some interesting and suggestive results in regard to the present question. Mrs. Holder gave rat Ss discrimination training in which another rat ("stimulus rat") was employed in one of these ways:

a. Consistently in association with the presentation of food--that is, as a positive discriminative stimulus (S^{D+}). These Group-R (reward) Ss were given an equal number of randomly inserted trials on which the stimulus rat was absent and they were not fed.

b. Consistently in association with nonreward--that is, as a negative discriminative stimulus (S^{D-}). These Group-F (frustration) Ss were treated in an exactly opposite manner from Group-R Ss. They were given an equal number of randomly inserted trials on which they were fed in the absence of the stimulus rat.

c. Inconsistently in association with reward and nonreward. The Group C (control) Ss were given an equal number of rewarded and nonrewarded trials, but half of each kind were associated with the presence and half with the absence of the stimulus rat.

-102-

The training apparatus consisted of two small starting boxes opening into opposite sides of a rectangular goal box. At the far end was a platform onto which a food tray was inserted during rewarded trials. The hungry stimulus rat was allowed to enter the goal box and go to the feeding platform simultaneously with the S.

Ss were 24 male albino rats approximately three months old at the beginning of training. They were placed in individual living cages at weaning and kept in individual cages during the training and testing procedure. Eight male albino rats approximately the same age as the Ss were used as stimulus rats. After the drive cycle was established and accommodation to the apparatus had occurred, a total of 40 training trials was given to all Ss. Two trials were given each day, spaced at least 30 minutes apart. Half of the trials were rewarded, and half were nonrewarded, according to the pre-determined random schedule. On rewarded trials, when S was on the platform, a tray filled with dry food was pushed into the apparatus. S was allowed to eat for five seconds. Time from starting box to the platform was measured on all rewarded and nonrewarded trials to determine the effectiveness of the stimulus rat as a discriminative stimulus for reward or nonreward.

Discrimination training was successful. Group-F rats ran significantly more slowly ($P < .01$) on paired or social trials than on individual. No significant differences occurred for Group-C rats. Group-R Ss learned the opposite discrimination ($P < .01$), but since their test behavior is not of interest in the present context, it is not presented.

Ss were first tested in a "one-sided" cooperative learning problem. S's task was to press a lever which would release a stimulus rat. When both rats were at the food tray position, they were allowed to eat for five seconds.

As shown in Figure 1, Group F was consistently slower

-103-

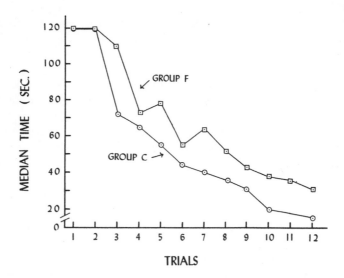

Fig. 1. Median Lever-Pressing Time for F and
C Groups on Cooperative Test Trials (E. Holder Study)

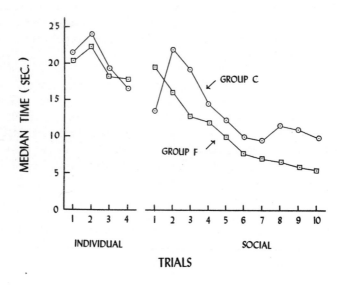

Fig. 2. Median Running Time on Individual and
Social Runway Trials (E. Holder Study)

than Group C. These differences were significant at
the .05 level. Data from one S in Group F are not included because it failed to respond on the last three
trials.

These results suggest a hypothetical "frustration"
state. However, it is obviously simpler to assume that
the Ss were simply transferring the slow-running habit
they learned in training to the test situation. This part
of the experiment is of interest, thus, in that it does
demonstrate quite clearly how a relatively simpler explanation of frustration effects in terms of past habits
can be sufficient.

A second test consisted of ten runway trials in which
each S was paired with another S from the same group
on the basis of closeness of running-time scores previously obtained in individual running trials in the same
apparatus. Ss were allowed five seconds of eating in
the goal box after each run. The two runways were
separated by hardware cloth.

The results are shown in Figure 2. The F rats ran
significantly faster than the controls on the paired or
social test trials, as predicted on the basis of an irrelevant-drive function of frustration-associated stimuli.
This result had also been found in an earlier similar
experiment.

Blocking of an Instrumental Avoidance Response

A doctoral dissertation by Ben Bernstein (4) was
aimed more directly at the problem of drive increment
following frustration. He first established a strong
wheel-turning response during shock-avoidance training in a modified Mowrer-Miller box. Ss were then
immediately extinguished under one of four response-
blocking conditions. Each group contained 18 or 19 rats.

Bernstein confirmed the prediction of the drive-increment hypothesis that S whose shock-avoiding wheel-

turning responses were blocked for two or four seconds during extinction would give significantly stronger responses after blocking and would show significantly greater resistance to extinction. Responses of Ss blocked for eight seconds were indistinguishable from those of controls. These results are shown in Figures 3 and 4.

The failure of the eight-sec. Ss to show more evidence of response vigor or greater resistance to extinction suggests a relatively rapid dissipation of the effect, at least in the avoidance type of situation. This result is in line with the findings of an experiment by Page and Hall (29).

Bernstein's experimental situation suggests some analytic procedures that could aid in the differentiation of drive and habit components, as earlier defined. For example, the stimulus characteristics of the apparatus--either the box itself or the manipulanda--might be systematically varied between training and test. This would make possible some experimental differentiation between the drive-increment and the associative process. On the basis of an associative prediction, an experimental group then tested in a situation more similar to that used in training would be expected to be more clearly separated from its control (no delay) group than would an experimental group tested under more varied conditions and compared with its control (that is, more varied conditions and no delay). However, a significant difference between the latter two groups would itself be an indication of some drive increment, provided satisfactory evidence could be obtained that significant transfer effects were eliminated.

Delay of Reward in a Runway

This experiment (16) was planned and performed by Wayne Holder under my supervision and with the assistance of Elaine Holder. After the Holders left the Missouri laboratory, George Collier completed the data analysis and interpretation.

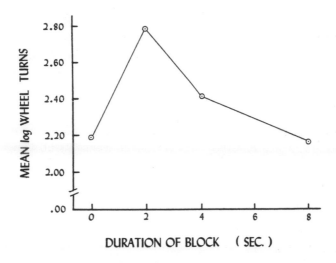

Fig. 3. Strength of Wheel-Turning Response during
Avoidance Extinction (Bernstein Study)

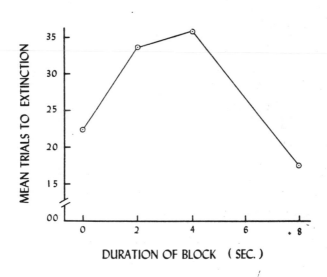

Fig. 4. Resistance to Extinction of Avoidance Response (Bernstein Study)

Most previous studies have investigated the effect of
delay of reward during acquistion when delay occurred
just preceding reward. The results have shown that
the rate and asymptote of learning are a decreasing function of delay. The present study was designed to examine
the effects of delay introduced when the response was near
asymptote and at a point midway in the response chain.
This enabled us to obtain post-delay response measures.

Thirty-nine albino rats were trained on a straight
runway, with each run interrupted in the middle of the
runway for one sec. Twenty-five trials were given, one
per day. All trials throughout the experiment were with
food reward.

Following training, the rats were divided into three
groups. The first group continued under the training
conditions, the second was delayed in the middle of the
runway for 15 sec., and the third was delayed for 45 sec.
Ten spaced test trials were given, one per day. A damped
buzzer was sounded during the delay period for the 15-sec.
and 45-sec. groups. It was introduced in connection with
a transfer test, to be described later.

Response strength, as measured both by starting time
(ST) and running time (RT), was a significantly decreasing function of the length of delay in the segment of the
runway preceding the delay and a significantly increasing
function of delay in the segment of the runway following
delay. The only exception to this was a single inversion
which occurred for the ST's from the start box between
the 15- and 45-sec. groups. The means of the last five
test trials for log (RT+1) and log 1/ST are presented in
Figures 5 and 6. These effects of delay did not appear
immediately but grew over test trials, a fact not shown
in the graphs.

These data appear to give strong support to the two-
factor theory (6) which originally stimulated the experiment. The results are readily explicable on the basis
of the hypothesis that delay produces an aversive state

-108-

("frustration"), the magnitude of which is a direct function of the length of the delay.   The decrease in response

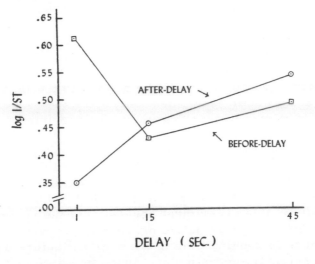

Fig. 5. Mean Starting Time before and after Delay
for Last Five Test Trials (Holder et al. Study)

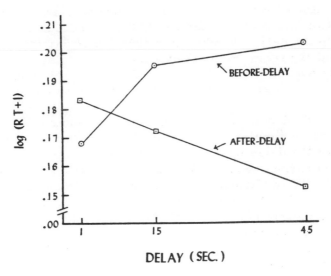

Fig. 6. Mean Running Time before and after Delay
for Last Five Test Trials (Holder et al. Study)

-109-

strength preceding delay results from the learning to avoid the noxious state produced by the delay (1, 6). The increased response strength after delay is explained on the basis of the predicted irrelevant-drive properties of the delay. The fact that we were able to obtain such clear-cut differences for the different delay groups, whereas earlier similar researches (e.g., 2) failed to do so, may well be related to the introduction of delay in our experiment only <u>after</u> the Ss were already well trained, rather than throughout training.

From the standpoint of the drive-increment hypothesis, a major difficulty is the failure of the supposed drive increment to manifest itself immediately. Also, it is important to note that the wide (24-hr.) spacing of trials in this experiment necessitates the assumption of some kind of associative process to account for the decrease in running time in the segment before delay. Amsel's (1) suggestion of a fractional anticipatory frustration response is an example of the kind of construct possible.

According to an associative interpretation developed by Collier, on the other hand, the decreased running time up to the delay chamber is a function of partial extinction resulting from the markedly increased delay of reward. This decrease is to be expected, in view of results which have shown running time to be longer with longer delays.

The decreased starting time and running time after the delay require a more complex explanation. The stimuli of the delay operation are assumed to elicit learned or unlearned responses incompatible with starting out of the delay chamber. The longer the delay, the more opportunity the animals have to extinguish or adapt these incompatible responses; the amount of decrease is therefore a function of the length of delay. The response of starting, on the other hand, is being rewarded and shows the expected decrease over trials.

Further, the delay is assumed to separate the second

half of the alley from the first half, so that the animals
in the longer-delay groups can be considered as making
two somewhat separate running responses. Hull's (17)
experimentation related to the goal-gradient hypothesis
indicates that running time will be less in comparable
segments of a short alley than in a longer alley. The
longer the delay, the more clearly we would expect the
two segments of the alley to be differentiated. Thus we
see the running time in the second segment decreasing
for the animals to whom the second segment now represents a short-alley situation, in which we regard the
delay chamber as a starting box; again, the amount of
decrease is a function of length of delay.

It is also possible that the drive-increment interpretation might account for the running-rate increment
of the 15-sec. group after delay, whereas the readjust-
ment interpretation might apply to the 45-sec. Ss. Of
course such a duplex notion is less acceptable because
more complex than either of the other ones by itself,
but it is reasonable to assume that the peak of drive
increment might be reached somewhere before 45 seconds.
Decisions among these theoretical alternatives must be
made on the basis of more data.

All of these interpretations assume that the very
mild buzzer, sounded while the 15-sec. and 45-sec. Ss
were in the delay box on test runs, was not an intrinsically noxious stimulus. Some support for this assumption is
afforded by the fact that the test effects definitely grew
over trials; if a simple avoidance of the buzzer were involved, it would seem that its effects should be evidenced
more quickly. In any case, verification of the results in
the absence of the buzzer is necessary.

Unique Frustration-Produced Stimuli

Early Evidence

This second factor of the "two-factor" frustration

theories (1, 6, 8) represents in some respects an even
more complex situation than that posed by the problem
of independent identification of the proposed drive-increment factor. Again, the early evidence is chiefly
from research on extinction. For example, Sheffield
(32) found that with massed training trials, partial reinforcement led to significantly faster running times
during extinction than did previous consistent reinforcement. No reliable differences occurred for spaced training. This result supported her hypothesis that trace
stimuli of nonreward, which presumably included stimuli
arising from frustration, are conditioned to a response
if rewarded responses in training follow quickly upon
nonrewarded ones. More recent research, however,
has failed to verify this result (37, 38; cf. also 6, 39).

The "internal stimulus" hypothesis was more directly
tested in a series of experiments by Amsel and Ward (3).
Rats were first consistently rewarded in a straight alley.
An intermittent reinforcement schedule was introduced,
with reward or nonreward in the first goal box as a cue
for a subsequent response: when there was no reward in
the goal box, a right turn out of it (the alley was now the
stem of a T-maze) was rewarded; when there was food in
the first box, a left turn out of it led to additional reward.
Ss were able to reach a mean of about 80% correct turns.

The authors interpret their findings as supporting
the view that frustration produces drive stimulation that
has directive properties. These results are certainly
interesting, but the interpretation presents difficulties.
It involves the tacit assumption that nonreward must produce frustration; furthermore, invoking a concept such
as "drive stimulation" seems gratuitous. The fact that
a rat can distinguish between reward and nonreward is
not a sufficient basis for hypotheses about either frustration or drive.

Consideration will now be given to two major aspects
of this problem in relation to some of the experiments
already described.

Frustration-produced Drive Increment as a Cue

This formulation is perhaps the simplest form of the hypothesis that such new and unique S-R relations are produced, since it does not require any additional stimulus characteristics beyond the drive increment already assumed. Of course it does depend upon the validity of the drive-increment hypothesis.

Bernstein's doctoral study (4) offers strong evidence in support of this form of the hypothesis. After extinguishing his Ss on the blocked shock-avoidance response previously described, he gave them a day of rest--under food deprivation--and then proceeded to run them in an entirely different kind of apparatus, a straight runway, to food reward. After 20 acquisition trials, all Ss were given 20 extinction trials, under the assumption that this new extinction would have stimulus ("frustration") properties in common with the first blocking. All trials were slightly spaced, with a four-to-six min. interval. In addition to the four groups carried over from the first part of the experiment, a control group of 15 naive Ss was used. No significant differences among the five groups occurred during acquisition.

Since some of Bernstein's animals exceeded the two-min. time limit on more than half of their trials, the mean and the median were not considered appropriate measures. The frequency measure used by Sheffield (32) and Stanley (36) was used instead. This measure is the number of trials on which the response time equals or falls below the median for all response times of all Ss.

A curvilinear relationship was found for both extinction measures for the four original groups. The distribution of means for all scores was significantly curvilinear ($P < .05$) and was very similar to the shape of the curve shown in Figure 3. The mean of the new control group was almost identical with that of the old zero-sec. group.

An even more pronounced curvilinear relationship ($\underline{P} < .001$) was found for trials to extinction. Again the new control group did not differ significantly from the zero-sec. group.

According to Bernstein's interpretation of these results, the greater resistance to extinction shown by the two-sec. and four-sec. groups was due to the transfer of response tendencies that had become associated with the frustration-produced drive increment. These results were in accordance with his prediction, which utilized the concept of a unique stimulus component (S_F) accompanying the frustration-produced drive.

Because the new control group failed to differ from the zero-sec. group, Bernstein dismisses the possible alternative interpretation in terms of fear from the earlier shock experiences generalizing differentially. Also, he holds that if differential transfer of fear were operating, it might be expected to act more strongly on the earlier acquisition trials, where only slight and insignificant differences occurred.

Two interesting suggestions for further more analytic experimentation are made by Bernstein. Use of a choice situation during extinction rather than a straight runway is suggested as a means of determining whether persistent goal-directed activity was learned during avoidance extinction and transferred differentially to the second test. Such a test would have relevance for the problem of differentiating between pure drive and the drive-association (motive) factors. Placement of a wheel in the goal box during the second extinction is also suggested as a test of the possibility that fractional antedating wheel-turning responses occurred and differentially reinforced the new running response through their accompanying s_g's. Apart from this problem, the transfer of such a response would itself be indicative of common stimulus elements.

A second part of the Holder et al. study (16) is also

relevant here. The three groups of rats differentially delayed for ten test trials were shifted to a second runway. The damped buzzer which had been previously associated with delay in the 15-sec. and 45-sec. groups was now sounded throughout each run. Ten reinforced runs were given, spaced one per day.

The two delay groups ran significantly faster than the one-sec. controls but did not differ significantly from each other. These results support the interpretation that the delay produced a conditioned drive increment that was then reinstated in the second runway. In the present case, the drive increment would be mediated by an obvious external cue, the buzzer, in the absence of any experimental manipulation of frustration; in Bernstein's experiment, the mediation would be via the drive increment directly arising in each case from the frustration operation. The presence of the buzzer cue in each situation in the present study makes it somewhat easier to interpret on a simple associative basis than is Bernstein's.

The two experimental groups differed more from the controls at the end of the test than at the beginning, so that external inhibition from introduction of the buzzer as an explanation of the slower control running is not indicated.

Noxious and/or Inhibiting Characteristics of Frustration

Slowing down of the experimental $\underline{S}$s in the runway segment preceding delay was cited as evidence for the noxious nature of frustration, although an alternative associative interpretation of this result was also described. There is a suggestion in Elaine Holder's research (15), already described, that frustration might produce cues of a noxious or aversive nature. That her "frustration" $\underline{S}$s increased their running rate to food more rapidly than controls in the social trials was interpreted as support for the irrelevant-drive, or drive-increment, hypothesis. It might also be interpreted, however, as evidence for the development of some noxious or aversive characteristic for the negative discriminative stimulus. A more adequate test of this view would involve a measure of behavior in direct response to the negative discriminative stimulus in the absence of any experimentally manipulated drive.

A related question concerns the role of frustration following a particular response as a determinant of subsequent response strength. This problem was posed as a consequence of some interesting results which I obtained in two experiments on food-hoarding in rats. In a first experiment (24) on the role of terminal reinforcement, only three of 20 animals deprived of their food pellets as they returned them into the home cage during ten training runs subsequently developed the hoarding habit; and each of these three had managed to eat small parts of the pellet before it was removed. Training was under 23-hr. hunger drive, test on the following day under relatively satiated conditions. Control animals subjected only to the presumably transitory emotional effects of removal of the pellet, followed by its immediate return, showed the usual hoarding development at test.

In a following experiment (25), all conditions were duplicated except that training as well as test was under satiation. These Ss, which were presumably not "frustrated" by the experimental removal of their returned food pellets, now showed the typical hoarding behavior characteristic of the control Ss in each of the experiments.

Consideration of these contrasting results suggested possible inhibitory effects of frustration following instrumental responses. The role of frustration as an inhibitor seemed to be indicated also by certain typical results from latent learning experiments, particularly the finding that satiated Ss apparently learn the location of an irrelevant incentive more readily than animals under some unsatisfied high-drive condition (cf. 22).

In one line of research, Lawson and Collier and I have explored the presumed inhibitory effects of inaccessible reward (food presented under wire guards) in the T-maze and the runway. I will not attempt a summary of the complex designs that we have used thus far, but I feel safe in saying that the inaccessible-reward operation as we have used it with the hungry rat has proved surprisingly resistant to the production of any inhibitory effects. We have not yet been able to show the positive results predicted by the original hypothesis. We have learned that this is a very complicated experimental problem, over and above the fairly obvious confounding of this kind of frustration operation with the secondary-reward concept.

It is possible that the difference in results thus far evident may be associated with the degree to which the consummatory response chain has been activated before blocking. In other words, the removal of food from the mouth may have a stronger frustration effect than the presentation of inaccessible reward (cf. 31). More direct experimental comparison of these operations is needed.

Theoretical Implications

Although the experiments that I have reported certainly do not provide any fully definitive answers to crucial problems of the frustration-drive relationship, they do offer some interesting leads for conceptualization of functions and formulation of theoretical relationships. I would like therefore to close this paper by making some tentative efforts toward a conceptual and theoretical integration of the material.

One way of attempting a clarification is to formulate some of the variables or dimensions along which critical questions can be asked. This will be done within the general framework of the three major products or effects of the frustration operation that have been covered: the two parts of the "two-factor" theories (drive and cue) and the inhibition suggestion. A final section will attempt

to amplify the strictly associative ("nonfrustration")
point of view.

The Nature of the Drive Increment

On the assumption that adequate positive evidence
for frustration-produced drive increment will be obtained, several important dimensions may be identified
with regard to its occurrence.

The learned-unlearned dimension

The production of drive can be thought of as a natural,
unlearned reaction of the animal to blocking. Some sort
of notion such as this seems to have underlaid the original
frustration-aggression hypothesis (12). The "vigor" research which I described was designed to investigate the
alternative possibility that learning is primarily involved.
This is the hypothesis that the more or less constant
struggle against deprivation and frustration that apparently
marks the natural life of most if not all animals might
well condition them to make vigorous responses as a kind
of generalized reaction to frustration situations. The
gradual acquisition of differential response times in the
Holder et al. experiment (16) also tends to confirm the
importance of learning. It is possible, of course, that
both differential learning of this kind and a natural unlearned tendency towards stronger responses occur.

It is interesting to note that the experiments showing the clearest support for a drive component to frustration are those in which the Ss were being rewarded
during all or most of the critical trials (e.g., 4, 15, 16).
In several other experiments, we rarely obtained conclusive or systematic differences among groups presumably being "frustrated" by methods that seemed intuitively,
at least, to differ in degree of frustration (inaccessible
reward vs. no reward vs. empty food cup). In these
latter studies, however, no responses made by S subsequent to an exposure to any of these conditions were rewarded.

-118-

This suggests that the presumed "drive increment" following frustration is very weak at best and is revealed by the direct building up, through reinforcement, of the behavioral consequences of this increment. It is also possible that the original slight increment in drive might itself be explained as the effects of transfer of training, as in the "vigor" analysis.

The relevant-irrelevant dimension

Most of the theoretical discussion on frustration has been with regard to an assumed "irrelevant" drive increment. The possibility of <u>relevant</u> drive increment seems to have been more or less overlooked. However, the Bernstein study (4) offers some interesting support for this latter notion, it seems to me, as well as the former. The increment in response vigor of wheel-turning in the main part of the experiment represents an increment in motivation--as I have distinguished this construct from drive proper--since the animal at test continues to make the same response on which it was trained. The apparent transfer of increased vigor to a different kind of extinction situation in the second part of Bernstein's experiment offers evidence for the irrelevant, generalized type of drive increment.

The results of Marzocco's (26) experiment on bar-pressing can be interpreted as evidence for relevant rather than irrelevant drive, if certain assumptions are made. Increase in mean force of bar-press from the first four to the second four responses during extinction was interpreted as indicative of a momentary increment in irrelevant-drive level. This effect on the first few responses during extinction can be interpreted as a kind of facilitation of the relevant drive rather than an irrelevant drive, since the learned response itself is involved rather than some other response. This effect would be somewhat analogous to pre-feeding sensitization (27), and perhaps also to the demonstration (31) of greater vigor following blocking after a moderate amount of consummatory activity had been permitted. What is obviously needed is a direct test of relevant vs. irrelevant drive factors within the same experimental setting.

As a matter of fact, it is interesting that so little information is available on the role of added or irrelevant drive directly manipulated. There are two recent studies (7, 19), the results of which might be interpreted as offering some support for this sort of dynamogenic notion.

The direct-indirect dimension

By "direct" production I mean the arousal of increased drive without any mediating function, such as that effected by "emotion." Although detailed treatment of the emotional variables is well beyond the scope of this paper, it may be assumed that emotions can be defined independently of frustration. Then the drive increment either could be a direct product of the frustration operation itself or could be a function of such frustration by-products as fear or anger.

In this respect, a comparison may be made between the relatively brief duration of the increased response vigor found in the Bernstein experiment (4), where fear of shock was involved, and the apparently longer duration of increased vigor in the Holder et al. experiment (16), where no such fear was involved, although the possibly noxious effects of the buzzer remains to be experimentally evaluated. Development of emotional factors seems to be, at least in part, a function of the extent to which more adaptive responses are extinguished or for some other reason are not available in the frustration situation.

The Nature of the Cues

The most important dimensions here may be outlined.

The drive-nondrive dimension

The degree to which a drive stimulus component acts as a cue is a controversial issue on which there is little direct evidence. As pointed out earlier, the drive-stimulus notion may be a relatively simpler one than the alternative view involving another type of frustration-associated stimulus. This would be true if some sort of drive increment does occur, since an additional stimulus component is not required. The transfer part of Bernstein's experiment (4) does appear to offer a strong support for such a view. However, that experiment does not clearly differentiate between an "emotional" and a "nonemotional" type of drive cue, since fear is involved. Both types are possible, of course.

Another alternative interpretation would be in terms of direct associative relations between nondrive stimuli and responses. An example of the potential usefulness of this view has been provided by Collier's suggested analysis of the Holder et al. data.

The generality dimension

The degree of commonality of cues, whether drive or nondrive in nature, represents another important dimension. The absence of experimental data bearing on this issue was noted in our literature review as one of the most critical present needs. Highly generalized frustration processes seem to be more assumed than demonstrated. Our "vigor" research is based upon an assumption of a high degree of commonality, or generality of cues. Bernstein's (4) transfer data may again be cited as an example where this notion seems to find experimental support.

The internal-external dichotomy

This distinction is well represented by a comparison of the Bernstein (4) experiment, in which no external cues were deliberately carried over to the transfer test, and the Holder et al. experiment (16), in which a mild buzzer was deliberately associated with the frustration operation and used as a stimulus in the transfer test. There is, of course, no reason why both kinds of cues cannot operate independently, but the absence of an external stimulus makes necessary the assumption of some kind of internal state, or at least self-produced cues.

This dichotomy also relates to the problem of generality of any assumed frustration state, or its independence of specific stimulus operations. Such generality would seem to require the assumption of some kind of internal state.

The Nature of the Inhibition

Should the inhibitory action of frustration suggested by comparison of the two hoarding studies be confirmed by the further experimentation which we are now conducting, its interpretation will constitute an interesting and important problem. Two alternative interpretations may be suggested.

First, the response decrement obtained might actually be a function of lower habit strength. This kind of direct effect during acquisition is not indicated on the basis of the results from investigations of "punishment," although there is some reason to doubt that the experimental situations are sufficiently parallel to justify much comparison. The bulk of the controlled nonverbal research on punishment of simple nonchoice responses (cf. 11, 13) has been concerned with its effect on responses that have already been acquired. Second, the response decrement obtained might simply be a function of the reinstatement at test of negative or interfering responses learned during training. This more indirect effect is somewhat along the lines of recent theoretical suggestions (e.g., 1, 10, 28).

The Strictly Associative Interpretation

One last theoretical position, which has been touched upon in the discussion, remains to be more fully explicated This is the view that the blocking operations involved in frustration produce no behavior which cannot be explained without assuming any special products, such as new drives or unique cues.

There are certain difficulties with each of the frustration theories. As already suggested, one is that the effects of frustration usually grow over trials. This fact suggests an associative factor, since, if frustration functioned purely as drive, its facilitation of established habits should be immediate.

Frustration sometimes results in facilitation, sometimes in inhibition, of the responses being measured by the experimenter. This suggests that the effects of frustration do not have unique response consequences but depend upon transfer of training or upon the various relationships between the other responses (interfering or facilitating) elicited by the blocking operation and the response being measured by the experimenter.

One example from our experimental work will illustrate the explanatory potential of this view. Consider the experimental Ss in the Holder et al. experiment as they are delayed 15 or 45 sec. for the first time during the test trials. As indicated earlier, their behavior can be interpreted as a function of the disruption in previously learned running responses now produced by the longer block itself; on this view it is not necessary to invoke a special drive concept. Moreover, the responses can be either learned or unlearned. Such responses to blocking are likely to be called "emotional," but they do not require the assumption of an emotion-produced drive as cue, as was hypothesized above in another connection.

The fact that such a strictly associative analysis is possible for an experiment yielding results which, at first appearance, seem so neatly to support a frustration-drive theory is provocative. Examination of experimental results within the frustration framework has indicated that there are few, if any, which cannot be as well explained, at least in an ad hoc manner, on the basis of an associative interpretation as on the basis of a frustration-

produced drive state. Whether results demanding the invocation of frustration-produced drive or of unique stimulus characteristics of frustration will accumulate is, of
course, an open question.

Certain suggestions may be made as to minimum requirements which need to be met before we can assume
any unique drive characteristics for frustration.

A first and fairly obvious point is that we should
examine closely the pre-experimental and prior-experi-
mental experiences of the organism to see whether there
was an opportunity to learn responses which transferred
to the frustration situation. We need more research of
the kind attempted in our "vigor" study in order to establish the possibility, conditions, and limits of such transfer.

Two considerations are especially important in connection with the transfer problem. Obviously we need
to consider the possibility of stimulus generalization and
of response generalization. The importance of response
generalization can be seen in the "vigor" study, where
strong responses seemed more similar to the original
responses learned in the situation. It may be that this
is true in many frustrating situations.

Also to be considered is the habit-family hierarchy
(18). Certain observed responses to frustration are related to the blocked response via a relatively high standing in the animal's hierarchy of responses. If the possible
responses that can be made are highly restricted, then,
after the animal's adaptive responses are at least partially extinguished, we may observe apparently new and mal-
adaptive responses which are attributed to frustration
per se, as in Maier's (23) experiments.

A second major point is that we need to examine very
closely the nature of the unconditioned reactions of the
organism to the operation. This position assumes that
we can distinguish between the direct responses to the
situational stimuli and the responses which ensue after
blocking of a previously established response. In many
-124-

cases, the observed results may follow simply from the presentation of the additional stimuli of the frustrating operation. We need answers to questions about what the animal would do in response to the frustrating conditions in the absence of frustration of an established instrumental response. Then we will be in a better position to test hypotheses about frustration-produced drive.

As has been indicated, decisions among these alternatives can be made only after a considerable amount of more analytic experimentation. Verbal identification of all blocking operations through a common term like "frustration" should not confuse the issue. The strictly associative view, if substantiated, would obviate the need for giving any kind of special status to the frustration concept. "Frustration" would become a synonym for blocking. Each blocking operation could then be investigated and explained independently of the others.

Summary and Conclusions

This paper has been primarily concerned with an analysis of some of the relations between the frustration (blocking) operation and drive. A conceptualization of certain of the basic constructs (frustration, drive, motive) was outlined. Recent unpublished research bearing on the problem was described.

The discussion was organized primarily around the evidence for the so-called "two-factor" theories of frustration--namely, the view that frustration results in (a) drive increment and (b) unique stimulus-response relations.

What final conclusions can now be drawn concerning this evidence? The case for the two-factor theory is in some respects convincing, but it is certainly not one that can be readily accepted, even on the basis of positive evidence predicted by the theory itself. That is, such positive results cannot be taken entirely at face value as conclusive evidence but are rather to be carefully examined in the light of alternative interpretations. This has been shown in some detail for one particular experiment that seems to offer new and exceptionally powerful positive data. The possiblility of alternative explanations not requiring the assumption of special "frustration" effects needs to be not only considered if proffered but actively solicited in order that a tighter case be made for any positive results. The issue certainly remains an open one.

What other implications can we now draw? Briefly, two methodological implications seem especially clear. First, we need to have more specific, analytic measures of what S is doing at critical times in order to differentiate among alternative hypotheses and to develop new ones. A number of examples of this need occurred throughout the discussion. Second, we need clear operational accounts of the experimental conditions in order that coordinating definitions may be soundly established among the many differing frustration operations. Generalization of results from one kind of frustration situation to another can be done only with the utmost caution. There does not seem to be any fundamental a priori reason to expect high correlations among data until the situational similarities are established.

References

1. Amsel, A. A three-factor theory of inhibition: an addition to Hull's two-factor theory. Paper read at the Southern Society for Philosophy and Psychology, Roanoke, Va., March, 1951.

2. Amsel, A., and Roussel, J. Motivational properties of frustration: I. Effect on a running response of the addition of frustration to the motivational complex. J. exp. Psychol., 1952, 43, 363-368.

3. Amsel, A., and Ward, J. S. Motivational properties

of frustration: II. Frustration drive stimulus and frustration reduction in selective learning. J. exp. Psychol., 1954, 48, 37.

4. Bernstein, B. Extinction as a function of frustration drive and frustration stimulus. Unpublished doctor's dissertation, Univ. of Missouri, 1954.

5. Brown, J. S. Problems presented by the concept of acquired drives. In Current Theory and Research in Motivation. Lincoln: Univ. Nebr. Press, 1953. Pp. 1-21.

6. Brown, J. S., and Farber, I. E. Emotions conceptualized as intervening variables--with suggestions toward a theory of frustration. Psychol. Bull., 1951, 48, 465-480.

7. Brown, J. S., Kalish, H. I., and Farber, I. E. Conditioned fear as revealed by magnitude of startle to an auditory stimulus. J. exp. Psychol., 1951, 41, 317-328.

8. Child, I. L., and Waterhouse, I. K. Frustration and the quality of performance: II. A theoretical statement. Psychol. Rev., 1953, 60, 127-139.

9. Crum, J., Brown, W. L., and Bitterman, M. E. The effect of partial and delayed reinforcement on resistance to extinction. Amer. J. Psychol., 1951, 74, 228-237.

10. Dinsmoor, J. A. Punishment: I. The avoidance hypothesis. Psychol. Rev., 1954, 61, 34-46.

11. Dinsmoor, J. A. Punishment: II. An interpretation of empirical findings. Psychol. Rev., 1955, 62, 96-105.

12. Dollard, J., Doob, L. W., Miller, N. E., Mowrer, O. H., and Sears, R. R. Frustration and Aggression.

New Haven: Yale Univ. Press, 1939.

13. Estes, W. K. An experimental study of punishment. Psychol. Monogr., 1944, 57. Whole No. 263.

14. Farber, I. E. The role of motivation in verbal learning and performances. Psychol. Bull., 1955, 52, 311-327.

15. Holder, Elaine. The role of learning factors in the development of social behavior in laboratory rodents. Unpublished doctor's dissertation, Univ. of Missouri, 1955.

16. Holder, W. B., Marx, M. H., Holder, Elaine E., and Collier, G. Response strength as a function of delay of reward in a runway. In prep.

17. Hull, C. L. The goal gradient hypothesis and maze learning. Psychol. Rev., 1932, 39, 25-43.

18. Hull, C. L. The concept of the habit-family hierarchy, and maze learning. Psychol. Rev., 1934, 41, 33-54.

19. Klein, G. S. Need and regulation. In Jones, Marshall R., (Ed.) Nebraska Symposium on Motivation 1954. Lincoln: Univ. Nebr. Press, 1954.

20. Lambert, W. W., and Solomon, R. L. Extinction of a running response as a function of distance of block point from the goal. J. comp. physiol. Psychol., 1952, 45, 269-279.

21. MacCorquodale, K. Learning. In Stone, C. P., and McNemar, Q., (Eds.), Annual Rev. Psychol., 1955, 6, 29-62.

22. MacCorquodale, K., and Meehl, P. E. Edward C. Tolman in Estes, W. K., and others, Modern Learning Theory. New York: Appleton-Century-Crofts, 1954. Pp. 177-266.

23. Maier, N. R. F. Frustration. New York: McGraw-Hill, 1949.

24. Marx, M. H. Experimental analysis of the hoarding habit in the rat: II. Terminal reinforcement. J. comp. physiol. Psychol., 1951, 44, 168-177.

25. Marx, M. H. Experimental analysis of the hoarding habit in the rat: III. Terminal reinforcement under low drive. In prep.

26. Marzocco, F. N. Frustration effect as a function of drive level, habit strength and distribution of trials during extinction. Unpublished doctor's dissertation, State Univ. Iowa, 1950.

27. Morgan, C. T., and Field, P. E. The effect of variable preliminary feeding upon the rat's speed of locomotion. J. comp. Psychol., 1938, 26, 331-348.

28. Mowrer, O. H. Two-factor learning theory reconsidered, with special reference to secondary reinforcement and the concept of habit. Psychol. Rev., 1956, 63, 114-128.

29. Page, H. A., and Hall, J. F. Experimental extinction as a function of the prevention of a response. J. comp. physiol. Psychol., 1953, 46, 33-34.

30. Roussel, Jacqueline S. Frustration effect as a function of repeated nonreinforcements and as a function of the consistency of reinforcement prior to the introduction of nonreinforcement. Unpublished master's thesis, Tulane Univ., 1952.

31. Sears, R. R., and Sears, Pauline S. Minor studies of aggression: V. Strength of frustration as a function of strength of drive. J. Psychol., 1940, 9, 297-300.

32. Sheffield, Virginia F. Extinction as a function of partial reinforcement and distribution of practice. J. exp. Psychol., 1949, 39, 511-526.

33. Sheffield, Virginia F. Resistance to extinction as a function of the distribution of extinction trials. J. exp. Psychol., 1950, 40, 305-313.

34. Spence, K. W. Theoretical interpretations of learning. In Stone, C. P., (Ed.) Comparative Psychology (3rd Ed.). New York: Prentice Hall, 1951.

35. Spence, K. W. Current interpretations of learning data and some recent developments in stimulus-response theory. In Learning Theory, Personality Theory, and Clinical Research: The Kentucky Symposium. New York: Wiley, 1954. Pp. 1-21.

36. Stanley, W. C. Extinction as a function of the spacing of extinction trials. J. exp. Psychol., 1952, 43, 249-260.

37. Tyler, D. W. Extinction following continuous reinforcement with control of stimulus-generalization and secondary reinforcement. Amer. J. Psychol., in press.

38. Weinstock, S. Resistance to extinction of a running response following partial reinforcement under widely spaced trials. J. comp. physiol. Psychol., 1954, 47, 318-322.

39. Wilson, Wilma, Weiss, Elizabeth J., and Amsel, A. Two tests of the Sheffield hypothesis concerning resistance to extinction, partial reinforcement, and distribution of practice. J. exp. Psychol., 1955, 50, 51-60.

COMMENTS ON PROFESSOR MARX'S PAPER

by
John P. Seward

Frustration is a slippery construct. Dr. Marx de-
serves high praise for the thoughtful logic with which he
has defined terms, formulated experiments, and analyzed
results in this forbidding but challenging territory. I can
appreciate the difficulties from my own brushes with a
closely related problem. Pereboom and I spent a winter
with activity wheels trying to demonstrate a general drive
property of incentive--just before Sheffield and Campbell
(6) succeeded in doing so with a stabilimeter type of cage.
It took us weeks more to formulate the problem in terms
of a two-part runway, only to find that Amsel and Roussel
(1) had already done the experiment.

One reason why frustration is hard to handle is because it has such a variety of effects on behavior. Under
some conditions it may amplify responses; under others,
suppress them: it may stereotype behavior or diversify
it. How can a common set of operations produce such
apparently chaotic effects? Marx points out that frustration is related to two other operations: deprivation and
extinction. But note that deprivation is commonly used to
produce a drive, while extinction is inhibitory. No wonder
the effects of frustration are hard to predict!

As a step toward reducing confusion to order, Brown
and Farber (3) presented the theory that blocking a response produces two factors: a general drive increment
(D_F) and one or more specific cues (s_F). They showed
that the interaction of these factors with other drives and
habits in Hull's system would lead us to expect different
outcomes depending on particular conditions. An inhibitory
effect does not follow immediately, but it can be deduced
with the aid of an additional assumption: that persistent
or severe frustration produces a diffuse "emotional" reaction (r_F) that disrupts activity in progress. Conditioning
of such a reaction would be equivalent to conditioned in-

hibition. No special inhibitory process is implied here; rather, a widespread invasion of central coordinating mechanisms.

Since Marx has evidently planned his experiments with the two-factor theory and its possible extension in mind, it may be useful to examine them as tests of three hypotheses: (a) Frustration produces a general drive increment. (b) Frustration produces a specific cue. (c) Frustration produces an inhibitory response.

(a) The first hypothesis calls for a definition of drive. Marx uses the term, like Brown and Farber, to account for the energy with which an organism does whatever it does. Since, in two-factor theory, drive appears as a general multiplier of habit strength, it does not include any stimulus already associated with the response in question. This qualification puts a severe restriction on the experimenter. To show that frustration has strengthened a response by way of D_F, he must show that it could not have done so by increasing the intensity of cues. Two classes of response are immediately ruled out as measures: (i) The blocked response itself cannot be used, since blocking may simply recruit proprioceptive impulses closely integrated with it. (ii) If a consummatory response like eating is blocked, any instrumental response in the sequence leading to it is disqualified on the ground that a fractional goal reaction, presumably conditioned to the response, may be exaggerated by blocking.

Of the earlier experiments cited by Marx, those of Sheffield (8), Marzocco (4), and Amsel and Roussel (1) fail to meet the second criterion. Of the later ones, consider Holder's experiment using a "social runway," in which rats that had been socially frustrated ran faster than controls (Fig. 2). Since the goal response, eating, was the same one originally blocked in the presence of another rat, the greater speed does not necessarily imply an irrelevant drive. The experiment by Holder, Marx, Holder, and Collier measured the same response, running, that was delayed, so it could not isolate a drive function. Bernstein's first experiment, in which he measured the strength of a blocked wheel-turning response, is open to the same criticism, not to mention the possible confusion of frustration effect with fear. His later experiment, however, to which I shall return in the next section, looks crucial in these respects.

But even if heterogeneous responses are used, Marx points out that a positive finding does not establish D_F. As Brown and Farber suggested, a habit of responding more vigorously to frustration may be learned. Lawson's exciting results on social rearing, if solidified, give added weight to the possibility. Of course he will want to see if competitive rats learn to intensify not only the blocked response but responses in general. If they do, we are faced with two further difficulties. One is the added factor of early experience that must be controlled in order to demonstrate D_F. The other is the conceptual problem of how a thing like general response energy can be learned.

A method of testing the D_F hypothesis that might avoid some of these obstacles would be to follow Miller's lead (5). Combine a neutral stimulus, e.g., a buzzer, with a blocking operation; then train the animal to make an instrumental response in order to turn off the buzzer. On a drive-reduction hypothesis of reinforcement, a positive result could be taken as evidence of D_F.

(b) For a direct proof that frustration produces a specific cue, we must show that it can produce a specific response not traceable to any other change in the environment. Since frustrating an animal necessarily changes its environment, this is not easy. Marx doubts--more than I do--that Sheffield (7) and Amsel and Ward (2) succeeded. Marx's own study with the Holders and Collier was admittedly disqualified by their use of a buzzer.

How could such a test be made? Suppose two groups of rats have been trained equally in four alleys, one all black, one all white, and the other two striped. Group E finds food only in the white (or black) and one of the striped alleys, never in the black (or white). Group C finds food

-133-

in <u>both</u> the white and black alleys (or neither) and in neither
of the striped ones (or both). The two groups are now given
a successive discrimination problem in which both arms of
a T-maze are either black or white: if black, a right turn
is rewarded; if white, a left turn. Preliminary training
has given both groups a set for color, but for Group E frustration has been differentially associated with black and
white, while for Group C it has been equally associated
with both. So if Group E learns the successive discrimination faster than C, we can attribute the result to cues
produced by learned frustration-responses.

Of the experiments described by Marx, only Bernstein's
seems to fulfill the requirements of the s_F hypothesis. In
fact Marx is right, I believe, in holding that this study con-
firms the D_F hypothesis as well. Bernstein, you recall,
blocked a shock-avoidant wheel-turning response for 0, 2,
4, and 8 seconds during extinction in different groups of
rats, and obtained more wheel-turning in the groups with
2 and 4 seconds of delay. He then gave all groups, plus a
control group, equal hunger-food training and extinction
on a runway. The same differences showed up in the second
extinction as in the first.

I can see only two reasonable interpretations. One
involves the assumption that s_F can produce D_F by conditioning. During the first extinction, blocking produced stronger
s_F's and D_F's in the 2- and 4-sec. delay groups than in the
other two. During the second extinction, equal s_F's were
aroused in all groups, but by stimulus-intensity generalization those in the 2- and 4-sec. groups evoked the strongest
D_F's. The other interpretation is that a fluke of sampling
occurred. A repetition of this truly remarkable experi-
ment--or one like it--would settle the matter.

The significance of Bernstein's study stems from his
choice of two such different tasks for training and testing.

(c) Two of the studies reported by Marx bear directly
on the hypothesis that frustration produces a characteristic
response with inhibitory properties. In one striking exper-

-134-

iment he showed that removing hoarded pellets from hungry rats prevented later hoarding under satiation, while similar treatment of satiated rats had no effect. He thereby isolated frustration from mere nonreward as the inhibiting agent. He did not, however, isolate r_F as the inhibiting mechanism; if frustration produced any response incompatible with hoarding, that response could have transferred to the later test. To implicate r_F, a conditioned stimulus must be shown to inhibit some quite different response.

This requirement was apparently met by Holder's first experiment on the effects of "social frustration." After giving her experimental animals discrimination training in which a stimulus rat was associated with nonreward in a runway, Holder taught them to press a lever that released another rat as a condition of receiving food. They took longer to press the lever than a control group (Fig. 1). These results impress me more than they do Marx. This is because I consider running and lever-pressing different enough to demand some mediating mechanism in order to explain the transfer of inhibition from one to the other. A frustration-response conditioned to the stimulus rat seems a likely candidate.

I look to experiments such as this ingenious series from the Missouri laboratory to increase our understanding of the nature of extinction.

References

1. Amsel, A., and Roussel, J. Motivational properties of frustration: I. Effect on a running response of the addition of frustration to the motivational complex. J. exp. Psychol., 1952, 43, 363-368.

2. Amsel, A., and Ward, J. S. Motivational properties of frustration: II. Frustration drive stimulus and frustration reduction in selective learning. J. exp. Psychol., 1954, 48, 37-47.

3. Brown, J. S., and Farber, I. E. Emotions conceptualized as intervening variables--with suggestions toward a theory of frustration. Psychol. Bull., 1951, 48, 465-495.

4. Marzocco, F. N. Frustration effect as a function of drive level, habit strength, and distribution of trials during extinction. Unpublished doctor's dissertation, State Univ. Iowa, 1951.

5. Miller, N. E. Studies of fear as an acquirable drive: I. Fear as motivation and fear-reduction as reinforcement in the learning of new responses. J. exp. Psychol., 1948, 38, 89-101.

6. Sheffield, F. D., and Campbell, B. A. The role of experience in the "spontaneous" activity of hungry rats. J. comp. physiol. Psychol., 1954, 47, 97-100.

7. Sheffield, V. F. Extinction as a function of partial reinforcement and distribution of practice. J. exp. Psychol., 1949, 39, 511-526.

8. Sheffield, V. F. Resistance to extinction as a function of the distribution of extinction trials. J. exp. Psychol., 1950, 40, 305-313.

THE STUDY OF CONFLICT[1,2]

Daniel R. Miller and Guy E. Swanson
University of Michigan

If a representative sample of psychologists, psychiatrists, and social workers, whose primary function is the modification of human behavior, were asked to name the theory that is most useful to them in their daily work, most of the respondents would unquestionably name the psychoanalytic theory of conflict. Today there is hardly a clinician who, regardless of his theoretical persuasion, does not try to interpret a symptom as an indirect expression of unconscious, incompatible needs. In textbooks on personality, few topics are stressed as much as is conflict. And with good reason. There is abundant clinical evidence that defenses are used so often and in so many situations that they tend to generalize to many reactions which have nothing directly to do with conflict. The literature is filled with cases which illustrate the relationship to conflict and defense of such varied forms of expression as the jokes a person appreciates, the content of his dreams and fantasies, the structures of his doodles, his vocational interests, his styles of physical expression, or his reactions to threat of failure. Because of the congruence among these many types of behavior, it has been claimed (10) that methods of resolving conflict become organized as a character structure--a general style of expressing oneself in one's relations with others.

There is no doubt that Freud struck a rich theo-

[1] We are grateful to J. W. Atkinson and U. Bronfenbrenner for their valuable help in clarifying some of the concepts.
[2] This paper was written at the Center for the Advanced Study of Behavioral Sciences.

retical vein when he began to interpret the symptoms of
conversion hysteria and obsessive-compulsive neurosis
as indirect expressions of repressed, conflicting needs.
Yet a current investigator who examines the literature
with a view to performing empirical research soon comes
to an unhappy conclusion. While some of the precious
ore has been refined by.clinical psychiatrists, most of
it is in the same state as when it was discovered. At
least it is not in a form which lends itself to objective,
empirical investigation. Such key concepts as needs,
moral standards, and defenses still remain to be clearly defined. While there is a general, but by no means
universal, agreement about the characteristics of some
of the defenses, no theory has been proposed to explain
the mechanisms by which the defenses distort perception,
the relationships among them, or conditions under which
they are learned.

Before such problems can be investigated, the basic
concepts must be defined and classified in a manner
which facilitates analysis of their inter-relationships.
The object of this paper is to propose a taxonomic system. In demonstrating the application of the system to
empirical problems, we shall cite examples from
studies undertaken by members of a project which we
directed. [3]

Let us consider a hypothetical conflict which introduces most of the basic concepts. Jim, a young man
in secondary school, has developed an avid interest in
baseball since joining the team. He has recently spent
so much time in practice that he has begun to neglect
his studies. He has been encouraged to practice by the
coach, a famous player in years gone by and the boy's
idol. Jim hopes that he may be good enough to play in
the major leagues. One day the coach has a talk with

---

[3]The project was supported by a grant from the National
Institute of Mental Health, U.S. Public Health Service.

Jim and tells him that he is not good enough to think of baseball as a career, that he should not have neglected his school work, and that at the end of the month he will be dropped from the team for his own good. Jim remembers all the encouragement he received previously and feels that the coach is being unfair.

Now, Jim probably experiences a number of conflicts. We shall concentrate on the one resulting from his aggression. If this were the only need, Jim might conceivably engage in some act which would annihilate the coach once and for all. But while Jim may even daydream about murder, physical assault, or insult, he probably will not engage in any of them. Even if he were not afraid of the consequences, his moral needs would be violated by such actions.

However, Jim is not without alternatives. There are a number of other methods which he may be impelled to use as a means of expressing his aggression. He might deliberately lose a game, spread malicious gossip, become irritated at the misplays of a teammate, or blame himself for the difficulty with the coach.

People tend to be consistent in the types of alternative expressions of the need which they select. The primary goal of any theory which describes the non-rational resolution of conflict is the prediction of substitutes. In this paper we shall devote a section to each of three factors which affect the selection of substitutes: moral need, expressive style, and defense. In a fourth section, the origins of the three will be traced to particular positions in society and to particular techniques of socialization. Before we begin, we shall identify each of the topics further and mention some of the reasons for our special interest in it.

Moral needs aim at the attainment of certain standards of performance which are defined in ethical terms. The standards may be phrased positively, in the form of ideals, or negatively, in the form of admonitions to avoid certain expressions of other needs. If an individual's moral aims define many kinds of behavior as evil, he is destined to experience many more conflicts than the man whose moral aims do not cut as wide a swath into his other behavior.

Our second concept, expressive style, refers to one's characteristic fashion of communicating his needs. Some people are most expressive with their bodies; others feel comfortable only if they can use concepts. Some people are customarily forthright in their expression of aggression; others must be devious and circumspect. Depending on a man's style, he should tend to favor certain alternative expressions of his conflicting needs.

Because defense mechanisms[4] facilitate the choice of a more permissible version of the need, they diminish anxiety. Although they result in self-deception, the distorted version often resembles the original sufficiently to give the alert observer a clue to the need. Slips of the tongue provide a good example. Freud (11) cites the case of a printer who made a "mistake" in setting type for a story about the crown prince, a man who was involved in some very juvenile escapades. Although the printer meant to refer to "crown prince," he inadvertently changed a letter so the term became "clown prince." When he set type for retraction, he again made the same error.

To review some of the common defenses, let us return to Jim's aggression toward the coach. If he were to displace his anger, he could attack a scapegoat and

---

[4]This is an unfortunate term because it connotes to some people a defense against external attack or against reified internal forces. Nobody uses defense in this sense. We continue to use the term because it is part of the technical vocabulary of the psychoanalyst.

retain his affection for his hero. He could displace the
anger to himself, in which case he would feel depressed.
Instead of turning the anger against himself, Jim might
project it. As a result, he might misinterpret the coach's
temporary irritation as unreasonable anger; this exag-
geration would enable Jim to deny that the aggressive
need was his. If he were to reverse the intended act,
he would not only avoid disliking the coach but would become extraordinarily eager to help him in some way.

Differences in social positions provide a key to variations in moral needs, expressive styles, and defenses.
Epidemiological investigations in the United States (9)
(16) and Europe (5) (13) have shown that patients with
certain disorders, such as conversion hysteria and
schizophrenia, usually grow up in working-class neighborhoods, while people suffering from such illnesses as
depression and obsession come from the middle classes.
Let us assume that symptoms are indirect expressions
of conflicting needs and that they are determined by
particular types of moral standards, expressive styles,
and defenses. In this case we can infer that patients in
contrasting social positions must develop different moral
needs, expressive styles, and hierarchies of defense.
Such a deduction suggests a way of studying the phenomena involved in conflict. Hypotheses may be phrased
in terms of the social categories which predispose a
person to develop one type of moral need rather than
another, one expressive style rather than another, or
the predisposition to favor one type of defense over another. Research on the social origins of conflict thus
requires three levels of variables. We start with differences in social position. From these, we infer techniques of child-rearing. And from child-rearing practices, we infer differences in moral needs, expressive
styles, and hierarchies of defense.

The Independent Social Variables

Inner conflict is an inevitable price of living in a

society. It is the price that we willingly pay in order to gain the advantages of group endeavor. But sharing in a group's effort requires inhibition. Not every impulse can be gratified immediately. In order for the group to survive, it must establish a code which defines certain actions as desirable and others as forbidden. The list of regulations in any society is very long. The child must learn to control his anger, his sexual impulses, and others which, if unregulated, might threaten the existence of the group. In time he learns some of the complicated variations of the rules, such as the permissible targets of anger. For example, he may criticize politicians and high-pressure salesmen, but not friends whose goals he shares--unless they violate the code by some act, such as spreading malicious gossip about him.

But self-control creates new problems. For example, men in most societies have sexual, aggressive, and status needs regardless of whether or not the societies forbid them. Conflict is therefore inevitable. Quite often every man is torn between two simultaneous and incompatible needs: between his forbidden promptings, on one hand, and his conscience or fears of rejection by his friends, on the other.

A random inspection of any population readily reveals considerable variations in characteristic moral needs, types of conflicts, expressive styles, and defenses. In selecting background factors, we were guided by the assumption that reactions to conflict are predominantly products of socialization. To the extent that most members of a given social group or of a given society have previously been subject to a common set of influences, we expected them to develop similar moral needs and similar repertories of defenses.

In order to obtain evidence about the differences in the methods used by various groups to resolve conflict, we first explored some of the literature on the cross-cultural incidence of personality disorders. When we found that a high incidence of depressive disorders is reported among the Hutterites (8), Koreans (2), and middle-class Americans (9), we conjectured that both the normal and abnormal members of such societies must have many experiences which reinforce the defense of turning anger on oneself. An adult patient's defenses are not likely to have developed full blown just at the moment when he is trying to resolve an overwhelming conflict. Considering the early ages at which most defenses are manifested, the patient must have used them for many years before his illness. We also speculated that learning conditions in societies with high rates of depression must be different from those of the African Negroes (3) and Chinese (12), who seem to have few depressives. Similarly we wondered whether the high proportion of obsessives among middle-class Americans does not indicate that both the normal and abnormal members of this group must mature under conditions which teach them to favor the defenses of undoing, isolation, and reversal. The low incidence of obsessions among African Negroes (6), Chinese (2), and working-class Americans (13) suggested that members of these groups must learn to avail themselves of defenses other than undoing, isolation, and reversal.

Social Class. While cross-cultural information helps us to phrase some of our questions, the research on the structure of our own society throws more direct light on the relationship between social position and reactions to conflicts. Of particular interest in Faris and Dunham's study (9) of the distribution of psychoses in the general Chicago area. Previous analyses of the organization of Chicago have indicated the existence of certain zones within each of which the residents are very similar in socio-economic status. For example, the poor factory workers live in a central business district. Next to it there is a district of rooming houses. Further on there is an apartment-house section. And finally there are the suburbs. Faris and Dunham report that the poorer the district, the greater is the incidence of schizophrenia. The central district produces

-143-

the largest amount. Next in frequency are the adjacent hobo and rooming-house neighborhoods. The lowest rates are reported for the outlying residential areas, which are economically the most prosperous. Unlike the schizophrenics, depressives have usually been reared in middle-class districts. It is necessary to examine the meaning of social status in order to speculate about the reasons for its relationship to symptoms and methods of resolving conflict.

Social strata differ from each other on such dimensions as prestige, power, and economic wealth. These tend to coincide, but not completely. For example, a manual laborer, as a member of his union, may have more bargaining power than a white-collar worker. Nevertheless, the middle class in American society generally have more power than the working class.

In our studies, we divided our subjects into social classes. We omitted the upper class because their number is small and they often are not available for study. Hence we compare the reactions to conflict of the middle and working classes.

Jobs held by members of the middle class require conceptual skills, afford a bargaining relationship to the employer on an individual rather than on a group basis, and earn incomes high enough to permit some saving after the essentials are purchased. Usually the American middle-class person can be optimistic about the possibility of improving his economic position, although the process may require considerable effort. The importance to the middle class of competent performance and individual advancement leads them to value hard work, saving, formal education, and socially respectable behavior. Those aspects of the middle-class style of life that seem most relevant to the resolution of conflict include an acceptance of responsibility for one's own conduct, rational self-control, self-denial when necessary, and the expression of feelings in complex, indirect, and often symbolic forms. In short, the member of the middle class must be able to discipline himself before he can leave his mark on the world.

Given these values, it is not difficult to make some guesses about probable moral standards, expressive styles, and defenses. Responsibility for one's conduct requires the development of moral prohibitions which apply to a wide range of behaviors, particularly those which may jeopardize one's social position. As for expressive style, the middle-class citizen should tend to seek indirect outlets for his aggression, since he is concerned with maintaining his respectability. Since he is not accustomed to working with his large muscles, he should not be inclined to express his anger in physical action. When he is in conflict, he should avoid guilt by defensive distortions which are compatible with the extensive prohibitions of his moral needs. Since he holds himself responsible for his own behavior, for example, he should be inclined toward such defenses as turning his aggression on the self, or reversal.

Because the member of the working class lacks the skills and the values needed for reasonably rapid advancement to white-collar jobs, he develops a very different style of life from that of the middle class. Since success is uncertain, the manual laborer tends to regard each act less as an investment in the future than as a source of momentary pleasure. He places a high value on his principal economic assets, physical strength, and skill. If he becomes physically impaired, he may be unable to support himself. In view of his limited potential for mobility, the working-class boy should have less need to internalize those aspects of the moral code which apply to aggression than the middle-class boy. We would not expect the working-class boy to engage in such defenses as self-blame and reversal, since they are not consistent with his moral standards and their use would not contribute to his economic advancement. He needs defenses which will help him to adjust to physical deprivation. He cannot do much to change his real world, but he can get solace from his daydreams: he can deny reality or with-

draw from the challenge of his problems. Because he
tends to communicate his needs physically and directly,
he should select as substitutes the action tendencies
which are most motoric and direct.

   Socialization. In stressing the importance of the
father's economic position, we assumed that it is associated with a style of life which the parents transmit
to their offspring. Type of material discipline is the
child-rearing practice which we felt would be most
closely associated with social position and with methods
of resolving conflict. If a mother is accustomed to reg-
ulating her son's behavior by appeals to guilt, she typically acts hurt when he misbehaves. When he identifies
with her, he too should tend to express aggression indirectly. In defending against conflicts involving aggression, he should be inclined to blame himself rather than
others, since she has always defined his misbehavior as
an attack on her. But if she uses corporal punishment,
then he identifies with an attacker and should express
aggression directly.

   We also studied other child-rearing practices, such
as methods of enforcing obedience, frequency of reward,
and harshness and timing of weaning and toilet training.
But this paper is not primarily concerned with the reporting of our experiments. That is the purpose of a
forthcoming publication. While I shall make some pass-
ing references to other child-rearing practices, I shall
stress discipline in reporting our results.

                 Selection of Subjects

   In chosing subjects for our studies, we took considerable care to develop criteria which would rule out
certain possible sources of error. I now summarize
these criteria in the hope that they will be of help in interpreting some of our results.

   Our primary object was the selection of an equal

sample from each social class. In obtaining these samples, we were motivated less by an interest in social class _per_ _se_ than by a desire to locate two groups which differed markedly in early backgrounds. We were confident from our reading of the literature on social classes that such groups would provide us with differences as great as any we could find within American society. In order to obtain data for classifying the family with respect to social status and child-rearing practices, we interviewed each mother in her home. Our class-typing procedure was that developed by Hollingshead and Myers.[5] Their method consists of a weighting of two scales. One is a seven-point scale of occupational status which ranges from higher executives, professionals, and proprietors at one extreme to unskilled workers at the other. The second is a seven-point scale of education, and it ranges from graduate work or professional school at one extreme to less than seven years of schooling on the other.

In our research we hoped to distinguish differences between the classes which would mirror the extent to which the families have taken over styles of life appropriate to their economic situations. Consequently, we rejected families which were moving up or down in the class system. Our criteria of social mobility included shift in status between grandparents' and parents' occupations, and contradiction between the family's actual class and the mother's description of the class status.

Our most complex problem in the selection of subjects involved the elimination of influences of conditions other than social position which might have affected our results in ways we would not have been able to interpret. Obviously the more controls we introduced the more difficult it became to obtain an adequate number of subjects who met our criteria. I now list the controls that we finally used.

---

[5]Personal communication.

We selected subjects for each of the studies that I
shall mention from among the pupils in the seventh,
eighth, and ninth grades of the cities of Detroit and High-
land Park, Michigan. If we had used higher grade levels,
we would not have been able to obtain an adequate sample
of lower-class subjects. If we had used lower levels,
our children would not have been able to read and write
well enough to take some tests in groups. To eliminate
sex differences, we restricted our sample to males. We
chose boys rather than girls because the theory about
psychological development is much clearer for males
than for females.

Because of the many reported class differences in
intelligence, we also controlled this variable. In order
to be chosen, subjects had to be classified as having an
intelligence score of low-average or above on the school
placement test, or an I.Q. score of 75 or above on any
of the several tests administered in the school system.
We also administered as part of the experimental procedure the Verbal, Reasoning, and Spatial Ability sub-
tests of the Chicago Tests of Primary Mental Abilities
(17). These variables were controlled for all significant relationships in the studies.

We eliminated subjects in certain special social
categories either because there is some question about
the meaning of their child-rearing practices or because
they have drastically fewer families in one class than in
another. As a result, we chose only white Christian
subjects whose parents were born in the United States
north of the Mason-Dixon line, and whose families originally came from northern and western Europe. In order
to eliminate the effects of complicating experiences which
might have resulted from divorce or the death of a parent,
we also required that each subject be in residence with
both of his biological parents.

Needs

Before one can study needs, he must have some basis for defining and classifying them. This is much easier said than done, since the number of current systems of motivation tends to approach the number of system-builders. However, there are some converging trends. In selecting from among these, we may be guided by the purpose of the taxonomy, the establishment of a frame of reference for analyzing such concepts as needs and defenses. This purpose is best served by the allocation of motivated behavior to a limited number of meaningful categories which I shall call aims or goal-states. A need is a disposition to engage in any of the actions which will achieve a particular aim. According to this definition, aim is the sole criterion for identifying a need. Need is not identified in terms of an act: there is no need to expel or to hurt. Need is not identified in terms of an object: there is no need for music or for new clothes. Need is not identified in terms of a stimulating condition, either internal or external: there is no hunger need. We identify needs only by their end-states, the goals of the action. We can speak of needs for satiety, for status, and for love.

Aim is a construct which we infer from observing behavior. A motivated person need not be aware of his aim. He may be conscious only of discomfort, of a desire to perform a particular act, or of a fascinating object. If he thinks of the aim, he pictures it as a desired goal whose attainment will change his affective state: he will feel better if he attains the aim. Subjectively, then, need refers to a discrepancy between current status and aim. The person expects that any of the actions which bridge the gap between status and aim should change his affective state. This description is obviously related to current expectancy theories (1) (15).

Aims give meaning to many possible implementing actions. The total number which may be used to achieve an aim is usually very large. A complex need, such as

increased social status, may be implemented by a myr-
iad of actions as varied as buying an expensive car, improving one's education, moving to a more prosperous
part of the town, and changing one's speech habits. While
the variety of potential actions is very great, it is reduced considerably by the actualities of a real situation.
The person's associations to the goal-state become organized as images of specific actions which are appropriate to the situation. We call these images action
tendencies. In a specific situation, only some of the
potential actions are applicable. It would not be meaningful, for example, for Jim to make sarcastic remarks
about the coach's low status if the coach comes from a
good family.

All of the action tendencies relevant to an aim may
be arranged in an order of preference. This hierarchy
is based on similarity to the most preferred action tendency. If there were no deterrent, Jim would probably
prefer to hurt the coach physically. But since Jim is
motivated by a conflicting moral aim, he has to resort
to an alternative action tendency. Given this description
of systems of hierarchically arranged action tendencies,
we can now define the primary goal of a theory of conflict as the prediction of the particular alternative action
tendencies which a person characteristically selects.

Moral Needs

As part of the child's early moral training, he learns
to avoid certain acts. In teaching their children, many
mothers tend to phrase moral precepts as ideals less
often than as prohibitions. The injunction, "Don't be a
tattle-tale," is probably more common than the offering
of rewards for keeping confidences. The admonition,
"This is not yours," is used more frequently than rewards for the return of other children's property.

In the course of internalizing moral standards, the
child becomes sensitized to certain dimensions of all

-150-

needs, since moral standards define the adults' rules
for rewarding and punishing his behavior. We may illustrate this learning process by some hypothetical experiences which are fairly representative of those of the
American middle-class child. If he hits his sister, the
repeated phrase, "Don't hurt your sister," which accompanies the adults' punishment soon makes him aware
that there is a class of objects which he may not hit, and
that his sister is a member of that class of objects. Such
questions as "Did you tease the cat?" similarily point up
the importance of avoiding a particular class of acts. The
sharp injunction, "Stop that temper tantrum," teaches
him that, regardless of the reason, this is one of a forbidden class of emotional expressions. The question,
"Did you mark up this book?" makes him painfully aware
that he would not have been punished if someone else had
committed this act. We shall refer to his awareness that
the initiative is his as the source. So defined, source
is the perceived origin of the action: whether a person
experiences the source of the need as being within rather
than outside of him. In short, the child learns that certain acts, objects, and affects are consistently forbidden,
and that he is punished when people learn that he is the
source. If the rules are applied consistently, he gradually comes to internalize them in the form of moral needs.

By defining certain acts as ethically unacceptable,
moral needs delimit the number of possible alternative
action tendencies available to a person in conflict. It is
therefore important to examine the nature of the limitations.

Some internalized moral standards apply only to a
specific act. Instances are the commandments, "Thou
shalt not kill" and "Thou shalt not steal." Other moral
standards forbid a range of acts, usually those which
are most preferred. An example is the middle-class
standard that it is wrong to attack someone unless he
attacks first. If this is part of Jim's code, he cannot,
without feeling guilty, hurt the coach or anyone else who
has not initiated hostilities. However, no other acts are

ruled out by this standard.

Some standards define a wide range of acts as immoral. If Jim's moral needs proscribe all acts except those which help one's enemies, he has no recourse but to help the coach in some way.

Some standards specify an object. If Jim's moral need proscribes the harming of helpless animals, he cannot use his dog as a scapegoat for the hated coach. Some standards apply to a range of objects. The commandment, "Thou shalt not kill," connotes "all living things." There are similar variations in ranges of prohibited sources. We can summarize the principles covered thus far by returning to Jim's conflict. Let us examine his aggressive sytem of action tendencies. The moral need can be analyzed similarly; therefore we need not describe it in further detail.

Figure 1

DIMENSIONS OF AN AGGRESSIVE NEED

Source	Act	Affect	Object
self	physical attack	rage	baseball coach
teammate	lose a game	indignation	basketball coach
schoolmate	insult	intolerance	teammate
teacher	protest	displeasure	strange adult
strange adult	criticize	impatience	child
student in another school	gossip	boredom	dog
member of other team	advise	indifference	automobile
rival coach	play a competitive game	warmth	self

Figure 1 describes four hypothetical dimensions of Jim's aggressive need. Depending on the particular situation in which Jim finds himself, he should develop action tendencies which consist of different combinations of elements in the four dimensions. If there were no conflict, Jim would select the first element in each of the four dimensions. He would wish to inflict physical pain on the baseball coach and acknowledge the rage and act as his own. But if there is a conflict, he can select a substitute from within one or more of the dimensions. He can make such substitutions as an insult for physical attack, boredom for a rage, a child for the coach, or a teacher for himself.

In each dimension the elements are arranged in terms of degree of similarity, and presumably in order of preference, to the one most preferred. If only the coach were barred as an object by the moral need, Jim should select for attack the basketball coach, the next object in order of preference.

The relationships of moral needs to conflict is aptly described by the common saying that "anything I like is either illegal, immoral, or fattening." Moral needs tend to define as sinful the most preferred elements in a particular dimension. Let us assume that Jim's moral aim is such that it is violated by not only the first order of preference in each of the four dimensions of aggression, but also by the second, third, fourth, and even fifth in some instances. Not only must he inhibit his aggression to the baseball coach; he must also avoid directing it at the basketball coach, the teammate, a strange adult, and a child. Only if Jim hurts a dog or an automobile will he be able to implement the aggressive aim in a manner which does not violate the moral one. Let us assume that Jim's moral standards also rule out the first five affects, the first two acts, and the first four sources. We will refer to these cutting points as moral thresholds. In choosing an action tendency which is compatible with the moral and aggressive aims, Jim must shift from the most preferred element of one of the

-153-

dimensions to another element which is below the moral threshold. But he need not displace within more than one dimension. If, for example, he shifts within the dimension of source from self to the rival coach, then he can retain the first choices in the other dimensions. Jim then believes that not he but a rival coach hates and wants to hurt the baseball coach.

A Study of Moral Needs. In discussing the theory, we have been attempting to describe a general frame of reference which has helped to clarify a number of hypotheses about the resolution of conflict. How did we jump from the context of theory to the selection of specific hypotheses and the development of techniques for collecting data? We shall try to answer this question by describing part of a study by Wesley Allinsmith, a member of our project. The purpose was to explore differences in degrees of guilt about an immoral wish which are expressed by subjects from different backgrounds. In order to determine moral standards with respect to the wish, it seemed necessary to obtain every subject's reactions to an incident in which someone has the actual wish. This was done with a story-completion test. In a typical story, the hero is unintentionally or regretfully hurt by an adult who previously has been an object of affection. The hero wishes the adult would drop dead and later learns that he has been in an accident. Allinsmith assumed that subjects with severe internalizations against aggression would tend to react to such a plot as though the hero were responsible for the mishap.

Intensity of guilt in the subjects' endings was ranked on a seven-point scale, depending on the degree to which the hero of the story attempted to confess or make reparation or was judged to experience any kind of pain, anxiety, punishment, or threat of punishment. Examples of extreme guilt are serious injury to the hero, long prison sentences, outlandish defensive distortions, or marked emotional states such as panic, terror reactions, or suicidal inclinations. Examples of low guilt include mild disappointments and occurrences which do not seem

-154-

of great interest to the hero.

We have previously explained our reasons for antici-
pating that members of the middle class would tend to
be more guilty about very aggressive acts than the working-class boys. However, it was difficult to know what
we would find in the case of the death-wish, since the
expression of such a sentiment would elicit considerable
condemnation in either class. Upon scoring the story
endings, we indeed find great guilt in so high a proportion of subjects from both classes that there is no significant difference in social status.

Next Allinsmith tested the relationship between type
of maternal discipline and the hero's guilt about his
death-wish. Again we were not certain about our prediction. However, we assumed that subjects whose
mothers try to regulate behavior mostly by psychological manipulation would show most guilt, and that subjects whose mothers typically use corporal punishment
would not express as much guilt.

We divided the mothers into three groups, depending on their reports of disciplinary practices. Those '
mothers who use predominantly psychological discipline
tend mostly to regulate their children's behavior by expressions of disappointment and appeals to guilt. Another group of mothers tends to resort to such measures
as spanking, slapping, and threatening. In addition to
the psychological and corporal group, there is a small
number of mothers who combine many behaviors, such
as restriction of children to their rooms, deprivation
of privileges, and occasionally one of the more extreme
types of discipline. We did not feel certain of the meanings of these mixed techniques; hence we eliminated
cases in which they had been used when we made our
predictions. In general we find a close relation between
discipline and intensity of guilt expressed in the story
endings. As predicted, the psychologically manipulated
show the most guilt.

Finally, we decided to make separate analyses within each social class of the relationships between type of
discipline and guilt over the death-wish. These analyses
were prompted by the suspicion that the content of the
specific action tendency, the death-wish, may be evaluated very differently within the two classes. We anticipated that such thoughts would be proscribed more in
the middle than in the working class. If this is true,
there is no reason to predict that working-class boys
whose mothers favor psychological manipulation should
be guilty about an impulse which is of little concern to
their parents. However, sons of middle-class mothers
who favor psychological manipulation, and presumably
use this technique to instill guilt about death-wishes,
should express more guilt than middle-class boys whose
mothers use corporal discipline. Upon testing the relationships between expression of guilt and type of discipline within each class, Allinsmith finds that the de-
ductions are corroborated. Sons of middle-class mothers
who use psychological manipulation tend to express more
guilt than sons of mothers who use corporal discipline.
However, in the working class guilt and discipline are
unrelated.

Expressive Style

Moral needs delimit the range of action tendencies
which can be substituted for the most preferred one.
But the range is usually still a broad one. We now consider another aspect of behavior which delimits the
range further. It is a person's customary style of expressing himself. I will describe studies of two types
of styles. One is the relative extent to which a person
is accustomed to express himself with his large muscles
and with symbols and abstractions. The second is the
directness with which he usually expresses aggression.

Motoric and Conceptual Expression. Our interest
in motoric and conceptual styles was kindled by the
characteristics of some of the personality disorders

which occur more often in one social class than in another. Conversion hysteria and catatonic schizophrenia, for example, are both associated with working-class backgrounds, and both disorders involve some malfunction of the voluntary muscles. Hysterics tend to express their conflicting needs indirectly by distorting a sensory or muscular function which is usually under voluntary control. Catatonic schizophrenics resolve some of their conflicts over aggression by immobilizing certain sets of muscles which might be used to express the forbidden needs.

As prominent as muscular malfunctioning is in the symptoms of the working class, it is conspicuous by its absence in the pathologies of the middle class. In fact the symptoms of this group seem to create muscular inhibition. Patients with the characteristic disorders of the middle class tend to express their problems conceptually. The obsessive ruminates. He worries, for example, that he has not been keeping his records in just the right way. Or he is concerned that he may have unintentionally offended a friend and tries to recall all the events that led to the presumed offense. The depressive broods about the causes of his guilt and wishes he could somehow cancel some of his past acts.

From the disorders of the two classes we can infer that the working class tend to express their needs motorically while the middle class tend to favor conceptual outlets. But styles of expression are probably not unique to patients. The normal member of each social class must also learn to express and to communicate many of his important needs in the manner characteristic of the patients from the same class. To test this deduction, Elton McNeil, another member of our project, compared the expressive styles of boys in the two classes. He anticipated that subjects from the working class would be dilated in expressing themselves by means of the large muscles of their body but constricted when required to use concepts. The middle class on the other hand should be constricted when communicating by physical means

-157-

but dilated when they can use conceptual approaches.
To create a natural situation requiring motoric communication, McNeil asked each boy to play a modified
version of the children's game of "statues." After the
subject was spun around, he was directed to "freeze"
in a pose that depicted an assigned theme. Then he was
photographed.

There were four themes. First the subject was told
to act "as if you are very, very happy; as if you had just
won a million dollars or got the one thing in the world
you have always wanted." Next, he was instructed to
behave "as if you are very, very frightened: as if the
wall of a building is falling over on you or a tiger is
jumping at you." Then he was told to portray great
anger, and finally profound sorrow. A person not ac-
quainted with our theory or our predictions rated each
photograph for presence and absence of six criteria of
motoric dilation: either hand waist high, both hands
waist high, either hand shoulder high, legs spread apart,
body not facing camera directly, and body not vertical.
On all but one criterion--shift in body from the vertical
position--the differences between the classes are significant and in the predicted direction. The exception is
not far from significant. There is little question but
that the working-class boys are more dilated than those
in the middle class in motoric expression as measured
in the game of statues.

Where a conceptual approach is required, we predicted a reversal of the results of the game of statues.
McNeil asked the children to make abstract paintings
of the same themes that had been portrayed previously.
A judge with no knowledge of our theory or predictions
rated the dilation and constriction of all paintings in
terms of criteria which we obtained from the literature
on interpretations of artistic production. Again our predictions are substantially confirmed, although the differences between the two classes are not as marked as those
obtained for motoric expression. On two criteria of dilation, lack of recognizable objects and four or more

colors, boys in the middle class significantly exceed those in the working class. On two criteria of constriction, small painting and structural use of black paint, the working class exceed the middles, as predicted, but the results are not significant. Finally there is one criterion of constriction, the use of pencil, which is significant but not in the predicted direction.

If motoric and conceptual are general expressive styles, it is necessary that their influence be demonstrated for many kinds of behavior. In another conceptual task, the Carl Hollow Square Test, which resembles a jigsaw puzzle, middle-class subjects significantly exceed those in the working class in the use of combinations of blocks rather than single ones. In addition, the middle-class group tends to give conceptual rather than motoric reasons for their choices of leisure activities and future jobs and prefer conceptual hobbies and conceptual jobs. The working-class boys, on the other hand, tend to pick the motoric alternatives in all four cases. However, only two of the differences between the classes are significant: choice of conceptual hobbies and games, and conceptual reasons for the importance of the job. The congruence of all these trends supports the original anticipation that the middle class would be conceptually oriented and the working class motorically oriented.

McNeil also analyzed the relationship of parental discipline to a single index of expressive style. In constructing this index, he arbitrarily picked as most conceptual those subjects whose paintings reveal the most dilation and who have low motoric scores in the game of statues. For the most motoric group, he chose those who are most dilated in the game of statues and have low conceptual scores in their paintings. The middle group consists of children who are not high in either their motoric or conceptual scores. We anticipated that mothers who favor corporal punishment would provide models of people who exert power by motoric means. Hence we expected their children to use predominantly motoric styles of expression. If the parents appeal to guilt, we expected their children to identify with the conceptual orientation involved in the communication of such abstract concepts as responsibility, guilt, and sin. The results support the predictions: subjects whose mothers tend to appeal to guilt are predominantly conceptual, and subjects whose mothers use corporal discipline are predominantly motoric.

Directness of Expression of Aggression. We have previously noted that if there were no conflict, Jim would carry out his first action tendency, which involves a physical attack on the coach. However, because of Jim's moral need, he inhibits this first choice. He inhibits not only the first but also a number of others which are so close to the original that they, too, fall within the purview of the moral prohibition.

There are considerable differences in the directness with which various people express a need in conflict. By directness we mean the closeness or similarity to the original within each of the dimensions of the aim. If Jim were to select another coach as an object of attack, he would express the aim more directly than if he vented his wrath on an automobile. Similarly, if he insulted the coach, this act would be more direct than trying to beat him in a chess game.

To measure directness of expression, Beverly Allinsmith, another member of our project, devised a story-completion test. The test consists of six story beginnings about boys who are frustrated or treated unfairly by older people. Since the adults are objects either of love or fear, the heroes are caught between simultaneous needs to retaliate and to seek love or protection. A typical theme describes the plight of Bill, who admires his older sister. But when something goes wrong, she always tells his parents that it is his fault.

The endings were rated on a scale consisting of eighteen degrees of directness. The scale was arbitrarily developed from a coding of the responses of a smaller number of subjects in a pre-test. Among the most direct responses are appeals to others to help in attacking the frustrator, and delays of direct action. Still relatively direct are substitutions of verbal for physical attack, and displacements of attack from the original object to another. In the middle of our scale are such categories as conscious but uncommunicated aggressive thoughts, and expressions of fears that the adult is angry at the hero. At the indirect extreme are feelings of sadness and of inordinate friendship toward the adults. These are substitutes which preclude the expression of aggression in either deed, word, or thought. Allinsmith added the scores on all six stories for each subject, and then divided the range of total scores into four categories, depending on degree of directness.

Because the control of physical aggression is required for social advancement, we expected directness of expression to be related to class membership. Middle-class boys are typically described (4) (7) as fighting only when attacked, as loath to hurt girls or supervisory adults, and as blinding themselves to the existence of aggression in others. Descriptions of the working class, on the other hand, suggest that direct expression of aggression is socially rewarded, and that parents teach children to fight peers of either sex as well as adults. Disturbances typical of the middle class, such as depression and obsession, usually reveal a preoccupation with aggression but an expression of it by tortuous indirection. In contrast, pathologies such as hysteria and catatonia are often characterized by direct expression of aggressive needs. However, when we compare the story endings of the two classes we find that social class is not significantly related to the projective measure of the directness with which aggression is expressed. There is not even a trend.

We next turn to the variable of parental discipline. If the parent uses corporal punishment, the child should express his aggression most directly. The mother is providing the model of a person who expresses her needs directly, and is also herself an obvious target of the child's aggression. Indirection should be the rule if the parent, instead of attacking, attempts to persuade by reason, acts hurt if the child misbehaves, and patiently pleads with him to control himself in the future. Since the mother reveals little or no anger and does not attack him, she provides no focus for his hostility. The relationship between discipline and directness of expression in story endings is very significant. The psychologically manipulated are indirect and the corporally disciplined direct in their expressions of aggression. The group with intermediate discipline are also intermediate in directness.

Let us review the material that we have covered thus far. To illustrate the forces which bear on the resolution of conflict, we have been considering a hypothetical conflict between Jim's aggression toward his coach and his conscience. Because of the conflict, Jim cannot use the most direct outlet for his wrath. Our primary problem is the prediction of his most probable substitute. We have proposed that the action tendencies provide different pathways to the aim of the need, and that their content be analyzed in terms of the four dimensions of source, act, affect, and object. Within each of these dimensions, the elements are organized in an order of preference based on similarity to the most preferred. An individual's moral needs usually preclude not only the first choice in each dimension but also a number of others. The study of moral needs indicates that Jim probably cannot face the idea of a death-wish if he comes from a middle-class family and if his mother has tended to use psychological discipline. The studies of expressive style suggest that Jim's choice among the morally acceptable elements in the four dimensions will also be influenced by his social class and his mother's discipline. If his class is middle, he will probably pick a conceptual alternative. He may, for example, marshal the evidence and protest to the coach. If Jim is from a lower-class family, he should be inclined

to pick one of the alternative motoric acts. If he pro-
tests, he will probably forego argument in favor of some
act such as defacing the coach's fence. If Jim's mother
has favored psychological discipline, he should pick a
conceptual and relatively indirect alternative. He may,
for example, try to advise the coach on the running of
the team. If Jim's mother has tended to use corporal
discipline, he will probably express his aggression directly.

Mechanisms of Defense

The range of alternatives within each of the four
dimensions--act, object, affect, and source--tends to
be narrowed down by moral needs and by customary
styles of expression. The range is delimited still further by defense mechanisms. The list of defenses in
the psychoanalytic literature is so long and varied that
it is necessary to classify them into groups before they
can be defined and become the objects of research. It
is possible to divide them into three families. Defenses
in the first family probably develop early in life and have
four characteristics in common: (1) they seem applicable to every type of conflict; (2) their use requires
little previous learning; (3) they distort reality markedly; and (4) they are of little help in solving real social
difficulties.

Denial is a representative example of the first
family of defenses. Almost anything can be denied,
since the mechanism results in the blotting out of large
segments of reality. Like dreaming, the defense requires little previous practice and is available quite
early, as we may see from observing the play of children. But while the stuff of which dreams are made is
consoling, it provides few practical solutions. The man
who believes that black is white cannot take any active
steps to help himself. In fact, if he is frequently unable
to estimate what is happening about him, he may not
even be able to carry on normal social relations.

Defenses in a second family differ from those in
the first on all the four characteristics just mentioned:
(1) these defenses seem applicable only to special kinds
of conflicts; (2) they require the previous mastery of
complex skills; (3) they distort a small area of the perceptual field; and (4) their use produces the fewest social
complications in societies which are realistically oriented.

Turning against oneself is a typical member of the
second family of defenses. When a person uses this
mechanism, he does not obliterate his problem. If he
is aggressive, he is still aware that he wants to attack
someone, that he feels angry, and that the need is his.
The distortion is confined to the target. Instead of being focused upon the original object, the anger is displaced to another target, himself.

The development of such a defense requires the previous acquistion of such knowledges and skills as an
image of one's body, a concept of self, the capacity to
grasp the distinction between self and others, the knowledge of approved and disapproved forms of aggression,
an understanding of the complicated idea of blaming, and
a high valuation of the recognition of others. Obviously
the turning of anger against oneself requires no major
distortion of reality, and does not create many social
problems if it is not used to excess. Not only does it
help to inhibit aggression, but it often leads to socially
rewarded behavior such as modesty.

Finally there is a third family of defense. Instead
of turning his eyes away from reality or shifting from
one action tendency to another, a person may deceive
himself about the strength of one of the dimensions of
a need. For example, Jim can defend himself by playing down the strength of his anger at the coach. In that
event, he need not convince himself that he is angry at
someone else. His perception of the action tendency is
accurate. All he distorts is its strength. "Sour grapes"
represents another well known example of this type of
distortion. Jim can salvage his self-esteem by thinking

-164-

that baseball is not a very attractive sport. Since he does not want to play very badly, his inability to make the grade is no great loss.

In the following discussion, we shall concentrate on defenses in the second family. They may be defined as dispositions to distort particular dimensions of the need: either the source, or act, or affect or object, or combinations of them. To illustrate this definition, we return to the diagram of Jim's system of aggressive action tendencies.

Figure 2

DEFENSES AGAINST AN AGGRESSIVE NEED

Projection	Reversal	Isolation	Displacement of object
Source	Act	Affect	Object
self	physical attack	rage	baseball coach
teammate	lose a game	indignation	basketball coach
schoolmate	insult	intolerance	teammate
teacher	protest	displeasure	strange adult
a strange adult	criticize	impatience	child
student in another school	gossip	boredom	dog
member of other team	advise	indifference	automobile
rival coach	play a competitive game	warmth	self

If Jim does not distort his preferred action tendency, he can report, "I wish to hurt the coach." He can acknowledge the source as being within himself; he knows that the intended act is to inflict pain; he feels the affect of hatred; and he is aware of the identity of the object. Figure 2 is similar to Figure 1 except that we have listed the name of a defense above each dimension. Let us begin with the dimension of objects. If Jim distorts his need by choosing not the preferred object, the baseball coach, but some other, then the defense is displacement of the object.

Jim may also defend himself by displacement within the dimension of affects. If instead of rage he experiences indifference, he can be aware of all the other aspects of the need except the affect connected with his wish to hurt. His isolation enables him to talk objectively about the wish because he lacks the feeling of hatred, and there is no threat that he will lose control. The hatred itself is displaced to some other object which he can safely hate to excess.

If Jim distorts the act by shifting from physical attack to helpful advice, and if this is accompanied by a comparable displacement of hatred by friendliness in the dimension of affect, the defense is reversal. While there are other possible displacements within the dimension of act, no names have been suggested for them.

Projection entails only the distortion of source. Jim need only reject the idea that the wish is his. If he believes that someone desires to hurt the coach, Jim can even feel righteously indignant. There are other possible combinations of distortions within the four dimensions, but we require no further examples to illustrate the nature of the second family of defenses. All of them involve a self-deception about the most preferred action tendency and a shift to another action tendency which still fulfills the original aim. The shift involves a displacement within one or more of the four dimensions of a particular aim.

Operational Definition. The construction of instruments for identifying defenses raises some methodological issues which are relevant to the validity of projective tests in general. In measuring the strength of a personality trait, the investigator customarily counts the number of signs of that trait in the subject's protocol.

This method requires a number of assumptions. For example, an investigator who is studying defenses must take for granted that the picture or inkblot elicits a conflict, and that the conflicting needs are strong enough to require defensive distortion. In addition, he must assume that the defense which he is studying is appropriate to the conflict and that the subject is using that mechanism rather than some others which may be equally appropriate. Our inclination to question these assumptions was strengthened by a pre-test of an unstructured projective instrument. Some subjects gave no evidence of conflict; some used no defenses; and some used defenses other than those in which we were interested.

Unstructured tests are poor research instruments because their stimuli contain so many attributes. The subject, depending upon his needs, selects from among these attributes and responds to the ones which he has chosen. The clinician is typically interested in gaining all the available information about one individual--his abilities, needs, symptoms, resistances, and defenses. Hence the clinician can use all the material in the protocol. But the researcher is typically interested in comparing not the different characteristics of one individual, but rather a group of individuals with respect to one characteristic. He wants to determine, for example, whether a subject, when compared to others, is high, medium, or low in the frequency with which he uses the defense of projection. The investigator can use only those data in the protocol which help him to rank the subject on that one variable. Even when a subject's predilection for a particular defense is strong, he may obtain a low score on an unstructured test because he is responding to irrelevant but salient characteristics of the stimulus. Such sources of error have to be eliminated by increasing the structure of the stimulus.

We chose the story-completion technique because it can be structured. We wrote story beginnings which phrase the conflict so specifically that all endings, even evasive ones, can be scored in a manner which is pertinent to the study.

A further methodological problem in identifying defenses involves the strength of the conflicting needs.
The use of defenses prevents the awareness of action
tendencies whose expression would create guilt. However, if the need is not strong so there is little or no
danger of expressing the action tendency, the person can
easily tolerate awareness of it. The strength of the need
must exceed a certain threshold to elicit a defensive distortion. There seems little reason to assume that the
reading of a story of the examination of a picture arouses
enough aggression to create a serious conflict about it.

We decided to create a real conflict in a study undertaken by Betty Beardslee. To control the effect of
experiences which the subjects may have had before
coming to the testing session, the examiner first obtained
their endings to three stories. Then she tried to stim-
ulate a real conflict between aggressive and moral needs.
Following the stimulation of aggression, she asked the
subjects to complete three other stories. She then compared the subjects whose defenses against aggression
increased from the initial to the second set of stories
with subjects whose defenses did not increase.

In order to arouse conflict, each boy was seen individually and told that most mothers report pleasant
facts about their boys to the interviewers. However,
they also mention some negative facts which they would
not admit to their own sons. Beardslee listed such confidences as the mothers' loss of patience with their sons'
humor, boredom with childish interests, embarrassment
caused by clumsy and tactless behavior, difficulty in
knowing how to react to "crushes" on girls, and inability
to respect certain impulsive judgments. After the subject
wrote the second set of story endings, the examiner said
she should have mentioned that the comments "about boys
being silly" were made not by mothers in Detroit, but by
a group in California. "Detroit mothers don't seem to
feel this way at all." Then the subject was asked to dis-

cuss his reactions to the opinions of some of the California mothers and his conjectures about the differences between mothers in the two states. Finally, the interviewer observed that all mothers mention more nice things than complaints, and that all the members of our project thought that the boys in this school were not silly or immature.

The six story beginnings all involve conflicting reactions to adults. In a typical plot, Paul, who loves his widowed mother, learns she is going to marry a man whom Paul has always hated. Presumably he has conflicting reactions to his new father. In scoring the results, we were particularly interested in the defenses of reversal and turning on the self. Reversal involves a selection by the hero of an act and affect opposite in meaning to the most preferred aggressive action tendency. Instead of hurting his father, for example, Paul ends up loving and helping him. It is necessary that the shift not result from a realistic ending such as one which describes a successful attempt by the father to win the boy's affection by kindness. Turning against the self requires the displacement of hostility from the original object to the self. Such is the case, for example, if Paul blames himself rather than the hated adult who is responsible for the difficulty.

Originally Beardslee had intended to analyze the two defenses separately. However, this was impossible because they occur together so often in the story endings. It is difficult to find instances of guilt which are not accompanied by explicit or implicit exoneration and affection for the adult. And, conversely, there is scarcely a case of reversal which is not accompanied by self-blame. We had originally assumed that the defenses would tend to occur together. However, we suspect that with the increased methodological sophistication which we have gained from this initial study, we might be able to write stories that would separate the two defenses. In any event, we treated them as a pair in this investigation. We labelled them the "expiating" defenses because they

-169-

are so pertinent to conflicts between aggression and moral needs.

Defenses which enable a boy to control himself rather than to attack others should be favored by the middle class, the group most concerned with control of aggression. Control, conscientiousness, and responsibility provide the path to a sound public reputation and social mobility. The working class, on the other hand, do not place as high a value on self-control and responsibility. The working-class child often lives in a hard world, a world with few rewards for self-sacrifice. His emergencies stem less from pressures to hide his negative feelings than from the vicissitudes of the difficult environment. For these reasons, we expected differences between the two classes in their shifts in the expiating defenses. The results support our predictions. Middle-class subjects tend to differ significantly from working-class subjects.

We reasoned that a relationship also would come to light between type of discipline and the expiating defenses. If a mother controls her own hostility, reasons with her son, appeals to his pride, and plays on his guilt, her son should find it difficult to hate her and easy to blame himself. On the other hand, if she uses corporal discipline so that she becomes the object of his hostility, he should be motivated to blame her rather than himself. We find, however, that the relationship between type of discipline and the expiating defenses is not significant. We suspect that the learning of these defenses depends less on punishment than on maternal incentives. Amounts of explanation given by mothers when requesting obedience and frequency of reward interact so as to relate significantly to the expiating defenses. These increase with the combinations of reasonable obedience and frequent reward and of strict obedience and infrequent reward. Apparently conditionality of love and amount of reward motivate the child to blame himself and to exonerate the adult much more than does type of threat.

Social Structure

Thus far we have attempted to describe a system for classifying the variables involved in the resolution of inner conflict. The system relates the concepts of needs, morals, defenses, and expressive styles. We also have proposed studies of the relationships of these three to independent variables selected from systems of stratification and socialization. We would like to conclude with a summary of the reasons for including such social variables in studies of psychological problems.

Without referring to an individual's relationships with others, it would not be possible to explain the content of his moral needs, the origins of his styles of expression, or the functional efficiency of his hierarchy of defenses. The relationship between behavior and group membership is not restricted to the topics which we have been discussing. Almost all the basic concepts of personality have been devised to explain interpersonal behavior, usually within particular social groups.

If we grant the inadvisability of studying an individual's predispositions, his skills, his expectancies, and his definitions of particular situations--all factors required to predict his interpersonal behavior--without taking his group memberships into account, then the omission of most social referrents from theories of personality is a serious error. It is my impression that the lack of progress in systematizing the many valuable observations of interpersonal behavior has resulted in great part from the absence of this external social frame of reference.

Most probably the lack of coordination between social and individual concepts reflects artificial separations between professions. However, the psychologist may be inclined to question the existence of social variables which can help him to organize his theory. A subject in a study is a member of many groups. Which memberships can contribute most to an understanding of his behavior? We would suggest that psychologists start with variables which refer to aspects of the total society and its larger sub-groups. All groups function in accordance with the general values of the total society. These general values pertain to such common goals as the rearing of children and the control of disruptive forms of behavior. Such values define the rights and obligations of individuals and help a person to know what to expect when he is participating in a particular relationship with a given person in a certain type of situation (14).

While theories of social structure are admittedly very imperfect, the empirical sociological literature demonstrates the fruitfulness of variables which refer to membership in various collective groups and to such categories as social class, ethnicity, region, and race. When such concepts are integrated with observations of individual behavior, we think we will take a long stride in the direction of constructing an integrated system of personality theory whose general outlines are acceptable to the profession as a whole.

REFERENCES

1. Atkinson, J. W. Exploration using imaginative thought to assess the strength of human motives. In Jones, Marshall R., (Ed.), Nebraska Symposium on Motivation 1954. Lincoln: Univ. Nebr. Press, 1954.

2. Beaglehole, E. Some modern Hawaiians. Uni. of Hawaii Res. Publ. 1939, 19, 156-171.

3. Benedict, P. K., and Jacks, I. Mental illness in primitive society. Psychiatry, 1954, 4, 337-390.

4. Bettelheim, B. Mental health and current mores. Am. J. Orthopsychiatry, 1952, 22, 76-88.

5. Cattell, R. B. <u>Personality.</u> New York: McGraw-Hill, 1950.

6. Carothers, J. C. A study of mental derangement in Africans and an attempt to explain its peculiarities more especially in relation to the African attitude to life. <u>Psychiatry,</u> 1948, <u>11,</u> 47-86.

7. Davis, A. Child training and social class. In Barker, R. G., Kounin, J. S., and Wright, H. F., (Eds.), <u>Child Behavior and Development.</u> New York: McGraw-Hill, 1943.

8. Eaton, J. W., and Weil, R. J. <u>Culture and Mental Disorders.</u> Glencoe, Illinois: The Free Press, 1955.

9. Faris, R. E. L. and Dunham, W. <u>Mental Disorders in Urban Areas.</u> Chicago: University of Chicago Press, 1939.

10. Freud, Anna. <u>The Ego and the Mechanisms of Defense.</u> New York: International Universities Press, 1946.

11. Freud, S. <u>Psychopathology of Everyday Life.</u> New York: The Modern Library, 1938.

12. Lin, T. Y. A study of the incidence of mental disorders in Chinese and other cultures. <u>Psychiatry,</u> 1953, <u>16,</u> 313-337.

13. Noyes, A. P. <u>Modern Clinical Psychiatry.</u> Philadelphia: W. B. Saunders, 1948.

14. Parsons, T. <u>The Social System.</u> Glencoe, Illinois: The Free Press, 1951.

15. Peak, Helen. Attitude and motivation. In Jones, Marshall R., (Ed.), <u>Nebraska Symposium on Motivation 1955.</u> Lincoln: Univ. Nebr. Press, 1955.

16. Schroeder, C. W.   Mental disorders in cities.
     Amer. J. Sociology, 1942, 48, 40-47.

17. Thurstone, L. L., and Thurstone, Thelma G.
     The Chicago Tests of Primary Mental Abilities.
     Chicago: Science Research Associates, 1943.

COMMENTS ON PROFESSOR MILLER'S PAPER

by
Richard L. Solomon

The most useful approach to problems of inner
conflict and the defenses erected to handle these problems is not readily evident.   The work done by Dr.
Miller and his colleagues shows a good deal of ingenuity and promise.   The association between the type of
defense employed in projective tests and social-class
membership is useful in that it raises many new questions to be explored.   The data seem to indicate, for
example, that parental child-training practices are
relevant to defenses, if we take into account social-
class membership.

One might ask whether this outcome is a product
of the methods usually used to assess child-training
practices as well as defenses.   These methods are indirect.   The child-training practices are discovered in
parental questionnaires.   The defenses are discovered
by projective tests.   As long as our methods remain
indirect, there is a chance for large errors, and such
errors will often be taken up by variance attributable
to such variables as social class.   This hunch is based
on the suspicion that the manner in which parents answer questionnaires and children respond to projective
tests are both related to factors associated with class
membership.   How are such indices related to actual
child-training procedures and actual defenses employed in everyday situations?   This is a problem which

-174-

Dr. Miller has, of course, considered. But a little uneasiness about such matters cannot do much harm at this stage of our explorations. The development of accurate and direct methods for describing child-training practices, independent of parental impressions, seems necessary. The development of situational tests for the objective assessment of characteristic defenses, independent of projective test responses, seems necessary. The more indirect are our methods of data gathering, the more we find interpretation substituting for a good description of actual behavioral and environmental events (which never can be directly ascertained from the interpretations). However, the most satisfactory and direct methods will be hard to invent. Meanwhile, the indirect methods can be of great value in helping us formulate hunches that can later be tested with greater and greater precision as new methods are developed. Dr. Miller's work has demonstrated this conceptual richness of the indirect approaches.

COMMENTS ON PROFESSOR MILLER'S PAPER

Sigmund Koch
Duke University

One can only admire the boldness of Professor Miller's aims. After decades of fashionable talk pointing to the need for introducing some kind of order into the allusively stated and complexly interlaced psychoanalytic doctrines of the defenses, Miller has had the temerity to move in this direction. After decades of pronunciamento-making and casual anthropological voyeurism with regard to the possible effects of social variables on modes of conflict resolution and other aspects of personality function, Miller has been among the few to ask questions which are at least accessible to research within a researchable society. Moreover, he has recognized that there are both contexts and times in science when one must seek a level of discourse adjusted to the terms of one's problems; he has not even found it necessary to purchase respectability by scaling his problems to the miniscule metric of current learning theory.

The translation of such aims into action -- any kind of action -- must at the present time be counted an achievement, even if as yet very little hard cash value, as measured by concrete advance, should prove to have accrued. Unfortunately, the mode of presentation imposed on Professor Miller by the range of his material makes evaluation of the concrete conceptual and research progress of his group very difficult. The paper leaves one with a desire to learn much more about the thinking of Miller and associates with regard to each of their main classes of variables, and about the details of their interesting but briefly reported experiments.

For instance, I should like to have a more careful spelling out of the senses in which social class is conceived as influencing moral needs, expressive styles, and defenses, other than as mediated by child-rearing techniques. I should like to have a surer understanding of the extent to which social class and child-rearing techniques were partialled out as independently variable effective factors in the reported studies. I should like to have a more differentiated analysis of child-rearing technique than that comprised in the distinction between "psychological" and "corporal" discipline. I should like to have a clearer definition of "moral needs," and one which at least makes plain whether the referent of this term is an independent system of entities having conceptual properties commensurate with those of other needs like aggression, or whether "moral needs" are equated merely with certain aspects of the socially learned patterning of non-moral needs. I should want fuller discussion of the concept of "expressive style." If expressive style is some kind of consistent attribute of the types of defense individuals tend to "use," then I am worried by statements such as: "Depending on a man's style, he should tend to favor certain alternative expressions of his conflicting needs." Further, I should like to be more confident that the illustrations of variations in expressive style are on commensurable continua. I see no grounds, for instance, for coherence between "motoric vs. conceptual" and "direct vs. indirect" expressiveness of aggression (or other needs), and, so far as I can tell from the reported evidence, there is nothing consistent with such an expectation in the actual findings.

Perhaps the central element in Miller's proposal of "a taxonomic system" for dealing with problems of conflict and defense may be found in his attempt to set up the concept of "need" in such a way as to preserve the flavor and utility of psychoanalytic instinct theory and yet permit more orderly analysis of the conditions governing substitute behavior. Despite the honesty and ingenuity of the attempt, I am sure that Miller would admit that there are currently grave indeterminacies in this reformulation. Thus, for instance, the "criterion for identifying a need" is defined in terms of "aim" -- a concept which in its Freudian form has never been very clear. Freud's usage varied from the very general ("satisfaction" of any instinct) to the highly specific (modes of consummatory activity associated with the "component" impulses of infantile sexuality). Miller apparently wishes to constitute "aim" at a generality level somewhere between these extremes ("satiety, " "status, " "love"), but he specifies no rule for bounding given "aims" and their correlative needs other than that "we infer [them] from observing behavior. " This introduces no trivial difficulty: If two needs are in conflict, what is in conflict with what? If the resultant behavior is the attainment of a "compromise" aim, in terms of an "action tendency" which is some function of the "preference hierarchies" corresponding to the four "dimensions" of each of the needs, then clearly the manner in in which the aim is specified will determine the composition of the corresponding preference hierarchies, and this in turn will determine the character of the "substitute" behavior predicted. Other severe difficulties are apparent, such as the need to explicate the meaning of "degree of similarity" as the ordering principle for

-177-

Miller's dimensional "preference hierarchies," but the enumeration of such difficulties is anyone's game, and I see no point in playing it.

Miller's experience with the problems involved in what is sometimes smugly called "tightening up" psychoanalytic formulations points up to me, and, I suspect, to him, a moral of some importance for psychological science. One obvious direction which such "tightening up" can take is to seek translation of psychoanalytic principles and findings into the construct language of some other presumably more rigorous formulation. When this is tried, the usual outcome is a selective and garbled translation in which the principle of selection is determined more by accidental features of the structure and developmental status of the "more rigorous" language than it is by the illumination-value or applicational utility of the psychoanalytic material translated. Furthermore, there is a strong possibility that the selectivity and garbling produced by such endeavors is no mere limitation in practice but one in principle. We must become willing to face the possibility that different problematic contexts create different universes of discourse and that the actual universe is large enough to contain universes of discourse which are incommensurable. A second direction for "tightening up" is, of course, to remain more or less within the <u>sui</u> <u>generis</u> level of psychoanalytic thinking; to preserve its conceptual grain, the "give" in its causal texture, and yet somehow achieve heightened clarity, consistency, and testability. It is in this direction that Miller has apparently chosen to go. And it would be an insult to the resources of the English language to assume that this is <u>not</u> a direction in which one can go a certain distance. But what Miller is probably finding is that the nature of the subtle historical and intra-personal connections of the broadly discriminated processes with which psychoanalysis deals is such as to set fixed limits to progress even in <u>this</u> direction. What, in short, he may be finding is that, quite independently of the content, truth value, applicational richness, or poverty of specifically <u>psychoanalytic</u> principles, <u>any</u> formulation directed towards

certain of the problematic and explanatory objectives
of psychoanalysis must inherit fixed determinancy limits
and other formal and methodological properties from the
character of those objectives. I would urge such considerations even on the psychoanalysts who are currently
calling on nonanalytic methodologists and theorists to
aid them in a conceptual housecleaning.

Though Miller's paper raises a very challenging
topic for anyone who holds a pre-theory of motivation,
I hope no one will accuse me of intellectual cowardice
if I reject the challenge to formulate a pre-theory of
conflict and the defense mechanisms. To my way of
thinking, the Freudian construct language is the proto-
typical example of an "extrinsic" grammar. No thinker
in the history of thought was more sensitive to phenomena
of intrinsic determination and to the descriptive isolation
of specific contexts which suggest intrinsic regulation:
witness the vast number of processes -- from infantile
fantasy content through libidinal organization and development to adult character formation -- for which Freud
adduced evidence for the clustering of events into stable
syndromes. Yet in the Freudian construct language such
syndromes are invariably referred to the joint interplay
of very generally and crassly defined end-determining
systems. These systems are uniformly extrinsic to the
detailed nature of the process-syndromes of which they
are the causal conditions. In fact, at the construct
language level, such process-syndromes have no finer
structure; they merely occur as "expressions of" or as
historically triggered by the end-determining systems.
Now it may be that as a kind of abacus on which to organize
and manipulate broad historico-causal generalizations of
the sort that Freud's problematic aims required, such a
use of extrinsic grammar is as indispensable as it is
convenient. But such problematic aims pre-empt but a
small part of the business of psychology; as I have tried
to show in my paper, many questions about vital conditions
of organismic performance are not entertainable until,
in some sense, we get within the process-syndrome and
study its laws of intrinsic relation.

A NEUROLOGICAL APPROACH TO MOTIVATION

John P. Seward
University of California, Los Angeles

Introduction

First of all, I feel that the title of my paper calls for some defense. It suggests that I seek to explain data gathered at one level by constructs drawn from another, and that is just what I shall attempt to do. Anyone so foolhardy today is almost certain to be attacked. He will be accused of reductionism and told that his undertaking is unnecessary, sterile, and a waste of time. It may even do more harm than good. So before proceeding I must say something to disarm my opponents.

The gist of my apology is that such critics may be right or wrong, but one cannot be sure until he tries. Even the critics will share my belief and hope that in some distant future there will be both a neurology and a psychology of behavior. When that goal is reached it will be possible, by coordinating definitions, to go from one conceptual level to the other with enormous increase in explanatory power. But if this much is granted the question becomes, not whether, but when to attempt a synthesis. We can only tell when the water is warm by testing it from time to time.

We are advised to pick our intervening constructs shorn of all "surplus meaning." A mature science, we are told, states the laws governing its own variables in the form of functional relations among them without borrowing from other languages. But if the intervening constructs of neurology and psychology must ultimately coincide, or at least run parallel, our guesses would seem to have more chance to survive if we made them with an occasional glance at what our fellow-scientists are up to.

Meanwhile the $100,000 question is: Does a theory lead to the discovery of new relationships? On the answer to that question the defense stands or falls. It stands if it can show that molecular theorems based on molecular facts imply new molar consequences that can be tested by experiment. If they cannot do so, the theory fails to pay off. This is a risky venture: its success or failure cannot be prejudged before it is tried.

As I see it, my contribution to this symposium is not a theory in any formal sense but an exploration--a detour, if you will--made in the hope of discovering a more direct route to a distant goal.

Motivation

Before selecting relevant neurological findings, we need to define the psychological problem more clearly. What do we mean by motivation? Psychologists are by no means agreed, as even a cursory reading of previous papers in this series will show. Brown (4) and Farber (10), for example, restrict the term to drive, to which they assign the general function of energizing any response in progress. Their purpose in making a drive completely nonspecific is to distinguish it from a cue or habit, to which they assign the discriminative and associative aspects of behavior. Since what a person does is usually more important than how vigorously he does it, this usage deprives motivation of most of our interest. But the crucial question is whether the authors, having taken the direction of behavior out of the category of motivation, are still able to account for it. Brown's treatment of acquired drives, such as that for money, still leaves the answer in grave doubt.

McClelland, et al. (17), and Atkinson (2), on the other hand, define a motive as the anticipation of affective change. Young's (37) theory of motives as hedonic processes, though developed in the context of food selection in rats rather than TAT protocols, is

-181-

essentially the same. In defining a motive, this type of
theory includes both cue and habit factors without confusing anyone. Its strength lies in its emphasis on
positive goals and its readier applicability to complex
human strivings. Its most obvious weakness, as it
stands, is the difficulty of stating objectively the conditions of affect, a lack which McClelland has made
some attempt to remedy.

For my present purpose I prefer Muenzinger's
frame of reference. Muenzinger (26) assumes that behavior can be more or less reliably marked off in units
of psychological movement, each unit characterized by
a constant direction from start to finish. By motivation
Muenzinger refers to the direction and strength of psychological movement, pointing out that while its direction remains constant within a unit, its strength, or
tension, may vary. Within this framework a motive
may be defined as an inferred process that determines
the direction of movement in a behavior unit. The definition implies the persistence of this process throughout the unit; it is noncommittal as to whether it involves
drive or goal, fear of punishment or hope of reward.
Assuming, as a working hypothesis, that such a process
exists, we seek possible physiological correlates. Actually, of course, we must do a great deal more than
find them; the important thing is to see how they mediate
response selection.

Behavior moves in many directions. For conven-
ience we may classify these in the two commonly used
categories of withdrawal and approach. The first group
tends, in general, to reduce stimulation; it includes
both escape and avoidance, whether due to pain, fatigue,
excretory functions, or other disturbances. The second
group may start with a bodily deficit or a specific appetite or a social need and typically leads to increased
stimulation from the environment. I recognize the short-
comings of this dichotomy; e. g., eating reduces (or escapes) hunger while it increases mouth stimulation. So,
too, exploring unfamiliar territory may reduce fear.

In such cases assignment is arbitrary, depending on what we consider the dominant instigator. At any rate the distinction will serve my purpose, which is to se- lect typical behavior units from each area and try to develop a theory to explain them. Briefly the units se- lected are as follows:

Withdrawal Behavior
    Escape
    Avoidance

Approach Behavior
    Appetite for Food
    Exploring

It will make the task easier if I represent each type of unit by a standard laboratory experiment. The princi- ples we use, however, if successful at this level, are to be applied much more broadly: my unattainable goal, like yours, is to understand why people make statues, climb mountains, watch TV, fight wars, and attend symposia.

Postulates

We are now ready for a brief excursion into neu- rology. We shall go only as far as we need to go to achieve our immediate purpose. In that sense our method is circular; quite frankly we are looking for properties of synaptic transmission between neurones that will "give" us the behavior we observe. A further search may turn up contradictions. But the method is only semicircular; rather than invent a neurology out of whole cloth I have tried to restrict myself to facts discovered by neurologists or to reasonable inferences therefrom. And there is always the hope that the con- structs hit upon will explain or predict behavior as yet unobserved.

Despite a vast amount of painstaking research, our

picture of the brain at work is sketchy at best. We
know it consists of an intricate network of millions of
cells in ceaseless activity, bombarded by volleys of
impulses and distributing messages from center to
center in constantly shifting patterns. We know that
these messages consist essentially of minute electro-
chemical action potentials varying in frequency, intensity, and periodicity. To bring order out of apparent
chaos, investigators have studied the mechanics of
transmission in relatively simple situations--sympa-
thetic ganglia, spinal and cranial reflexes--where afferent stimuli could be controlled and correlated with
outgoing impulses. These studies have yielded a few
principles which, applied to the higher cortical and
subcortical centers, enable certain hardy souls to con-
jecture plausibly, though vaguely, about how the brain
performs its functions. Hebb's (13) doctrine of the
ontogenesis of adaptive behavior is one of the most
persuasive attempts. He showed how uniformities of
stimulation in early life might organize cortical cells
into assemblies that tend to fire together in more or
less regular sequences. Olds (28) showed how the same
model could be used to derive a typical motivated behavior unit. This is the sort of conceptual nervous system I have in mind.

The principles we need can be stated as four
postulates:

Postulate 1. Successive Inhibition. After a neurone
has fired, there is a brief period of relative refractoriness (20-100 milliseconds in the spinal cord (25)) during
which it can be rearoused only by a stronger stimulus.
Its excitability is further depressed by later shocks
delivered within a few milliseconds ("summation of sub-
normality" (Lorente de No (15)). This property, cutting
down the number of interneurones bombarding motor
cells, is commonly accepted as the cause of depression
or failure of response when the same reflex is repeatedly evoked (11).

-184-

Postulate 2. Spatial Summation. If two or more impulses arrive at neighboring synapses on a nerve cell body within a brief period (0.15-0.5 ms. in the oculomotor nucleus (16), as long as 13 ms. in the cord (3)), they may fire the neurone although a single impulse fails to do so. Far from an exception, spatial summation is considered the rule in synaptic transmission. The fact that it usually takes a group of nerve endings firing simultaneously to discharge a cell is given a major role in the selection of pathways through the central nervous system (CNS).

Postulate 3. Circular Excitation. Neurones in the CNS are so arranged that a volley of impulses once initiated may re-excite the same units for a brief time without further input, provided these have recovered between cycles. Lorente de Nó has made a strong case for this "principle of reciprocity of connections" (14). Besides presenting anatomical evidence of the abundance of such closed chains in the CNS, he argued that their functioning was necessary to account for cases of long after-discharge (16). Although he believed that short chains, due to successive inhibition, depended on outside support, he pointed out that long chains might maintain their own activity. Even here Lorente de Nó was presumably thinking in terms of milliseconds. Hebb (13), however, showed how multiple pathways made it possible to think of alternating circuits persisting as long as a half-second or a second. A further extension of reciprocity from neurones within assemblies to several assemblies firing in unison or sequence might provide even longer periods of perseveration.

You may remember how some theorists impulsively seized on reverberating circuits as a possible physiological basis for long-time retention. Their hopes were quickly abandoned, but we are properly sensitized to the risk of making a similar mistake. It is still possible, however, that circular excitation may play some part in producing structural changes at synapses that outlast the activity itself. With this idea in mind, consider the next postulate.

Postulate 4. Presynaptic Plasticity. Rapidly repeated stimulation increases the effectiveness of synaptic transmission by the stimulated fibers for some
time thereafter; prolonged disuse decreases the capacity of fibers to transmit impulses. Post-tetanic potentiation, as Eccles (8) calls it, has been observed in
spinal cord reflexes as well as in peripheral ganglia.
Its size and duration vary with the duration of the tet-
anizing stimulus. In normal fibers the excitatory increase lasts several minutes, but special procedures
have revealed longer lasting changes. By severing
dorsal roots beyond the ganglia, Eccles and McIntyre
(see 8) showed that prolonged disuse depressed reflex
effectiveness. Potentiation, however, could still be
induced by stimulating the severed roots, and it now
lasted several hours. Moreover, adjacent fibers showed
"compensatory potentiation" that apparently decayed
much more slowly. Eccles sees here a possible basis
for the roles of use and disuse in learning and forgetting.

The observed effect is confined to presynaptic endings. Eccles attributes it to the swelling of synaptic
knobs, for which there is other evidence. It is not subject to spatial summation nor revealed by antidromic
stimulation, as it would be if the receiving neurone became more excitable. At first glance this seems to
disqualify it for a theory of association. Since each afferent fiber makes contact with many efferent ones, how
can the effect of exercise be at all specific to the response
made? This is not the place to argue the question, but
I can say that after wrestling with the problem for some
time I believe the difficulty is not insurmountable. [1]

---

[1] One might assume, for example, that the one-sided
"Eccles effect" takes place only if the receiving neurone
is actually discharged, an assumption that should be open
to experimental test. Or one might refer response specificity in learning to the same mechanisms that are used
to account for fractionation in the reflex (15).

As to the second part of the postulate, the loss of conductivity with disuse, that is certain to meet with solid resistance. "Disuse" as an explanatory concept is as obsolete as "instinct," and most psychologists agree to ignore it as a factor in forgetting. Since the proposition cannot as yet be put to a crucial test at the behavioral level, its usefulness may well be questioned. At the same time it has neither been proved nor disproved. It is even conceivable that neurology may bring it in again by the back door.

An alternative, and in some ways more attractive, interpretation of Eccles's evidence is that it provides a basis for a form of immediate memory to be distinguished from long-time retention. Such an interpretation would take account of the short time intervals so far reported and might obviate the dubious concept of disuse. But in the absence of a more suitable mechanism it seems desirable to apply this one to a wider range: if it is more likely to be refuted, there is more to be gained by confirming it.

We are now ready to try, with the aid of these four postulates, to derive the elementary phenomena of motivation. Rather than attempt any formal proof, I shall merely point out the line of argument such a proof might take. This is inescapable with a theory in such a rudimentary stage as this one. For one thing, the postulates refer to properties of single neurones and synapses, while the behavior to be "derived" is mediated by the interplay of thousands of such units. The steps leading from one descriptive level to the other are by no means clear.

Derivations

Withdrawal Behavior

Escape. Take as an example May's (18) demonstration of fear-learning in rats. His first step (Part 1) was

to put the rat in one half of a long box with a fence in
the middle and grid floors on each side that could be
separately charged. The shock was turned on in the
rat's half until he went over the fence; after an interval
the same thing was repeated on the other side, and so on.
A typical rat reacted to the shock by varied responses--
freezing, jumping, standing, running--but in the course
of training he scrambled over the fence with less and
less delay. How is this trend to be explained?

Three stages may be distinguished, each of which
will be represented by a diagram. First is the stage of
varied responses shown in Figure 1. Here we see two
cross-sections of time, each containing a different response. The rectangles, drawn in perspective, represent

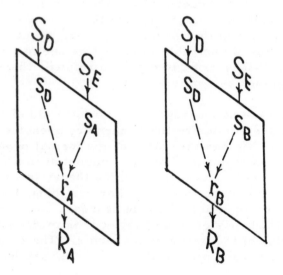

Fig. 1. Shock-escape. Stage 1: varied responses.
S_D = shock; S_E = box interior; s--→r = perceptual-motor
pattern in CNS; R_A, R_B = successive responses (e.g.,
hop, freeze).

the CNS, with peripheral stimuli, internal or external,
indicated above and overt responses below. The small

s's and r's inside stand for perceptual and motor patterns, respectively, but are not meant to be clearly demarcated. Broken arrows are used for relatively new central connections, solid arrows for older ones.

Why does the rat vary his responses under continuous shock instead of repeating the same one over and over?[2] I attribute this behavior to successive inhibition. By Postulate 1 each response produces a brief period of subnormal excitability in its constituent neurones. Although this period, in a single neurone, is measured in milliseconds, it does not occur at the same time in all elements but overlaps in different parts of the total pattern. It is conceivable that it may take a second or two for enough units to recover normal excitability at the same moment to permit the same response to be repeated. But by this time, under constant shock, some other response will already be started.

The second stage is reached when the rat climbs the fence and puts an end to the shock. Neurologically the significance of this event is that the cell assemblies involved in the last response are the only ones that can recover without further disruption. They are therefore free to reverberate briefly, as described in Postulate 3 and shown in Figure 2. Here $s_c \dashrightarrow r_c$ denotes the cell assemblies for hurdling the fence; the divergent rectangle is used to suggest a backward look at the circuits reactivating themselves after R_C.

Thirdly, we have the situation on a later trial, shown in Figure 3, when the rat goes across at the onset of shock. This result is attributed to the presynaptic plasticity inferred from Postulate 4. I assume that the circular excitation noted in the preceding stage provided the re-

---

[2]Some rats do adopt quite early a stereotyped reaction to shock such as freezing to the grid. Such cases call for a different explanation; e. g., the simultaneous arousal of antagonistic responses.

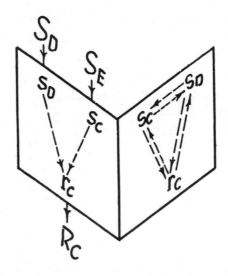

Fig. 2. Shock-escape. Stage 2: first success.
R_C = correct response of crossing fence; double arrows
on reversed panel indicate reverberating circuits.

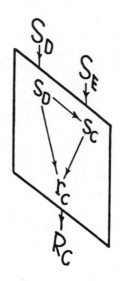

Fig. 3. Shock-escape. Stage 3: response learned.

peated stimulation necessary to potentiate synaptic knobs. So the shock becomes most strongly attached[3] to the response that removes it.

Students of learning theory will recognize in Postulates 3 and 4 a possible mechanism of reinforcement, one that smacks of both Guthrie and Thorndike. In Guthrie's postremity principle (Voeks, 35) a change of stimulation protects the last response from being unlearned. In our postulates the stimulus change protects the last response from having its own reverberation disrupted. And in the circular excitation of Postulate 3 we have a neural counterpart of Thorndike's "O.K. reaction" (34).

Avoidance. In Part 2 of his experiment, May put his experimental rats in a section of the box with the fence removed and gave them a series of buzzer-shock pairs. Figure 4 shows the hypothetical neural events during the series, including the re-exciting chains set forth in Postulate 3. Since in this case no one response

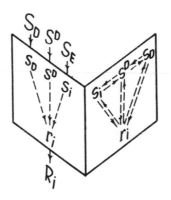

Fig. 4. Shock-avoidance. Stage 4: buzzer paired with shock, fence removed. S^D = buzzer; R_i = any of varied responses to buzzer and shock.

---

[3] "Attached" is a more suitable term than "connected"--which implies a two-way coupling--to refer to the asymmetrical process described in Postulate 4.

consistently turned off the shock, the cell combination most strengthened by tetanic stimulation (Postulate 4) was presumably the one linking buzzer with shock.

The third and final step (Part 3) in May's demonstration was to put the rat back in the original box with the fence and sound the buzzer. He gave 12 experimental rats 25 test trials each; they crossed within 10 seconds on 70% of trials. Twelve control rats that had been shocked without the buzzer crossed on only 9%.

Here is a striking example of avoidance behavior; how can it be explained? In Part 1 shock stimulation became potent to arouse crossing. In Part 2 the buzzer became potent to arouse some part of the stimulation due to shock. So in Part 3, by way of this mediating shock-surrogate, the buzzer was able to evoke crossing. Figure 5 depicts the theoretical situation. It shows the buzzer (S^D) producing fear (S_D) and thereby the hurdling response.

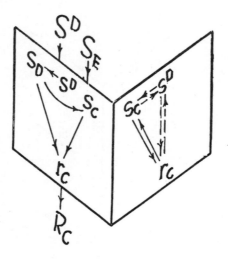

Fig. 5. Shock-avoidance. Stage 5: tests with buzzer alone, fence present. R_C to S^D mediated by pattern already learned (cf. Fig. 3).

Postulates 1, 3, and 4 do more than explain May's finding; they also lead us to predict a further decrease in latency of crossing to the buzzer in Part 3, since the response turned off the buzzer. May did not obtain this result, but his rats may have already approached a limit in Part 1. In a similar experiment with no initial shock-escape training, Brown and Jacobs (5) did confirm the prediction.

Approach Behavior

So far we have relied mainly on a principle of reinforcement by drive reduction deduced from neurological postulates. Turning to approach behavior, we face a knotty problem in learning theory: will the same drive-reduction mechanism suffice? Will it, for example, explain the development of behavior toward food?

Appetite for Food. Consider first the question of how the infant of any mammalian species learns to suckle. Take the human, for a change, and assume, for the sake of argument, no innate responses but the suckling and swallowing reflexes and suppose a minimum of help from the mother.

We start with a hungry infant making a variety of restless movements. The situation parallels that of a rat on a charged grid in Figure 1 with S_D referring to hunger instead of shock; the restless behavior is equally accounted for by our first postulate. In the course of moving about, the infant happens to touch the mother's nipple with his lips; he squeezes it, producing a flow of milk, and swallows. He squeezes again and soon his whole behavior changes; the restlessness has gone while he devotes himself to rhythmic sucking and swallowing, rarely interrupted even by a burp.

This dramatic change could be explained by the establishment of a powerful cycle of reflexes dominating central pathways and inhibiting other activities (Postulate 1). But what happens if soon afterwards the nipple

-193-

is suddenly removed? The change is even more dramatic: now his movements are more agitated, his
cries louder than before he started to nurse.[4] "That's
easy," you say. "The infant is frustrated." But precisely what does this mean? His hunger drive is, if
anything, weaker than before. Since the adequate stimulus to sucking (viz., the nipple) is no longer present,
how can that reflex exert any further influence?

I suggest that the basic neural mechanisms of frustrated behavior are the circular excitation and spatial
summation of impulses. As the infant nurses, much of
the sensory context becomes highly potentiated, or conditioned, to the act of suckling. When this response is
broken off, the motor or premotor center is still strongly bombarded by conditioned stimuli; moreover, since
these stimuli can fire only a small fraction of its cells
at any one time, the center can be partially excited
again and again. (Here I follow Old's (28) argument.)
Each returning volley of impulses summates with incoming ones to recruit new fibers; as motor thresholds
are passed, muscles contract and add their proprioceptive feed-back to the bombardment. It is this heightened
"central excitatory state" (cf. 9) that arches the back
and raises the decibel level.

If such a mechanism exists, it must be recognized
as an energizer, found in connection with approach behavior, over and above the drive stimuli from which one
withdraws. There remains to be seen whether it quali-
fies as a motive in the sense of directing a behavior unit
toward a specific goal.

To explore this possibility we might take a hungry
rat in a Skinner box and analyze the process of learning

---

[4]This description is admittedly hypothetical. It goes
beyond the published evidence and should be verified by
controlled observations (cf. 31). If it turned out to be
correct only under certain conditions, a study of these
should prove illuminating.

to press a bar for a pellet. But since this process is complicated by hunger drive and its reduction, it would be simpler if we could minimize these factors. I propose instead a hypothetical experiment in which a non-hungry, non-thirsty rat is rewarded for bar-pressing by a few sips of sugar solution. The assumption that the rat would exceed his operant level under these conditions is not too far-fetched in view of the results reported last year at this symposium by Young (37) and published elsewhere by Young and Shuford (38). They kept rats constantly supplied with food and water so that hunger and thirst were at a minimum. Nevertheless when these animals were given one trial a day in a runway to a sugar solution, they progressively increased their speed and more so for stronger concentrations than for weaker ones. Their speed was apparently determined by the properties of the goal object rather than by their internal state. If, as seems likely, the same sort of thing were to happen in a Skinner box, it could be derived as follows:

Ignoring preliminaries, we start with the occasion when the rat first presses the bar and sips the forthcoming solution. The situation is represented in Figure 6. On the left side the instrumental response occurs.

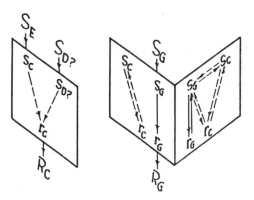

Fig. 6. Food-approach. Trial 1: non-deprived rat presses bar and sips sugar. R_C = bar-pressing response; S_G = sugar solution.

The drive stimulus is left unspecified because up to this point the motive is probably exploratory and we have yet to analyze its mechanism. On the right side the taste of sugar starts the chain of drinking reflexes. This response serves two functions: (a) it displaces s_E permitting $s_c \rightleftarrows r_c$ to reverberate, and (b) it includes the bar-pressing sequence in its own repetitive cycle, as indicated in the figure. By Postulates 3 and 4 we can deduce a strengthening of connections $s_c \dashrightarrow r_c$ and $s_c \dashrightarrow s_G$, among others.

On finishing the liquid, our subject again explores the box. But this time he will press the bar with less delay. We predict this because (a) s_c will be more readily aroused,[5] and (b) it will tend to bring with it the tasting-drinking activity ($s_G \dashrightarrow r_G$). Without the liquid itself, this activity can be only incipient, but its impulses can circulate, and, by Postulate 2, they can summate with s_c to orient the rat to the bar and facilitate pressing. Figure 7 tries to illustrate how subminimal excitation of the consummatory pattern (indicated by the interrupted cycle and dotted lines to s_G) may serve to motivate the instrumental response.

To recapitulate, our search for a physiological motive process has uncovered two candidates for the role: the persistent drive stimulus and the re-exciting circuits of the fractional goal response. Either mechanism alone appears capable of both energizing and directing a behavior unit, but ordinarily they may be expected to combine. Such combinations could be made explicit for escape and avoidance, where the drive stimulus is more conspicuous, and for approach behavior, where the goal seems to play a major part. Instead of doing so, however, I wish to underline another outcome of our search; viz., the two functions assigned to reverberating circuits in these derivations. First, through

---

[5] To show the basis of this inference, Figure 6 should be drawn in more detail; specifically, s_E should be included in the $s_c \rightleftarrows r_c$ circuit.

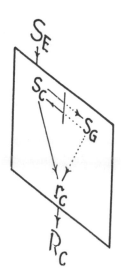

Fig. 7. Food-approach. Trial 2: rat presses bar sooner. Dotted lines indicate partial arousal of and facilitation by s_G.

the presynaptic plasticity described in Postulate 4 they help to integrate the cell assemblies that mediate responses. This is an associative function; by virtue of it the closed chain provides a possible mechanism for Hull's concept of reinforcement as habit strengthening. It depends on drive reduction insofar as a continuous drive stimulus inhibits circular activity (Postulate 1). Secondly, through the spatial summation recognized in Postulate 2, recurrent impulses increase excitatory potential. This function is energizing; it, too, may be called reinforcing, but only in the pristine meaning of the term, to facilitate, the meaning that Sheffield (33) has happily resurrected with his drive-induction theory of reinforcement. Note that both functions are directive. We have already seen that the final responses of behavior units are freest to perseverate and are therefore most strongly conditioned to contiguous stimuli. Similarly, since fractional s_G's are most intensely aroused by the patterns most recently active, these patterns receive the bulk of facilitation. So again final responses are favored over early ones, which means that successful responses, on the whole, are strengthened and errors eliminated.

Exploring. So far we have developed a mechanism to handle a few simple forms of withdrawal and approach behavior closely related to bodily needs. The question remains whether the same mechanism will handle those goals, so typical of higher species, that have no apparent organic basis. To make a start toward answering this question, I have chosen a type of behavior almost universally observed in species as diverse as rat and man, yet apparently quite independent of organic deficit or disturbance (23).

But is there an exploratory motive? Harlow (12) assures us that there is, that it has its own built-in drive-reward mechanism, and that it is as powerful as the viscerogenic drives if not more so. The tendency to explore is strong enough to produce crossing of an obstruction box (27), learning at a choice point (24), and solution of a visual discrimination problem (6). It probably plays a part in goading our own efforts to understand it. Certainly it presents a challenge to the present theory of motivation.

Before meeting this challenge, I should like to acknowledge again my indebtedness to Hebb. As readers of his book (13) are already aware, his theory of motivation as "the persistence and stability of the phase sequence" (p. 223) has strongly influenced my thinking. The following discussion of exploring will bring out even more clearly the close affiliation between the two theories.

To define exploration in a preliminary way, take an example from one of Montgomery's experiments (21). He put rats on an unfamiliar T-maze consisting of three 30-in. elevated sections and observed them for 10 minutes. He found that locomotor activity as measured by the number of 15-in. units traversed in successive 100-sec.

-198-

periods decreased progressively. He also found that at the choice point new sections were chosen in preference to those just traversed significantly more often than chance. In another experiment, Montgomery (20) showed that the percentage of alternating place-choices decreased as time between trials increased. At the same time he has presented cogent evidence (22) that these characteristics are due to the temporary satiation of an exploratory motive rather than to "reactive inhibition." Generalizing from his findings, we may define exploratory behavior by three properties: (a) it is aroused by and directed toward novel stimuli; (b) it is diminished by its own exercise; and (c) it recovers during a period of disuse. Our task is to account for these three properties in terms of our theory.

First, what is a novel stimulus? Hebb (13) has shown that certain emotional reactions, such as surprise and fear, presuppose learning. I make the same assumption for curiosity. A novel stimulus, that is, is not completely new; it consists of unfamiliar elements in a familiar context. It is, in short, unusual. What one has already learned determines both what stimuli are novel and how he will react to them.

Consider one of Montgomery's rats, neither hungry nor thirsty, at the choice point of his T-maze. Suppose he has never been on an elevated maze before. Still, he has had some weeks in which to integrate perceptual and locomotor reactions to lights and shadows, walls and floors not altogether unlike his present surroundings. To explain his initial response we must try to reconstruct part of that earlier experience.

Assuming that both paths are equally unfamiliar, we attribute his first choice to "chance." Suppose he chooses the left-hand path (S_L). We now assume that on an indefinite number of previous occasions he reacted to slightly similar spatial arrangements ($S_{L'}$) by moving into them as far as he could go ($R+$). When he reached the end ($S_{K'}$) he stopped and eventually withdrew

-199-

(R-). Figure 8 represents one such hypothetical sequence. Note that S_D stands for whatever motivated

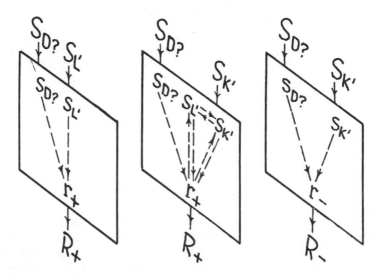

Fig. 8. Pre-exploratory behavior assumed by
theory. $S_{D\,?}$ = unspecified motive; $S_{L'}$ = situation
resembling left path of T-maze; $S_{K'}$ = dead end; R+ =
approach; R- = withdrawal.

the animal before he was able to "explore" (according
to our definition); the drive is left unspecified but was
presumably too weak to interfere with the recurrent
impulses shown in the middle panel. The significant
outcome is the attachment of $s_{L'}$ to $s_{K'}$ by Postulates
3 and 4.

With this background in mind, we are ready to
picture the choice-point situation in more detail. Figure 9 shows our subject choosing the left-hand path.
The dotted lines to $s_{K'}$ in the left panel represent the
partial arousal of expectancies based on previous experiences, partial because S_L is, by hypothesis, partly new to the animal. It is the summation of these abortive cycles (Postulates 2, 3) that motivates him to move

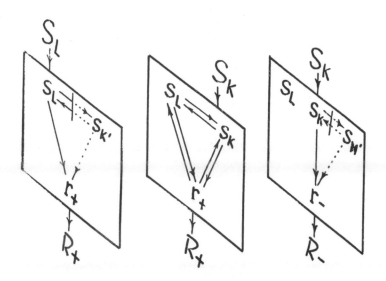

Fig. 9. Exploration. Rat at choice point chooses, explores, and leaves left path. S_L = left path; S_K = end of left path; $s_{K'}$, $s_{M'}$ = partly aroused, facilitating expectancies from previous occasions (cf. Fig. 8).

ahead until he reaches the end of the path (S_K). There he stays until increasing refractoriness of s_K--$>$r+ (Postulate 1) combines with further expectancies (here introduced as $s_{M'}$ and derivable in the same manner as $s_{K'}$) to impel him to withdraw. The result is a circuit joining s_L and s_K in a new integration.

The next time the rat arrives at the choice point from the same direction, provided the interval is not too great, we know he is much more likely to enter the right path than to re-enter the left one. With Montgomery I believe this is due to selective satiation. An attempt to interpret satiation is illustrated by Figure 10, showing a later reaction to the left-hand path. Here you will see that the partly inadequate and therefore recurrent impulses that helped to evoke R+ are missing. In their place is the recent and therefore available expectation (s_K) of the end of the path with its associated tendency to withdraw (r-). Since the tendencies to approach and

-201-

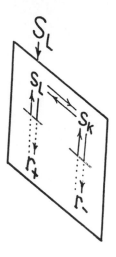

Fig. 10. Satiation of exploratory motive. Approach
pattern (r+) blocked by incipient withdrawal (r-) from
anticipated dead end (s_K).

withdraw are mutually incompatible, neither response
is likely to occur.[6] The right-hand path is still unexplored, so it provides the same incentive that it
formerly shared equally with path L. But after the entire maze has been explored, we may expect the rat's
general activity to decline.

A simpler explanation, not involving approach-
avoidance conflict, is available if we can assume that
after one trip down the left path the $s_L - r \rightleftarrows s_K$ network
is so completely fired at the choice point that it cannot
maintain circular excitation, becoming refractory instead. This is essentially Hebb's theory of satiation
(13, p. 224-231) applied to exploration and supplemented by a suggestion of Olds (28). A decision between the
two theories could be reached at a molar level by a rel-

---

[6]Mutual blocking of antagonistic responses does not
follow directly from the present postulates, although it
may eventually be shown to follow indirectly from Postulate 1 among others.

atively straight-forward experiment.

One more finding remains to be accounted for: the decrease of spontaneous alternation with increase of time between trials. The longer the delay between exploring path L and returning to the choice point, the less predictable is the rat's next choice. This is to be expected if we can assume that the traces acquired on the previous trial become weaker with time. With loss of control over s_K and r-, stimuli from path L will again stir up a self-maintaining process, recruiting impulses to R+. Ground for the assumption is provided in the controversial second part of Postulate 4, the neurological counterpart of a law of disuse.

Now that we have started, I should like to go on to other motives--likes and dislikes, sociability and solitude, excitement and peace, security and risk, money and love--and see how far the proposed theory will carry us. But time forbids, and anyhow it would not be worth while until the basic postulates have met more rigorous experimental tests. And here we face the crucial question for any theory: does it lend itself to empirical verification?

At this point I can see four places where the theory invites attack at the behavioral level:

1. Postulates 3 and 4 identify it as a perseveration theory. Conditions that favor the circular excitation of impulses should favor learning and retention. Experiments designed to test the perseveration hypothesis (7, 19) bear directly on the present theory as well.

2. The same postulates imply backward conditioning. If conditioning involves recurrent activity in a closed circuit between CS and US, the process should work both ways. The theory does not imply that the connection formed will be equally strong in both directions. Backward conditioning has suffered dubious status for some years (29, 36), but Razran's (30) recent

review, pointing to the reality of the phenomenon, should lead to a revival of experimental interest.

3. Postulates 2 and 3 offer a neurological basis for incentive motivation; they provide for the possibility that behavior can be energized as well as directed in the absence of specific drive states and drive stimuli. In short, the theory implies <u>functional autonomy of motives</u> (1). Some of the difficulties and possibilities of research on this problem have been discussed elsewhere (32).

4. The theory holds that exploratory behavior is evoked neither by the unknown nor the familiar but by a ratio between the two. To test this inference we might conceive of an experiment like the following, although the details might be hard to work out: An animal--rat, cat, dog, or monkey--is raised from birth in a closed box, with visual experience limited to its interior. It is then tested in a multiple-choice apparatus with three compartments, A, B, and C, A being identical with the subject's living quarters, B differing in some respects, and C differing as completely as it is possible to imagine. Our theory predicts that the subject will first explore B. If in later trials it is allowed to spend time in C, its readiness to explore C will first increase and then decrease.

This sample of possible experiments may be enough to suggest that a neurological approach to motivation has some empirical potential. It gives ground for hope that it is not too early to combine theory with experiment in this area.

Before closing, let me point out one implication of the theory for a basic educational problem, the development of interests. We have seen that incentive motivation depends on two conditions: (a) present stimuli must be able to initiate a response tendency; (b) that response must be delayed. The response may be to eat a grape or get a token, or it may be to know the outcome of a novel. Like the curiosity of the exploratory rodent, interest de-

pends on incomplete knowledge, on expectancies aroused
but unfulfilled. Before a child can develop an interest
in an activity or a subject matter, he must learn something about it. The failure of old-time pedagogy was
that the attempt to force that initial learning often de-
feated its ultimate purpose by building up more aversion
than intellectual appetite. The danger of progressive
methods is that by refusing to direct the child at all we
let him pass one closed door after another without stop-
ping to open it.

References

1. Allport, G. W. Personality: A Psychological Interpretation. New York: Holt, 1937.

2. Atkinson, J. W. Exploration using imaginative
   thought to assess the strength of human motives.
   In Jones, Marshall R., (Ed.), Nebraska Symposium
   on Motivation 1954. Lincoln: Univ. Nebr. Press,
   1954. Pp. 56-112.

3. Brink, F., Jr. Synaptic mechanisms. In Stevens,
   S. S. (Ed.), Handbook of Experimental Psychology.
   New York: Wiley, 1951. Pp. 94-120.

4. Brown, J. S. Problems presented by the concept
   of acquired drives. In Current Theory and Research
   in Motivation: A Symposium. Lincoln: Univ. Nebr.
   Press, 1953. Pp. 1-21.

5. Brown, J. S., and Jacobs, A. The role of fear in
   the motivation and acquisition of responses. J. exp.
   Psychol., 1949, 39, 747-759.

6. Butler, R. A. Discrimination learning by rhesus
   monkeys to visual-exploration motivation. J. comp.
   physiol. Psychol., 1953, 46, 95-98.

7. Duncan, C. P. The retroactive effect of electro-shock on learning. J. comp. physiol. Psychol., 1949, 42, 32-44.

8. Eccles, J. C. The neurophysiological basis of mind. London: Oxford Univ. Press, 1953.

9. Eccles, J. C., and Sherrington, C. S. Studies on the flexor reflex. V. General conclusions. Proc. roy. Soc., Ser. B, 1931, 107, 597-605.

10. Farber, I. E. Anxiety as a drive state. In Jones, Marshall R., (Ed.), Nebraska Symposium on Motivation 1954. Lincoln: Univ. Nebr. Press, 1954. Pp. 1-46.

11. Fulton, J. F. Physiology of the Nervous System (3rd Ed.). New York: Oxford Univ. Press, 1949.

12. Harlow, H. F. Motivation as a factor in the acquisition of new responses. In Current Theory and Research in Motivation: A Symposium. Lincoln: Univ. Nebr. Press, 1953. Pp. 24-49.

13. Hebb, D. O. The Organization of Behavior: A Neuropsychological Theory. New York: Wiley, 1949.

14. Lorente de Nó, R. Vestibulo-ocular reflex arc. Arch. Neurol. Psychiat., 1933, 30, 245-291.

15. Lorente de Nó, R. Analysis of the activity of the chains of internuncial neurons. J. Neurophysiol., 1938, 1, 207-244.

16. Lorente de Nó, R. Transmission of impulses through cranial motor nuclei. J. Neurophysiol., 1939, 2, 402-464.

17. McClelland, D. C., Atkinson, J. W., Clark, R. A., and Lowell, E. L. The Achievement Motive. New York: Appleton-Century-Crofts, 1953.

18. May, M. A. Experimentally acquired drives. J. exp. Psychol., 1948, 38, 66-77.

19. Miller, N. E., and Coons, E. E. Conflict versus consolidation of memory to explain "retrograde amnesia" produced by ECS. Amer. Psychologist, 1955, 10, 394-395. (Abstract)

20. Montgomery, K. C. "Spontaneous alternation" as a function of time between trials and amount of work. J. exp. Psychol., 1951, 42, 82-93.

21. Montgomery, K. C. The relation between exploratory behavior and spontaneous alternation in the white rat. J. comp. physiol. Psychol., 1951, 44, 582-589.

22. Montgomery, K. C. A test of two explanations of spontaneous alternation. J. comp. physiol. Psychol., 1952, 45, 287-293.

23. Montgomery, K. C. The effect of hunger and thirst drives upon exploratory behavior. J. comp. physiol. Psychol., 1953, 46, 315-319.

24. Montgomery, K. C. The role of the exploratory drive in learning. J. comp. physiol. Psychol., 1954, 47, 60-64.

25. Morgan, C. T., and Stellar, E. Physiological Psychology (2nd Ed.). New York: McGraw-Hill, 1950.

26. Muenzinger, K. F. Psychology: The Science of Behavior. New York: Harper, 1942.

27. Nissen, H. W. A study of exploratory behavior in the white rat by means of the obstruction method. J. genet. Psychol., 1930, 37, 361-376.

28. Olds, J. A neural model for sign-Gestalt theory.

Psychol. Rev., 1954, 61, 59-72.

29. Osgood, C. E. Method and Theory in Experimental Psychology. New York: Oxford Univ. Press, 1953.

30. Razran, G. Backward conditioning. Psychol. Bull., 1956, 53, 55-69.

31. Sears, R. R., and Sears, P. S. Minor studies of aggression: V. Strength of frustration-reaction as a function of strength of drive. J. Psychol., 1940, 9, 297-300.

32. Seward, J. P. How are motives learned? Psychol. Rev., 1953, 46, 99-110.

33. Sheffield, F. D., Roby, T. B., and Campbell, B. A. Drive reduction versus consummatory behavior as determinants of reinforcement. J. comp. physiol. Psychol., 1954, 47, 349-355.

34. Thorndike, E. L. The Fundamentals of Learning. New York: Columbia Univ., Teachers College Bur. Publ., 1932.

35. Voeks, V. W. Formalization and clarification of a theory of learning. J. Psychol., 1950, 30, 341-362.

36. Woodworth, R. S., and Schlosberg, H. Experimental Psychology (Revised Ed.). New York: Holt, 1954.

37. Young, P. T. The role of hedonic processes in motivation. In Jones, Marshall R., (Ed.), Nebraska Symposium on Motivation 1955. Lincoln: Univ. Nebr. Press, 1955. Pp. 193-238.

38. Young, P. T., and Shuford, E. H., Jr. Quantitative control of motivation through sucrose solutions of different concentrations. J. comp. physiol. Psychol., 1955, 48, 114-118.

COMMENTS ON PROFESSOR SEWARD'S PAPER

by
Melvin Marx

I share with many others, including Professor Seward, a certain feeling of skepticism with regard to neurophysiological speculations. The value of such thinking may certainly be challenged unless some new theoretical or experimental products occur, either with regard to the influence of the neurophysiological speculations on behavioral theories, or vice versa.

One aspect of Seward's presentation that might qualify for such an achievement is his suggestion concerning the neurophysiological basis of frustration in terms of reverberating circuits and the spatial summation of responses. The contribution, if made, would certainly seem to be with regard to new behavioral observations suggested by this notion. Offhand, I do not see any very obvious suggestions of this sort, but it is certainly possible that such could be derived. One comment that I would like to make along this line is that the distinction between relevant and irrelevant drive factors must be kept clearly in mind as behavioral experimental designs are considered.

To take a somewhat less optimistic view of this matter, the review of the frustration literature that Lawson and I recently completed gave us convincing evidence of the looseness and inadequacy of the great majority of theoretical formulations. To attack such an inadequately understood phenomenon with equally uncertain neurophysiological speculations is a brave enterprise but perhaps not a particularly promising one. Compounding of ignorance may have some profits but needs, I think, to be prosecuted with considerable caution.

In view of the critical discussion of Seward's general position by Beach, I will refrain from any further comments of this nature.

An aspect of Seward's presentation that I would like to comment on very briefly is his treatment of appetite. Here it seems perfectly apparent to me that we need to assume some kind of latent motive--such as for sucrose or milk--that is more or less independent of the more general "drive" state of the organism (that is, his general "hunger"). Certainly this will be true after an $\underline{S}$ has had sufficient experience with various incentives. Appetites then come to be aroused by external stimuli.

This point is relevant to Seward's statement that there is a reduced hunger drive in the Sears' frustrated infant (bottle removed after some nursing). But here it must be recognized that all of the eliciting cues are active, and more so than at the initiation of the nursing. This situation brings to mind the condition of the male rat during successively more rapidly consummated copulatory sequences within an experimental session, which I commented on in regard to Beach's paper.

The role of practice as a potentially very important variable is again suggested. I would like to see observations such as these made with this variable clearly manipulated. If learning is important in this respect, one would expect that the vigor of such reactions to blocking of nursing would grow over nursing sessions.

COMMENTS ON PROFESSOR SEWARD'S PAPER

by
Frank A. Beach

I want to begin by complimenting Dr. Seward on an exceedingly ingenious line of analogical reasoning. But in the next breath I feel compelled to point out what seems to me to be several rather serious weaknesses in the argument, although I am certain that they have all occurred to Dr. Seward.

As he noted, the situations which produced the four postulates he has mentioned were inevitably exceedingly simple ones. The experimental preparations involved sympathetic ganglia, more or less isolated spinal reflexes, and the like. Therefore I am dubious of the generality of these principles and question the legitimacy of leaping verbally from simple reflex arcs to imaginary "cell assemblies."

Equally disturbing to me is the fact, pointed out by Dr. Seward, that his interpretation cannot be put to crucial test at the behavioral level. If this is true, and I believe that it is, then one might reasonably ask just what the diagrams concocted by Dr. Seward actually tell us about either behavior or the nervous system. They bear a suspicious resemblance to what several psychologists have called "neurologizing." I may be completely missing an important point, but unless this is the case, I see no value whatsoever in schematic representations of the sort Dr. Seward has presented. They do not illuminate the behavioral data, and they do not suggest, at least to me, any experiments by which their validity can be checked.

EXPERIMENTALLY DERIVED CONCEPTIONS OF
ANXIETY AND AVERSION

Richard L. Solomon   and   Elinor S. Brush
Harvard University   McGill University

Introduction

In the most general common-sense terms, aversive stimuli are unpleasant; most Ss work hard to terminate or avoid them and are emotionally aroused by
their presence. The specific stimuli that will prove to
be functionally aversive may differ across species, and
they may differ within species. However, one type of
aversive stimulation, electric shock applied to the skin,
appears to be reliable both between and within several
mammalian species, and so it has been widely used by
experimenters.

Electric shock, when it arouses strong skeletal
activity and high intensity autonomic responses, is
usually called "painful." It is also defined as an "unconditioned stimulus," referring to the fact that certain
reflex reactions occur with a very high probability in its
presence. It may also be defined as fear-arousing, the
term "fear" referring to a poorly defined constellation
of emotional-type behaviors of a skeletal and autonomic
sort. In mammals such as dogs, cats, and rats, onset
of electric shock (with a current flow of about 2 ma.)
is usually accompanied either by vigorous locomotion or
by immobility and "freezing," together with reactions such
as high-pitched vocalization, piloerection, defecation, uri-
nation, pupillary dilation, gasping, drooling, and trembling.
These symptoms constitute a pain-fear reaction pattern;
the unconditioned response (UR), a so-called respondent,
is elicited by the unconditioned shock stimulus (US).
Transfer of control of many of these fear reaction components can be easily achieved. If a previously neutral
stimulus, such as an innocuous tone, is repeatedly paired

closely in time with the onset of the US, conditioned fear reactions will eventually appear at the onset of the tone alone. We call such acquired reactions <u>conditioned fear</u> or <u>anxiety</u>. The tone is called the CS, the conditioned stimulus; or perhaps it may be called the cue or signal.

It is a striking fact that the successful use of electric shock as a potent US and aversive motivator has led to the virtual neglect of other noxious stimuli in the experimental study of aversion. A few exceptions may be mentioned, such as the employment of bright light, intense sound, or cool water--all of which can be used as motivators. But even in these exceptional cases, systematic conditioning and avoidance training experiments are, for the most part, lacking. Two generalizations may be made in this regard. We psychologists have barely scratched the surface in locating aversive stimuli for the various species we use as Ss in our experiments. And when we do locate a type of aversive US which is especially potent in a species, we do not experiment with it unless it is as controllable as shock stimulation. To make the point, pressure stimulation of the back of the tongue is a strong US for the gag reflex, reverse peristalsis, and the induction of nausea. Conditioning and avoidance learning based on this type of aversive drive state probably takes place in a variety of ways in many societies. The prevalence of voluntary vomiting and the low threshold for involuntary vomiting in the Navaho is a case in point. One might ask whether anticipatory CRs for the conditioning of this particular reflex pattern are distinctively different from those for shock conditioning. Are all aversive anticipatory states alike? In reading some motivation theorists today, one obtains the impression that the anticipation of <u>anything</u> "bad" is anxiety or fear or dread. But perhaps each aversive US breeds its own type of conditioned anticipatory reaction pattern, qualitatively and quantitatively different from any other. We cannot provide information on this matter because most of our detailed knowledge comes from experiments using shock as the aversive US. And, therefore, our analysis of aversion will mainly be an analysis of electric shock aversion, a study of the psychology of shock-induced pain and fear. There is certainly a great need to broaden the base of study of aversive motivation.

The psychological importance of aversive stimulation lies in its functionally motivating properties. As Miller (91, p.436) has stated: "Fear is an important drive because it can be learned so readily and can become so strong. Fear is called learnable because it can be learned as a response to previously neutral cues; it is called a drive because it can motivate the learning and performance of new responses in the same way as hunger, thirst, or other drives." The kinds of learning which can be motivated by an aversive US, or by a CS which elicits conditioned anxiety, are called, respectively, escape and avoidance. An escape response is one which results quickly in US-termination. An avoidance response is one which prevents the onset of the US. Escape and avoidance responses are often called instrumental, or operant. When we refer to aversive behavior, we refer to a class of behavioral events which includes escape responses, avoidance responses, innate fear reactions, and acquired fear or anxiety reactions, as well as various types of "startle patterns."

There are many experimental techniques of establishing aversive behavior, and each of these is interesting in its own right. However, by far the most influential techniques for theory-making have been those designed to establish avoidance behavior. Therefore, we shall sacrifice, because of limitations of time and space, a thorough review of all work on aversive behavior; we shall emphasize anxiety and avoidance phenomena at the cost of exhaustiveness. However, in order to point out the many approaches to the study of aversive motivation, we shall list, in a sketchy way, the most widely used techniques.

The general purposes of this essay will be: (a) to outline the methods which experimenters have used to establish aversive behavior; (b) to review the anxiety

and avoidance experiments which were critical in the
evolution of theories of aversion; (c) to review the better known parameters of avoidance training situations
and their consequent effects on behavior; and (d) con-
comitantly to relate, wherever important, the outcomes
of parametric studies of avoidance behavior to current
theoretical conceptions. For prior reviews of these
topics the reader is urged to refer to Schoenfeld (126),
Miller (91, p. 436 ff.), Mowrer (100), Woodworth and
Schlosberg (169, p. 668 ff.), and Solomon and Wynne
(138).

The Avoidance Phenomenon

The avoidance behavior phenomenon is of great interest to many theorists. There are many reasons for
this, but three stand out: (a) the emotion and motivation theorist sees the fear and anxiety concomitants of
avoidance behavior as possibly relatable to complex
emotional disturbances in human Ss; (b) the student of
higher mental processes sees the "anticipatory" character of avoidance responses as a simple prototype of
forward-looking or purposive behavior; and (c) the
learning theorist sees the avoidance experiment as a
critical testing ground for divergent theories of conditioning and learning. A description of a typical avoidance training sequence and its consequent behavioral
outcomes will, we believe, help to demonstrate the conceptual richness therein.

First, an introductory note of caution. We often
take the avoidance phenomenon itself for granted. We
somehow assume that it is natural for organisms to
"anticipate" noxious events in an "adaptive" fashion.
But it is only after we set up certain special types of
environmental event sequences that the avoidance phenomenon emerges. Failures of Ss to learn to avoid are
not rare, but they are less apt to be reported in scientific papers than are the successes. And the conditions
surrounding failures to learn to avoid are as instructive

to the investigator, in many cases, as are the optimum conditions for producing the avoidance phenomenon. With this warning in mind, let us look at the avoidance phenomenon and one of the more successful ways in which it can be experimentally produced.

The S, a dog, is harnessed into a rubber hammock, his chest, abdomen, and chin firmly supported, and his legs hanging down. On either side of his head are two aluminum panels mounted on a wooden framework which surrounds S's head. Strapped to S's hind toe pads are two large electrodes. Behind S is a loud-speaker. [1] After a 10-min. acclimation period, during which S initially struggles some and then later remains almost motionless, S appears alert, orients toward sounds, may bark intermittently, and often wags his tail. Then E, controlling the experimental apparatus in an adjoining room and watching S through a one-way mirror, presents a musical tone through a loud-speaker behind S. S pricks up his ears and looks around. After the tone has persisted for 5 sec., an intense electric stimulus is applied to S's rear toe pads, so that current flow through S is 4.0 ma. S is immediately thrown into a great surge of activity which includes skeletal and ANS responses. He thrashes about, waves his legs, hunches his back against the harness straps, bites at the rubber hammock beneath his chin, screeches, defecates, urinates, shows pupillary dilation, piloerection, and profuse salivation. After 21.4 sec. of struggling and thrashing, a violent turn of the head ends in S's pressing the aluminum panel to his right. Both tone and shock are terminated immediately by this act. S has finally es-caped from both tone and shock.

During this whole sequence, E has recorded S's EKG. Before the tone went on, the resting heart-rate

[1] This example is taken from a recently completed experiment by A. H. Black (7), who has very generously allowed us to use his observations prior to their publication.

level was 100 beats per min. This did not change during the 5-sec. period between tone onset and shock onset. When the shock went on, the rate climbed abruptly to 240 beats per min. and maintained this level until the panel-press by S terminated shock. Then the EKG became erratic and dropped precipitously to an average rate of 70 beats per min., characterized by great irregularity of heart action. Even after the overall rate returned to normal, the beat-by-beat rate was at first more variable. Three minutes later the variability had disappeared.

On succeeding presentations of the tone-shock sequence we note that S escapes more quickly. His escape latencies decrease. After 16 presentations, averaging 3 min. apart, S turns his head quickly after the onset of the tone and pushes the right-hand plate with his nose. This terminates the tone and prevents shock from being applied. (The first avoidance response has emerged. Its latency was 2.1 sec.) S goes on to avoid shock perfectly, trial after trial, after a long series of trials on which he sometimes fails to avoid and sometimes succeeds.

While S's aversive action was thus becoming more regular, his EKG was changing. On the third trial the heart did not hold its resting rate during the tone-shock interval. Instead, it jumped to a rate of 180 beats per min. in response to the tone onset, and further increased to 260 beats per min. after shock onset. Clearly, S's heart, along with his head, was responding quite differently to the tone than it had before the avoidance training procedures were instituted.

Why did the first avoidance response emerge on the sixteenth trial? Why did it emerge at all? Why did S finally come to respond quickly to the tone without failure? There are many ways that the psychologist talks about these questions, and it is this fact which surrounds the avoidance training experiment with a rich aura of theoretical significance.

Watching the procedures and behavioral phenomena we have just described, one psychologist says, "The dog anticipated the shock, and so he responded quickly to the tone." Another psychologist says, "The dog was afraid of the tone, and so he tried to terminate it as quickly as possible." A third psychologist says, "The tone became symbolic of shock, and so the dog responded to it in the way he had successfully terminated the shock." A fourth psychologist says, "The tone aroused anxiety, which is unpleasant or motivational, and the dog responded to the tone in order to terminate his anxiety." A fifth psychologist says, "The dog is now being frightened by inactivity, by doing those things which are associated with onset of shock; he now turns his head because it is rewarding; he likes head-turning -- it is reinforcing in itself." And a sixth psychologist says, "The dog demonstrated a negative attitude toward the tone which was once neutral." A seventh says, "The dog knows what will happen if he doesn't press the panel, so he presses it." An eighth says, "The dog has developed a panel-pressing compulsion that has generalized widely to new stimuli because of libidinal overflow." A ninth says, "The tone has a negative valence and panel-pressing increases its psychological distance." A tenth says, "It's just conditioning." These statements represent a wide variety of psychological languages. Each of the statements is represented, in one way or another, in leading conceptions of avoidance behavior.

However, lest the reader assume that we have exaggerated the richness, subtlety, and heterogeneity of the various conceptions of avoidance behavior, remember that we have so far described only one class of aversive training procedure and its consequent behavioral phenomena. The ten comments above are not limited merely to this one type of procedure. Let us now look at the variety and complexities of several classes of aversive training and their correlated behavioral phenomena.

Types of Aversive Training Procedures

There are at least nine distinct types of training procedures used to establish anxiety, escape, and avoidance behavior. Each has led to its own particular and suitable conceptualizations, and the welter of theories about aversive behavior cannot be adequately interpreted without some sense of these procedural differences.

(1) The method of gradual emergence. This is the method outlined above in our description of a typical avoidance experiment. The tone is the previously neutral CS or signal, and it is paired with the shock, a noxious or aversive US, without S having had specific prior experience with either. A specific instrumental response, like head-turning (or panel-pushing), will terminate the CS and shock; it will also terminate the CS and prevent shock if it is emitted during the prescribed CS-US time interval. Thus, when S has learned to avoid the US, he has also learned to escape from the CS. While S cannot control the onset of CS, he can control its "offgo"; S can control the onset of the US and can prevent it, and he can control US offgo. Good examples are found in Hunter (67), Mowrer and Lamoreaux (103), Brogden et al. (17), and Solomon and Wynne (137). A variation on this method is the trace-conditioning procedure used by Kamin (69), in which the CS terminates automatically several seconds before the US is presented.

The typical behavioral outcome of this type of training procedure is the gradual emergence of short-latency escape responses and then the gradual increase in frequency of occurrence of avoidance responses. However, abrupt emergence of avoidance can occur under some conditions. Fear is presumably conditioned to the CS before avoidances emerge. Often the stable avoidance response differs from the escape response in its morphology and latency characteristics. In addition, failure to learn to avoid can occur, under conditions not very well understood at present. When training is successful, early trials are characterized by a high level of "emotional" ANS and skeletal reactions, while, in contrast, the well learned avoidance response usually is not accompanied by high-intensity emotional reactions. Extinction is often difficult to obtain by ordinary omission of the US.

-219-

(2) <u>The method of prior response shaping</u>. This
method pretrains S to perform the escape response without a controlled, discrete, phasic CS. The US is presented at irregular intervals, and the proper escape
response will terminate the US. (During this phase S
cannot control or prevent US onset.) After the instrumental escape response becomes stereotyped and of
short latency, a CS can be introduced on each trial
several seconds' prior to US onset. A CS-US relation is
thus established after the escape response is quick and
reliable. The onset of the US is prevented by a short-
latency response to the CS. Good examples are found
in Warner (157), Zeaman (173), and Church and Solomon
(27).

The typical outcome of this procedure is, first, the
development of anxiety, then stable escape responses,
and then the quick acquisition of avoidance behavior after
the CS is introduced. The avoidance response is very
much like the escape response in its morphological and
latency characteristics. Fear of the signal often develops
before avoidance does.

(3) <u>Escape training with a short CS-US interval</u>.
In this method, the CS-US interval is short, and S cannot prevent the US by responses occurring during the
CS-US interval. Often E uses simultaneous onset of
CS and US. The specific escape response terminates
both CS and US but cannot control either CS onset or US
onset. S can avoid the US only if it is omitted when he
responds quickly to the CS on certain <u>test trials</u>. Test
trials are infrequent. In this method, <u>extinction</u> procedures (consistent omission of US) serve to allow
avoidance of the US along with escape from the CS. Good
examples are found in Hunter (67), Brogden, Lipman and
Culler (17), Schlosberg (124), Sheffield (127), and Sheffield
and Temmer (128).

The typical behavioral outcome of this type of procedure is a decrease of escape latencies during shock
trials, a gradual decrease of avoidance latencies on

test trials, and an increase in the frequency of anticipation responses occurring during the CS-US interval
up to a maximum of about 50% of responses to the CS.
Thus, responses during the CS-US interval are unstable.
High intensity fear reactions occur to the CS. Extinction is easy to obtain.

(4) The method of prior anxiety conditioning; the
"acquired drive" experiment. In this method, first
the CS and US are paired closely in time, but there is
no escape or avoidance response by which S can either
prevent or terminate the CS or US. The CS-US sequences
are repeated, regardless of S's behavior. Then the procedure is changed. The S is allowed to terminate the CS
by the performance of some specific instrumental response, and the US is not presented. The specific instrumental response, which E allows to terminate the CS, is
arbitrary, but it cannot be too unlike the responses elicited on prior trials by the US. Good examples of this type
of procedure are found in Miller (90), May (88), and
Brown and Jacobs (19).

The typical behavioral outcome of this training procedure is, initially, the development of "emotional" reactions to the once-neutral CS. Sometimes "supersti-
tious" skeletal responses also emerge. When the second
stage of the procedure is introduced, S will often emit
a wide variety of "flight" and "attack" responses, any
one of which can be chosen by E to terminate the CS.
However, if a specific type of response is prescribed
prior to its occurrence, it may never occur, and there
will be no learning to terminate the CS. Such failures
are quite apparent in the work of May (88) and Brown and
Jacobs (19). In some recent unpublished studies of Kamin
(70), this method was almost a total failure in producing
stable, learned instrumental responses in dogs. Extinction is usually obtained if the US is never again paired with
the CS.

(5) The Pavlovian method. In this method, E presents to S the CS-US sequence with either a long or a

-221-

short CS-US interval, no matter what behavior S demonstrates. The US is only omitted on certain test trials.
E measures the development of conditioning by the magnitude of aversive responses on such trials; or, if the
CS-US interval is long enough, E can measure the development of conditioned "anticipatory" responses occurring
during the CS-US interval, before the US appears. The
response studied is that which has the morphology of the
particular type of URs elicited by the US itself. Good
examples of this procedure are found in Bechterev (3),
Liddell et al. (81), Schlosberg (123), and the various
eyelid-conditioning experiments, such as those of Hilgard
and Marquis (59), Kimble (74), and Bernstein (5). Also,
the method is well illustrated in the measurement of
sensory thresholds in animals by Upton (155) and Wever
(161). In this conditioning method, the test trials, on
which the US is omitted, are like the avoidance trials
in other methods. On such trials the CR is not followed
by the US, and the CS is terminated without too much
delay.

This type of procedure produces unstable motor
learning. Anticipatory responses during the CS-US interval often interfere with the CR itself. When the US
is quite noxious, there is much struggling and diffuse
emotional reactivity. Gibson (47) has described this
vividly. Extinction of the motor response is easy to
obtain.

(6) The method of temporal pacing. This method
is reminiscent of Pavlov's (114) temporal conditioning.
No specific CS need be used (although one can be used).
The US is presented at regular intervals if S does nothing.
If S performs the designated avoidance response, the next
presentation of the US is delayed a fixed number of seconds.
The US-US interval can be controlled independently of the
interval between an avoidance response and the next US
presentation. If a CS is used, it can come anywhere in
the US-US interval (as a "warning signal"). Usually the
avoidance response terminates the CS. There is no response which terminates the US. Instead, the onset of

the US is prevented by the avoidance response. The US
is usually of short duration. This method was studied
recently by Sidman (129, 130). It is especially interesting because there need be no escape response which is
consistently effective; only an avoidance response is
necessary.

Learning can be successfully obtained by this procedure. Usually the avoidance response persists for
long intervals without shock reinforcement.

(7) The method of prior anxiety conditioning; the
appetitive inhibition experiment. In this method, no
particular avoidance response is established. Rather,
the S is given several CS-US pairings; and then, when
the CS is capable of eliciting an "anxiety reaction, " it
can be used to interfere with on-going behavior. For example, presentation of the CS while S is eating may inhibit ingestion. Or if S has learned to lever-press when
hungry in order to get food pellets, presentation of the
CS may depress the rate of lever-pressing. This latter
variation has been called the CER method (conditioned
emotional response) by Hunt et al. (63, 64, 65, 66) and
Brady et al. (8, 9, 10, 11, 12). It appears to be a particularly useful method and has been adopted by Mowrer
et al. (102, 106) in some recent experiments of widespread theoretical importance. This method has had a
long and interesting history, starting with the work of
Masserman (87) on neuroses in cats, and including Estes'
(41) important monograph on punishment, as well as
Lichtenstein's (79) work on feeding inhibitions in dogs.
Actually, the operations are very much like the acquired
drive experiment where CS and noxious US are paired
without S being able to interfere. The difference lies in
the test situations: in the acquired drive experiment the
aversive CS is tested for the reinforcing properties of
its termination, while in the appetitive inhibition experiment the aversive CS is tested for the disorganizing or
interfering properties of its onset.

(8) The punishment method. In the various avoidance

and escape training methods, the experimenter employs
aversive signals and noxious stimuli for the purpose of
establishing new behaviors. However, the methods used
in escape and avoidance training can be used to reduce
the probability of occurrence of previously established
and reliable responses. When this is done, we usually
call the operation "punishment." The history of this
method is too extensive to be dealt with here. However,
recent articles by Dinsmoor (37, 38) may be consulted
for this material. Some typical recent examples of this
method are found in Estes (41), Gwinn (53), and Solomon,
Kamin, and Wynne (135).

There are as yet no general principles derived from
this method. The technique has produced temporary
avoidance of a previously established response, followed
by revival of the response; it has produced complete
termination of consummatory responses and death by
starvation; it has produced both rigidity and increased
variability in different experiments; it has facilitated,
in some cases, the response it was intended to suppress.
The technique is unpredictable in its outcome at the present state of our knowledge.

(9) The method of contrast. This is a mysterious
and relatively unexplored technique. S is accustomed
to certain stimulus patterns which surround the important
events of his existence. Then, without prior warning,
some salient aspect of his environment is radically altered. Pavlov (114) referred to this type of event as an
external inhibition. But with the more recent observations
of Hebb (55) on the reactions of chimpanzees to the de-
capitated head of another chimpanzee, and with many supporting clinical observations on startle, it appears that
aversive reactions of high intensity can be induced by
such stimulus alterations. To call the phenomenon "fear
of the novel or unfamiliar" doesn't explain it. But perhaps experimenters will some day use this technique in
avoidance experiments with the purpose of discovering
the laws governing such dramatic instances of aversion
for unfamiliar stimulus patterns.

We have outlined, in sketchy form, the procedures often used to produce aversive behavior in laboratory experiments. The diversity of techniques is at one and the same time a strength and limitation for scientific thinking in this area of knowledge. Many of the "crucial" experiments devised to test conflicting theories of aversive behavior have been carried out in different experimental settings. Some results are a product of the particular methods used, and a shift in method seems in many cases to throw doubt on prior observations. There are cases where the reproducibility of specific behavioral phenomena is in dispute, due to the widely differing techniques used by different experimenters. One need not fear at present the "stifling" effects of increased demands for operational uniformity and standard measuring devices. If one were to hazard a guess about the present state of affairs, it would be in the opposite direction: we probably could profit by some judicious standardization of procedures and measures.

We must therefore temper our interpretations with a realization of the fact that where the results of various experiments do not agree, the reason _may_ be that there were variations in the experimental procedures used. With this limitation in mind, let us turn now to a somewhat selective survey of the experimental literature on anxiety and avoidance behavior.

The Experimental Study of Anxiety and Avoidance Behavior

Historical Orientation

The avoidance learning paradigm has important precursors, I. P. Pavlov and V. M. Bechterev. One might justifiably say that the history of the study of anxiety and avoidance begins at the point where Pavlov, having observed what he called the "psychic secretion" of the salivary glands, turned from observation of this phenomenon to an experimental investigation of it. Because conditioned or acquired anxiety can be established with Pavlov's techniques, Pavlov's work is still of great interest to motivation theorists.

The paradigm for classical or Pavlovian conditioning is as follows: An unconditioned stimulus (one which always evokes a given response) is preceded closely in time by a stimulus which never evokes the response. If, after a number of such paired presentations, the unconditioned stimulus is omitted, it will be found that the previously neutral stimulus is now capable of evoking the response. There is one crucial difference between this paradigm and that for avoidance learning: in avoidance learning, the US is _omitted_ if the subject makes the appropriate response to the CS, while in classical conditioning the presentation of the US is _not_ contingent on the behavior of the subject but is determined solely by the experimenter.

Pavlov worked exclusively with one response, that of salivary secretion; the US was the placement of a small amount of meat powder or acid powder on the tongue of the canine subject. A variety of conditioned stimuli were used, and a variety of parameters of the situation, many of them temporal ones, were investigated.

While reports from Pavlov's laboratory were published in Russian as early as 1899 and in English in 1906, Hilgard and Marquis (59) regard the 1913 translations of Bechterev's _Objective Psychology_ (3, 4) as the most influential on American psychology. Bechterev applied Pavlov's experimental procedures to the study of withdrawal and respiration responses in dogs and humans, using electric shock as the unconditioned stimulus. His work gained the interest of J. B. Watson, who proceeded to study conditioned motor reflexes at Johns Hopkins. After a year of experimentation, Watson introduced the conditioned motor reflex to American psychology in his presidential address at the 1915 convention of the APA, saying: "The conditioned motor reflex, while familiar in a general way to everyone, has not, so far as I know, en-

-226-

gaged the attention of American investigators. This is
not surprising in view of the fact that all of the researches have appeared in Russian and in periodicals which are
not accessible at present to American students. At least
we have not been able to obtain access to a single research
publication. The German and French translations of
Bechterev's 'Objective Psychology' give the method only
in the barest outline. Bechterev's summary was the only
guide we had in our work at Hopkins" (158, p. 94). After
outlining the results of his own investigations, he ended
his address with a statement expressing " ... a bias in
favor of this method ... " (158, p. 105).

Hilgard and Marquis state, "It is probably to
(Bechterev) more than to Pavlov that we owe the bold
acceptance of conditioning by psychologists, although the
details of conditioning which came to be accepted were
Pavlov's" (59, p. 9). This statement, although obviously
true in part, seems to over-emphasize Bechterev's role,
which we would limit to that of providing psychology with
a demonstration of the fact that Pavlov's method could be
applied to motor responses; once this demonstration had
been made, and had been repeated in America by Watson,
it was Pavlov to whom the American psychologists turned,
and it was his procedures and terminology which they proceeded to use and change.

One of the ways in which Pavlov's procedures were
altered by American psychologists is illustrated in an
experiment published by Hamel (54) in 1919. Hamel
called his paper "A study and analysis of the conditioned
reflex," but he deviated from the procedure outlined by
Pavlov in one important respect: he omitted the US if
the subject responded to a CS with finger withdrawal! The
reader will immediately see that this is an avoidance-
training procedure. The interesting point here is that
neither Hamel nor any of his contemporaries recognized
this change at the time; he and they thought he was doing
a pure experiment on classically conditioned reflexes.
What Hamel did was to give the S an "indefinite number"
of "touches" on the arm (this constituted the neutral CS)

-227-

and then a single touch in a different spot on the arm.
If the S did not respond to the latter (positive) CS with
finger withdrawal, he received a shock on the finger.
Hamel measured the latency of the response under conditions he deemed appropriate for "reflex" response and
under conditions he thought conducive to "conscious discrimination." The difference between these conditions
seems to have been whether he asked the subject for his
introspections only at the end of the experiment or also
during the course of it. He found no differences in latency
of finger withdrawal under these two conditions, and concluded that since the "reflex activity" was "related to
the conscious fear of being shocked," this was not a true
conditioned reflex. Two other studies of avoidance learning, one by Carr and Freeman (23) and one by Yarbrough
(171), also were reported many years before anyone
identified the phenomenon.

The next American psychologist who set out in ear-
nest to study conditioned reflexes was Liddell. In 1926
he announced the establishment of "a laboratory for the
study of conditioned motor reflexes" (80). However, he
promptly became interested in the emotional concomitants of the conditioning process, and most of the studies
published by Liddell and his associates were primarily
concerned with the establishment of "experimental neuroses" in sheep and other animals, rather than with the
extensive systematic study of important parameters of
conditioning. However, the techniques used to induce the
"neuroses" were, for the most part, classical conditioning
procedures.

Then Schlosberg reported in 1928 (122) that he had
successfully used classical conditioning procedures to
establish a conditioned patellar reflex in 44 of 49 human
subjects, using as the CS a bell, click, buzz, or tactual
pressure; he also varied the CS-US interval. He found
no significant differences in ease of conditioning when
the interval was varied from .20 to .44 sec., but conditioning was more difficult when the interval was less
than .11 sec. A general finding was that the CRs were

-228-

unstable in both amplitude and certainty.

An interesting application of the classical conditioning technique was made to the measurement of thresholds. In studying auditory thresholds, for example, a
tone would be paired with shock; if the subject developed
a conditioned response to the tone, he obviously could
hear it. Upton (155) used this technique on guinea pigs
in 1929; Wever (161), in 1930, applied it to the cat; and
Culler, Finch, Girden, and Brogden (31) used it on dogs
in 1935. It has also been used to test the hearing of in-
fants suspected of being deaf (1). Upton, Wever, and
Culler et al. unwittingly deviated from the Pavlovian
paradigm in the same way Hamel had, namely, by omit-
ting the US when the subject responded to the CS. Avoidance training was thus part of the experimental repertory
by 1930, although it had not actually been formally "in-
vented" yet.

The Comparison of Aversive Classical Conditioning with Instrumental Escape and Avoidance Training

The comparison experiments were important because they created interesting theoretical problems for
those who experimented with aversive behavior. They
generated most of the important theoretical positions
concerning negative motivation or aversion.

The first experiment explicitly designed to compare
aversive classical conditioning procedures with those
employed in avoidance training was carried out by
Schlosberg in 1934 (123). He noted that both procedures
had been used by various experimenters, apparently
without any suggestion that they might be fundamentally
different. Using an ingenious apparatus composed largely of cardboard, rubber bands, paper clips, and thread,
Schlosberg set out to condition tail withdrawal in the rat,
under classical and instrumental escape conditions. The
conditioned stimulus was either a buzzer or a light; the
US was shock near the end of the tail. The CS was pre-

sented alone for 335 milliseconds before the shock came on; after 165 msec. of CS and US, both were terminated. The responses recorded were tail movements, breathing changes, and squealing. The conclusions of major interest to us are, first, that there were no significant differences between the shock-escapable and -inescapable groups, and, secondly, that since the CRs were not like the URs, they may have represented the development of partially successful instrumental escape responses. Schlosberg concluded from this that it was probable that conditioning constituted only one, rather than the only, type of learning. One other finding, the relevance of which will become apparent later, was that the first response to appear with training was a shift from slow to rapid breathing.

The following year, Hunter (67) reported the first experiment in which the avoidance procedure did produce learning superior to that of the classical procedure. In this study, the CS and US, buzzer and shock, were of .20-sec. duration, and the CS-US interval was 2 sec. The rats in the instrumental group could escape or avoid shock by running to another quadrant of an octagonal runway. Of the thirty rats in the shock-inescapable group, only four met the criterion of ten successive CRs; the others all learned to jump up and cling to the ceiling. Of the 43 rats that could escape or avoid shock by running, 38 met the criterion in less than ninety trials, and none of them jumped to the ceiling. Two additional findings concerned ease of extinction. One was that rats conditioning quickly may extinguish either quickly or slowly; rats conditioning slowly extinguish quickly. The other finding was that rats punished for making the avoidance response by being shocked for running, once they had met criterion, took a mean of 6.8 trials to reach an extinction criterion of five successive failures to respond to the CS; rats run through ordinary extinction procedures took, on the average, 63.6 trials to reach the extinction criterion.

Schlosberg repeated his earlier experiment in 1936 (124), but changed the locus of the shock from the tail

-230-

to the foreleg and the required response from tail withdrawal to leg flexion. He found, this time, that inescapable shock was more effective than escapable, as
regards stability of the CR; however, the avoidance procedure produced greater resistance to extinction. As
in the 1934 experiment, his "groups" were extremely
small. A monograph by Hilden (56) in 1937 substantiated
Schlosberg's findings.

The following year, Kappauf and Schlosberg (72)
published another study of conditioned leg-withdrawal
in the rat. They varied the CS-US interval from 1/3 of
a sec. to 7 sec., using a delayed-conditioning procedure
--that is, one in which the CS was present throughout
the CS-US interval. Within each interval, one rat could
escape shock, and the other could not. The CS-US interval did not seem to have very much effect on the
learning of leg withdrawal, which was not learned very
well in any group. However, breathing changes, which
were also recorded, showed much better conditioning
and a pronounced CS-US gradient--that is, learning was
better with shorter CS-US intervals.

In 1938, Brogden, Lipman, and Culler (17), in a
widely cited study, reported conditioning guinea pigs to
avoid shock by running in an activity cage in response to
a tone. A delayed procedure was used, with a CS-US
interval of 2 sec. For four guinea pigs, the shock could
be escaped or avoided; for the other four, it could not.
The difference between these two groups was dramatic--
the subjects in the instrumentally trained group made
an increasing number of CRs on successive days of training and soon reached a level of 100% CRs. The guinea
pigs conditioned with the classical procedure made conditioned responses on no more than 50% of the trials,
and the mean rate of conditioned responding was considerably lower than that; furthermore, there was no
consistent increase in the level of CRs among animals
in the classical procedure: the slope of their "acquisition curve" was approximately zero. The results of this
experiment are thus like Hunter's and are different from
Schlosberg's.

Mowrer published a comparison of aversive classical conditioning and avoidance training procedures in 1938 (98). The response conditioned (in human subjects) was the galvanic skin response (GSR); the CS was a light of 5-sec. duration, followed by a 200-msec. shock. His choice of the GSR was based on the fact that it would not be complicated by voluntary factors present in the striped-muscle responses used by Hunter and Schlosberg. The lack of difference between his groups, however, was completely overshadowed by the fact that the presence or absence of a GSR response, before as well as after conditioning, depended entirely on whether or not the shock electrodes were attached. He therefore analyzed his results in terms of expectancy, or preparatory set.

The relative effectiveness of the two aversive procedures was again tested by Munn in 1939 (109). A rat was put into a tambour-mounted cage, where it was presented with a CS and US, each of 1 sec. duration, at an onset-onset interval of 2 sec. The response was an increase in activity, which seemed to take the form of "getting ready" for the shock. Although the rats in the shock-avoidable group took significantly fewer shocks to reach criterion and made more CRs during acquisition (though not significantly more), they took more trials to reach criterion (not reliable). Munn pointed out that the acquisition curves of the two groups were parallel and thought that this consistency suggested two things: first, a true difference, and, secondly, that similar processes were involved in conditioning by the two procedures. Although Munn used 27 rats in each group, his non-significant results are, we think, readily explainable. The response he chose to condition was of the nature of "getting ready" for the shock. It should not, therefore, be surprising to find that the rats who received shock on every trial took fewer trials to learn to make this particular type of response consistently.

In 1946, Whatmore, Morgan, and Kleitman (162) reported a rather complicated experiment designed to test the influence of avoidance training on non-avoidance conditioning. In doing this, they first trained the dog to make a leg-flexion response, with one foreleg being conditioned by classical procedure to a hum CS, while the other was trained to <u>avoid</u> shock by responding to a bell. After this had been accomplished, they carried out further operations, such as switching the conditions to the opposite legs and dropping out the avoidance part (all of which must have been very confusing to the dog). However, the main finding of interest to us here is that the avoidance leg reached a level of 90% CRs, while the non-avoidance leg gave CRs only 20% of the time.

An experiment which shed much light on the divergent results of such experiments was that of Sheffield (127), in 1948. He pointed out that an important difference between the instrumental and classical procedures lay in what the animal was doing when the shock came on. In the avoidance group, the animals would not have been shocked had they been running; therefore, they were shocked for not running and started to do so when shock came on. But in the classical group, the animals might be running when the shock came on; an animal was therefore shocked for making the running response and so would <u>stop</u> running. Sheffield therefore repeated the Brogden <u>et al.</u> experiment, but paid closer attention to what the animal was doing when the shock came on, and what changes in behavior were brought about by the shock. His results, in general, were the same as those of Brogden, Lipman, and Culler, but his detailed analysis of the effects of shock revealed that when an animal in the shock-unavoidable group was running when the shock came on, he often responded to shock onset with behavior incompatible with running. Furthermore, the probability of the animal running in response to the CS on the next trial was <u>decreased,</u> whereas for those animals that had continued running when the shock came on, the probability of a conditioned run on the next trial was <u>increased.</u> In the shock-avoidable group, Sheffield found that successive avoidances led to extinction rather than to further strengthening of the conditioned response.

Although the question of the relative efficacy of classical conditioning instrumental training procedures would seem to have been exhaustively explored by this time, Traum and Horton included it as one more variable in a factorially designed experiment reported by Mowrer in 1950 (101). The difference found between the effects of avoidable and unavoidable shock was in the same direction and of the same magnitude as that found by Brogden, Lipman, and Culler, and by Sheffield. But to complicate matters again, Logan (82), in 1951, reported significant results in the opposite direction. He trained human subjects, using avoidable or non-avoidable shock near the right eye to condition the eyeblink. A delayed procedure was used, with a CS-US interval of 450 msec. The Ss conditioned with the classical procedure were significantly ($p = .01$) superior to Ss trained in instrumental avoidance in per cent CRs during acquisition; the avoidance group was more resistant to extinction.

By far the most elegant and exhaustive experiment comparing the Pavlovian procedure with the avoidance training procedure was that of Gibson (47), in 1952. She summed up the important theoretical problems posed by previous experiments in a simple, cogent, and challenging manner. She said: "Does electric shock act as a reinforcing agent to strengthen a conditioned response? This purely experimental question has far-reaching implications. Shock may be regarded as punishment. The effects of punishment are of intense interest to social and child psychologists; but there are as yet no commonly accepted, well-founded principles of the operation of the effects of punishment . . ." (47, p. 18). In participating in many of Liddell's conditioning experiments at Cornell, Gibson watched ". . . the relentless succession of metronome beats followed by shock . . ." (47, p. 18). She asked, "Why should the animal flex its foreleg to the sound of the metronome? The reaction yields it nothing, apparently, but another shock. Yet this routine has been a traditional method of establishing conditioned responses. From a Pavlovian standpoint, a conditioned response (leg

flexion) is predicted. The shock regularly produces the
flexion; hence, in terms of a contiguity-substitution theory, the metronome should do so after a number of paired
stimulations. But such an expectation is wholly con-
tradictory to effect theory. From the standpoint of the
traditional law of effect, shock is unpleasant and is therefore a negative reinforcement; it should tend to suppress
any action preceding it. If the animal begins to lift its
leg to the metronome, and the shock follows, the action
should be discontinued" (47, p. 18). In order to elucidate
this problem further, Gibson performed a series of experiments in which young goats were trained in a free
locomotion situation under three conditions: (1) the
Pavlovian aversive conditioning procedure, with shock
inevitable, (2) the shock could be avoided by a particular
uniform response, and (3) shocks were randomly delivered.

Gibson's results were complex. She observed at
least ten different aversive response patterns to the CS
in the Pavlovian situation, and the subjects shifted response type frequently. In the avoidance training group,
there was uniformity of responding. After an animal had
learned a uniform avoidance response, subsequent introduction of the Pavlovian procedure increased response
variability, and then a new avoidance response could be
established by again shifting the training procedure.
Gibson's most important conclusion was that her data
gave ". . . no support for the Pavlovian view that shock
acts to reinforce a withdrawal movement, in the sense
of increasing the probability of the same motor reaction;
it had, instead, a tendency to suppress a preceding action,
with the result that another took its place" (47, p. 30).

Recently, Wickens and Platt (165) have contrasted
classical conditioning and avoidance training procedures
in a finger-flexion experiment on human Ss. In the same
experiment, the two groups of Ss were further subdivid-
ed into two groups, one in which the finger flexion immediately terminated the CS and one in which the CS
continued for 450 msec. after the flexion occurred. It
was found that the groups with no delay in termination

of the CS acquired flexion at a more rapid rate. The
Pavlovian group was slightly inferior to the instrumental avoidance group.

We are led to conclude from the experimental studies concerning the relative effectiveness of classical
aversive conditioning and avoidance training procedures
that the latter produces better and more stable aversive
motor behavior, while the former produces more anxiety or emotion.

But, while the evidence is heavily loaded in this
direction, there are exceptions. How are these to be
explained, along with the generalizations? We have
been describing experiments and their data so far. Now
let us see what the behavior theorists were doing with
these findings.

Competing Theories of Anxiety and
Avoidance Learning

In 1932 and 1934, with the scant data available,
Tolman (151, 152) applied cognition theory to the data
of classical conditioning as well as to instrumental or
trial-and-error learning. While he did not have aversive behavior especially in mind, his analysis was certainly applicable. Simplified, his point was that conditioning and learning were characterized by perceptual
reorganization, by changed associations among sensory
events. He felt that the CS-US relationship in Pavlovian
conditioning established in S expectations, as well as
knowledge, about what is followed by what. The CR is
an index of the strength of the expectation that the US
will always follow the CS. The CS comes to symbolize
or forecast the US, and so it achieves some of the functional properties of the US. This analysis was also applied by Tolman to instrumental training situations. It
worked especially well for avoidance learning as far as
the building of expectancies was concerned. Anxiety for
Tolman is not a drive state but a negative expectation, a

knowledge of bad things to come. This type of theory
was weak only because it did not have any provision for
predicting the development of a specific instrumental
avoidance response. Almost any skeletal locomotor response was accepted by Tolman as an index of negative
expectations, as S's knowledge of what is to come. To
a marked degree, early cognitive theory left the S knowing what was going to happen, but it did not provide him
with a mechanism for doing anything useful about it.
Nor did it emphasize the motivating properties of emotional conditioning. It was pretty dispassionate; too
much so for such a dreadful process as avoidance train-
ings!

Early cognitive learning theory was not well e-
quipped to handle the results of experiments contrasting
classical aversive conditioning with avoidance training.
There is a CS-US relationship in both. Expectations
arise therefore. But what is the process which fixates
the particular motor response? In Pavlovian conditioning, the CR is there as the index, because it is recog-
nizably like the·UR. This does not apply, however, to
the emergence of an avoidance response, where the CR
and various prior URs may bear little resemblance to
one another. In 1934, Tolman could only use the instrumental avoidance response as an index of expectations
(or knowing) after it emerged, because the specification
of processes selecting out the response to be reinforced
was missing. Therefore, monistic cognition theory, depending heavily on perceptual reorganization, was lacking an important ingredient. (See Osgood (112) for a
good discussion of this problem.)

While Tolman was trying to make a simple cognitive,
perceptual learning theory account both for the facts of
classical conditioning and instrumental learning, others
felt that the problem was more complex. Skinner (131)
in 1935 published a paper on two types of conditioned
reflex, which he called type I and type II. Later, in 1938,
they were called types R and S, respectively. Type R
involves the process of operant learning, in which we do

-237-

not specify the original stimulus for a response. The law of type R learning is: "If the occurrence of an operant is followed by presentation of a reinforcing stimulus, the strength is increased" (132, p. 21). Type S conditioning is the Pavlovian paradigm, where we are dealing, not with operant or instrumental behavior, but rather with reflexes which have a clear and definable eliciting stimulus. Skinner's law of conditioning of type S was: "The approximately simultaneous presentation of two stimuli, one of which (the 'reinforcing' stimulus) belongs to a reflex existing at the moment at some strength, may produce an increase in the strength of a third reflex composed of the response of the reinforcing reflex and the other stimulus" (132, p. 18).

Applied to phenomena of aversive learning, Skinner's formulation had appeal. In the first place, in avoidance training experiments, certain respondents were conditioned, such as autonomic reactions of the anxiety type. Conditioned breathing reactions, squealing, heart-rate elevation, and diffuse skeletal reactions had all been observed in the course of avoidance learning. These reactions often accompanied the acquired avoidance response, and thus the whole pattern could be considered to be Skinner's "third reflex." But what, in avoidance training, is the reinforcing stimulus for the type R learning of the operant? Here is where the formulation may have appeared weak. In avoidance learning, when S is avoiding regularly, can absence of the US be a reinforcing stimulus? Or is its absence a condition for quick extinction? Clearly, the nature of the reinforcing stimulus posed a problem in the explanation of stable avoidance responses, such as those demonstrated in the Hunter (67) and Brogden, Lipman, and Culler (17) experiments, where shock was omitted for a "correct" response.

A most important theoretical paper for students of aversive behavior was that by Schlosberg (125) in 1937. Using much the same scheme as Skinner's, Schlosberg expanded the idea of the respondent to include "diffuse preparatory responses" (125, p. 379), and he further described operants to be precise, "adaptive" responses. The development of diffuse preparatory responses takes place both in classical aversive conditioning and in avoidance training. However, in the classical conditioning situation, such reactions cannot modify the unconditioned stimulus. They extinguish when the US is omitted. In the avoidance training experiment, a response which avoids the US is often fixated. In the latter case, omission of the US does not seem to be a potent condition for extinction of the learned avoidance response. Schlosberg here invoked the conception of "success," an adjunct of the law of effect, in order to account for the reinforcement of avoidance responses.

Such a law of effect process, he maintained, is "clearly irrelevant" for the establishment of conditioned reflexes of a "tonic or diffuse" kind. He stated: "It is these responses that seem to condition most readily and regularly as has been proven in the conditioning of breathing, glandular secretions and galvanic skin responses" (125, p. 388). However, like Skinner's treatment, Schlosberg's was weak in specifying the nature of "success" or Thorndikian "effect." He referred to the avoidance situation as one in which a particular response can modify the unconditioned stimulus; such a modification he labelled as successful, as giving reward or avoiding a punishment. But we still have no reinforcing stimulus; and further, we have no spelling out of a mechanism or process which would render "avoiding a punishment" as a "satisfier" in Thorndike's terms. How can absence of the US be a reward? Despite this unsolved problem, Schlosberg's paper made it easier for later theorists to handle the differential characteristics of classical aversive conditioning and avoidance learning; he left the door open for "anticipatory" respondents.

Interestingly enough, Hullian learning theory offered the mechanism whereby this problem could be handled; yet in doing so, it sacrificed theoretical clarity in explaining the facts of classical aversive conditioning.

Hull and his colleagues adopted <u>drive reduction</u> as the reinforcing state of affairs for all types of organismic responses, both operant and respondent. There was no reinforcing stimulus postulated. In pushing drive-reduction theory to its logical conclusions, Mowrer (99), in 1940, adhering closely to the Hullian constructs, pointed out the role of <u>anxiety reduction</u> as a reinforcing event in aversive learning. This reinforcing mechanism for the avoidance response was one possible solution to Schlosberg's unsolved problem. But in order to hold a unitary Hullian theory together, Mowrer (99) felt that drive reduction had to be the reinforcer for classical aversive conditioning too. It was, therefore, termination of the US which reduced drive in the Pavlovian aversive experiment. This position was clear in Miller's writings too.

Before the publication of Hull's <u>Principles</u> in 1943, Miller (89) had demonstrated the utility of the concept of <u>acquired drive.</u> In 1941, he orally reported experiments in which a previously neutral stimulus, after being paired with shock, could later in its own right <u>serve functionally</u> in the way prescribed by D, or drive, in the Hullian system. Its onset would increase activity, and its termination would reinforce instrumental responses. Miller's criterion for the presence of an acquired drive was that it should function in the same way as other drives. The fact that the new learning took place in the presence of fear, but <u>not</u> of shock, meant to Miller that his criterion had been satisfied, and that fear was playing the functional role of a drive by motivating new learning.

A similar experiment by May in 1948 (88) also demonstrated the acquisition of a fear drive. In this study, rats were trained to escape shock by crossing from one half of a Mowrer-Miller shuttle-box to the other half. They were then confined in the middle of the box and given inescapable shocks paired with a buzzer. When they were later presented with the buzzer alone, they crossed the barrier in response to it. Since the buzzer terminated when they did so, the response was presumably

reinforced by fear reduction. The much greater number
of correct responses produced by the experimental group
(as compared with controls that received both buzzer
and shock, but not paired) was presumably due to this
reinforcement. Then Brown and Jacobs (19), in 1949,
suggested that the drive for the new learning in the Miller
and May experiments might have been frustration of the
running response which had been learned as a means of
escape from shock. Therefore, they _first_ paired a buzzer with shock without allowing any escape response.
They then tested the rats on the learning of a hurdle-
jumping response, with buzzer present but no shock.
The measure of learning was latency of jumping. When
compared with a control group which had received buzzer stimulations but no shock, the experimental group
showed shorter latencies and a decrease in latency over
successive blocks of trials. These results were not
significant until freezing behavior was controlled; when
this was done, the superiority of the experimental group
was significant at the .01 level, showing again that fear,
once acquired, can function as a drive by motivating
new learning. In 1951, Brown, Kalish, and Farber (20)
performed an experiment based on the Hullian assumption
that any response tendencies present in a given situation
will be enhanced by the presence of a drive. They reasoned that if they could demonstrate the enhancement of a
response tendency in a situation designed to condition
fear, they would have shown that fear has drive properties. Thus,

> In broad outline, the experimental procedure
> described below was designed to develop a con-
> ditioned fear reaction in an experimental group of
> animals and to make it possible to determine whether
> the presence and magnitude of this anxiety state
> could be inferred from changes in the strength of a
> startle reaction which was itself never conditioned
> during the experiment (20, p. 30, authors' italics).

They therefore presented rats with a CS paired with
shock for seven trials a day, interspersed with three

trials on which the CS was followed by a loud noise which elicited a startle response. When the magnitude of the startle response in this group was compared with that of a control group (in which the CS was presented <u>after</u> the shock on half the trials), it was found that the experimental group showed an increasing startle response as training continued, while that of the control group remained fairly constant. Brown, Kalish, and Farber concluded that the increasing magnitude of the startle response in the experimental group reflected the increasing strength of a learned fear drive.

These results would seem to demonstrate that fear can be learned and that it can, if the experimental conditions are designed to allow for this, act as a drive to motivate new learning.

Miller's 1941 experiments were later published (90) in 1948, and were, along with the May and Brown <u>et al.</u> experiments, the point of departure for his fine review of <u>learnable drives</u> in 1951 (91). In this latter article, Miller postulated that learned fear drives are strong response-produced stimuli. The responses which produce the drive stimuli are parts of the fear reaction elicited by the acquired drive stimulus (or CS). He stated: "At present learnable drives, such as fear, cannot be observed directly and have not been studied thoroughly. On the basis of what we do know, two related hypotheses are advanced: (1) that learned drives, such as fear, obey the same laws as do overt responses; and (2) that they have the same drive and cue properties as strong external stimuli" (91, p. 439). This was a succinct statement of the drive reduction hypothesis generalized to cover the conditioning of fear.

Clearly, two theoretical trends were becoming incompatible. For Schlosberg and Skinner, most of the reaction components of fear were conditionable without the assistance of reward, a reinforcing stimulus, or "success." The CS-US relationship was all that was required in order for a CS to acquire the function of arousing fear reactions. As Miller strove to maintain the integrity of a Hullian view of the reinforcement of fear reactions, some difficult and contrived explanations became necessary. For example, Miller maintained ". . . we must also assume that fear is reinforced by a reduction in the strength of the pain rather than by its onset. According to this hypothesis it does not matter whether or not a response, such as fear, causes the drive reduction as long as it is contiguous with it" (91, p. 446).

This position leads one logically to the expectation that the removal of fear by a successful avoidance response will increase fear's own strength; fear is a response pattern followed by drive reduction, and so the ability of the CS to evoke fear reactions should be increased in this case. How, then, can fear extinguish in experiments in which shock is avoidable?

While Hull and Miller struggled with ingenuity to handle the problem of classical aversive conditioning, Mowrer (100), in 1947, left the fold. He had many reasons for doing so, but most of them reduce readily to the reasons Schlosberg had given ten years earlier for maintaining a dualistic view of learning. However, Mowrer elaborated to some extent on Schlosberg's two-process position. He held that an important distinction between classical aversive conditioning and instrumental avoidance training was not only the type of law which explained the two classes of events but also the type of responding organ to which the law applied (visceral versus skeletal responding units). For Mowrer, conditioned anxiety reactions were established on the basis of laws derived from Pavlovian conditioning experiments; the important variable here was the contiguity of CS onset and US onset. The establishment of the escape and avoidance responses, in contrast to the anxiety reactions, obeyed laws of Hullian theory, such as reinforcement through pain reduction and anxiety reduction. Mowrer's interesting addition was the assumption that the Pavlovian laws applied to autonomic-nervous-system responding members, while the Hullian laws applied to the escape

-243-

and avoidance responses--the responding members of the skeletal nervous system.

This distinction, made both on the basis of type of law and type of responding member, was not what Schlosberg had in mind. In fact, Schlosberg described many cases where laws of stimulus contiguity, not "success," covered skeletal aversive conditioning. These cases were the conditioned knee jerk, diffuse bodily tension or tonus, vocalization, and various kinds of "flinching" reactions. These reactions to a CS were obtainable with inescapable shock. Mowrer's classification could not handle such phenomena. (And, indeed, in cases where "voluntary" control of autonomic nervous system responses has been achieved, the classification is again severely strained.) However we may feel about these limitations, by bringing anxiety reduction and drive reduction conceptions into dual process theory, Mowrer created a strong and interesting alternative to Hullian theory as modified and elaborated by Miller.

These years, 1945 to 1951, were certainly characterized by widespread references to the concepts of anxiety, acquired drive, and drive reduction. But there were in evidence some important critics, employing different conceptions of the aversive learning process.

Sheffield (127), in 1948, pointed out that S-R contiguity theory as developed by Guthrie (52) could explain the differences in stability of performance found between shock-escapable and shock-inescapable training conditions. In analyzing his experiment, which roughly duplicated the Brogden, Lipman, and Culler (17) experiment (see above), Sheffield pointed out that often the onset of the US in the Pavlovian group elicited behavior incompatible with the measured running response. In the shock-avoidable group, Sheffield reported that successive avoidances often led to response decrements rather than to strengthening of the instrumental response. He concluded: "The results are interpreted as showing that omission of shock has no strengthening effect and

that the results obtained by Brogden, Lipman, and Culler
are consistent with the contiguity theory of learning"
(127, p. 176). Any condition which tends to break up an
S-R correlation in time will lead to extinction. Any
strong stimulus eliciting a response incompatible with
an existing response under study will tend to weaken an
existing S-R correlation in time. The implication is
that the classical aversive conditioning procedure would
be quite effective if shock onset did not itself elicit reactions incompatible with the occurrence of the running
response. It is important to note that Sheffield's skill-
ful account of both classical aversive conditioning and
instrumental avoidance learning did not require inferences
about anxiety or acquired drive or drive reduction.

Somewhat similar to Sheffield's position, yet growing out of a different experimental and theoretical tradition, was the position outlined by Schoenfeld (126) in
1950. Schoenfeld felt that the concepts of anxiety, fear,
emotion, anxiety reduction, and acquired drive were
all quite useless at present. However, unlike Sheffield,
Schoenfeld did not reject the conception of reinforcement
in discussing the growth of operant escape and avoidance
behavior. His attack on the concepts of fear, emotion,
and anxiety was sharp and masterfully argued. Schoenfeld
said: "A word is no better in science than its clarity and
unity of meaning, and by this token anxiety in its multi-
farious non-operational meanings is a perfectly bad
word. . . . Certainly we do not understand from the
clinical standpoint precisely what anxiety is in man,
whereas the laboratory worker can specify a meaning"
(126, p. 74). Then he argued: "Our definition of anxiety
is a descriptive or positivistic one: anxiety is the relationship between the presentation of S_1, after the $S_1 \rightarrow S_2$
operation has been sufficiently performed, and certain
measurable behavior changes. Both the changes and
the operation for obtaining them figure in this statement
containing no theoretic terms peculiar to itself. One
may feel that such a definition shows conceptual poverty,
but on the other hand we may be sure that it does not lack
precision" (126, p. 74 ff.). Furthermore, Schoenfeld

claimed: "It is the failure to adhere to a descriptive statement of anxiety that causes confusion. Calling anxiety 'fear,' 'fearful anticipation,' 'emotion,' and so on, involves terms that are themselves ill-defined and that bear a heavy psychological and conversational burden of inextricable connotations" (126, p. 75).

Schoenfeld then went on to spell out his own descriptive system and to introduce his theoretical conception of anxiety, escape, and avoidance learning. The CS acquires, in the avoidance training procedure, secondary negative reinforcement properties by action of the law of secondary reinforcement. This law holds that the association of a neutral stimulus with primary reinforcement results in the neutral stimulus acquiring reinforcing properties. If the primary reinforcement is negative, i.e., shock, then the CS becomes a negative secondary reinforcer. Responses that <u>terminate</u> a negative secondary reinforcer are strengthened. The CS also elicits respondents; and it can depress on-going behavior.

Then Schoenfeld made his big point: "In avoidance, the organism learns to make a response which prevents the onset of a noxious stimulus, and the seemingly natural question is how the <u>non-occurrence</u> of an unconditioned stimulus can act as a reinforcement.... We have, however, the alternative possibility, which we shall adopt as the more reasonable, of denying the question and holding that the non-occurrence of the noxious stimulus is <u>not</u> the reinforcement for the avoiding response" (126, p. 83). Rather, the reinforcement comes from the <u>termination</u> of tactile and proprioceptive stimuli which have been paired in the past with the US and now share some of its properties. Furthermore, the "proprioceptive stimuli produced by the avoidance response may, because they are correlated with the termination of noxious stimuli, become secondary positive reinforcers and hence strengthen the tendency to make the response which generates them" (126, p. 88). Schoenfeld felt that the concepts of positive and negative secondary reinforcer, proprioceptive secondary positive reinforcer, and "secondarily noxious compounds" were superior to Mowrer's and Miller's concepts of anxiety reduction, emotion, and fear, mostly because his concepts invoked ". . . no new assumptions about intervening variables . . ." (126, p. 88).

However, it proved difficult for Schoenfeld to convince the anxiety-reduction theorists that a proprioceptive secondary reinforcer was any more descriptive or objective or less inferential than anxiety reduction. After all, proprioception is "under the skin, " along with anxiety and anxiety reduction. However, it should be pointed out that Schoenfeld's descriptive formulation emphasized two sets of operations, one for the conditioning of respondents and one for the strengthening of operants; and thus, while anxiety and anxiety reduction were rejected, the duality of avoidance training was recognized and utilized in much the same manner as is found in Skinner's, Schlosberg's, and Mowrer's prior treatments of the subject.

Starting in 1950, Solomon and Wynne (137) and their associates (21, 22, 26, 27, 69, 135, 136) performed a series of experiments on traumatic avoidance training in dogs; they felt that a modification of Mowrer's position was more useful for the handling of their data than were other conceptual alternatives. Solomon and Wynne put forth their position in 1954 (138). They rejected Mowrer's ANS-CNS typology, retained Schlosberg's conception of two processes, and retained Mowrer's and Miller's conception of anxiety as an acquired drive state and anxiety reduction as the reinforcing state of affairs for strengthening instrumental avoidance responses. While for Schoenfeld the avoidance response is, in reality, an escape response, getting S out of the presence of secondarily noxious stimuli, for Solomon and Wynne the avoidance response was also an escape response, but it got S out of a state of anxiety. Whether this distinction is significant remains to be seen.

Solomon and Wynne elaborated on prior two-process theories. They invoked a principle of anxiety conservation

which claimed that the procedures most efficient for
bringing about the extinction of anxiety reactions (previously conditioned to the CS) are incompatible with
conditions most efficient for bringing about the extinction of instrumental avoidance responses. Elicitation
of anxiety reactions by the CS, without presentation of
the US, is the condition needed for the extinction of anxiety. But if anxiety reactions are elicited by a CS, and
an avoidance response allows escape from the CS, en-
suing anxiety reduction will further strengthen the
avoidance response. This poses a dilemma for the de-
signer of therapeutic procedures. Solomon and Wynne
felt that a further development of the usefulness of the
anxiety construct would involve much psychophysiological
research in the future, and they suggested several lines
of approach to this problem. They recognized that the
weakness of their conception was the fuzzy status of
"traumatic stimulus" and the poorly understood attributes of anxiety.

These conflicting theoretical views leave us with a
number of unsolved problems. All of the theoretical
positions reviewed seem to us to have their inadequacies,
and we have tried to indicate them as we went along. It
appears to us that systematic parametric studies are
required, involving both behavioral and physiological
methods, in order to choose among the existing theories
or to develop better ones.

In particular, since avoidance learning seems to
occupy an important place in theoretical divergences,
studies of the important parameters of avoidance training are in order. Some of these have already been done,
and we shall turn now to a survey of them, with the following questions in mind. What are the currently known
important parameters of avoidance training? What do
their behavioral effects tell us about the inadequacies
of current theoretical concepts? What new relationships
need to be studied?

Parametric Studies of Avoidance Training

(1) Non-temporal parameters. The non-temporal parameters of a learning situation are those involving the numbers (or frequencies) of events, and the intensities of stimuli.

(a) Frequency of US. Although the number of shock reinforcements (Hovland, 60) and the frequency of reinforcement (Brogden, 13) (Humphreys, 62) has been varied in the classical aversive conditioning situation, the very nature of avoidance learning makes it difficult to study these factors in the instrumental paradigm. Whether the experimenter continues training for an arbitrary number of trials or until an arbitrary number of successive avoidances has been made, the number of shocks received and the distribution of them are up to the subject and not to the experimenter. However, the experimenter can correlate the number of shocks actually received by S with consequent behavioral data. For example, Solomon and Wynne (137) found the correlation between the number of shocks required to produce the first avoidance response and the later alternations between avoidances and failures to avoid to be -.42. Thus, "difficulty" early in training reduced later sequential response variation in their dogs. Such an outcome can be predicted by all the theories we have mentioned.

(b) Intensity of the US. Although the effect of US intensity on learning was examined as early as 1908 in the classic study by Yerkes and Dodson (172), the first study of this variable in an avoidance training situation was not carried out until 1955. However, several earlier studies were similar enough to the avoidance paradigm to be mentioned here.

The first of these earlier studies was one by Passey (113) in 1948 which varied the intensity of an air-puff used as the US in a study of human eyelid conditioning. Although the procedure used was the classical one, there is the possibility in eyelid conditioning that receiving

-249-

the air-puff on the lid instead of on the cornea can be construed as constituting an avoidance; certainly it is **less** noxious. Passey used four intensities of stimulation, intensity being measured in pounds of air pressure per square inch. He found that the higher the air pressure, the more rapid the learning (as measured by amplitude of response) and the higher its asymptote (as measured by both amplitude and frequency of CRs).

Miller and Lawrence (93), in an unpublished study, varied shock intensity in establishing fear of a CS. The animal could not avoid the shock: it was placed on an electrified grid in the white compartment of a Mowrer-Miller shuttle-box. After a certain number of escapes to the black compartment, the rat was placed in the white compartment with no shock present, but now with a door between the two compartments. The measure of strength of fear was the speed with which the animal learned to open the door and escape to the black compartment by performing a lever-pressing response. Miller reported that: "The stronger shock produced a stronger learned drive, presumably fear" (91, p. 447).

Spence and Taylor (143), in 1951, studied eyelid conditioning in humans as a function of both strength of air-puff and degree of manifest anxiety (as determined by Taylor's modification of the Minnesota Multiphasic Personality Inventory). Although the classical aversive conditioning procedure was used, there is the same possibility here as in Passey's experiment, namely, that a CR might be "successful" to the extent that it reduced the impact of the US. In any event, both independent variables were found to produce a significant effect on the amount of eyelid conditioning, with a stronger US and higher anxiety level leading to better conditioning.

The first study of shock intensity in a true avoidance training situation was performed very recently by Kimble (75). He trained rats to escape or avoid shock by performing a wheel-turning response in a Skinner box. The shock intensities used were 0. 2, 0. 5, 1. 0, and 2. 0 ma.; a control group was run without shock. The CS was a buzzer, which came on 5 sec. before the scheduled onset of shock and terminated with the response. The only measure of acquisition reported by Kimble was the asymptotic latency of the wheel-turning response, and this he found to be an inverse function of shock intensity. When the curve plotting asymptotic latency against shock intensity is examined, however, it becomes apparent that its significance is due to the performances of the 0. 2-ma. group, whose latency asymptote was longer than the CS-US interval; if this group is excluded, the function is a virtually horizontal line. Either the mean latency of the 0. 2-ma. group was not really asymptotic or there were two kinds of asymptote in that group, one comprising those rats learning nothing more than the escape response, and one including rats whose response latencies were similar to those in the other three groups. Kimble found no difference between groups in resistance to extinction; this finding was unexpected and led him to make the following statement:

Such a failure for extinction measures to reflect differences obtained during the training presents a problem. The usual assumption is that avoidance responses are mediated by a learned fear. On this assumption, the better performance of the Ss trained under very strong shock can be explained in terms of a greater fear. But, on the same assumption, one would suppose that the greater fear would persist into the extinction period and that resistance to extinction would be greater after conditioning with a strong shock. The usual theorizing about avoidance learning thus encounters difficulty in treating these extinction data. It may be that studying the extinction of avoidance responses will provide a means of arriving at a more exact statement of the role of fear in the mediation of behavior (75, p. 283).

There are three points to be raised about this conclusion. First of all, we have noted that the magnitude of the acquisition differences may well be slight. Secondly, the only response measure Kimble reported for the acquisition data was asymptotic latency; in the next study to be presented, a larger number of indices of acquisition were obtained, and asymptotic latency differed significantly between groups, although many of the other indices did not. Finally, as will be pointed out in our section below on temporal parameters, Kimble's results may be due to the fact that the response was always followed immediately by termination of the CS. That is, in all groups, the experimenter terminated the CS as soon as the subject performed the instrumental response; this similarity between groups may have been potent enough to counterbalance the effect of the different shock intensities and produce the obtained absence of differences between groups in resistance to extinction.

A more exhaustive analysis of the effects of shock intensity on avoidance learning was recently completed by F. R. Brush (21). His apparatus and procedure were those employed by Solomon and Wynne (137); five groups of dogs were run, one with each of the following shock intensities: 0.34, 1.57, 2.57, 4.29, and 5.78 ma. The indices of acquisition obtained included trial number of the first avoidance and of the last shock, number of shocks, latency of the first avoidance, latency of the criterion trials, and asymptotic avoidance latency (mean latency over 200 extinction trials). The only one of these indices to vary significantly with shock intensity was asymptotic latency, which was a U-shaped function of the shock-intensity parametric. There was no effect of shock intensity on the number of trials to extinction. One of the few indices significantly related to shock intensity was the percentage of animals learning: this index increased as a function of shock intensity. These largely negative results, like Kimble's, may well have been due to the action of a response-terminated CS.

Our survey of studies of the effects of intensity of

the US in classical aversive situations had led us to expect that avoidance learning would be influenced by the shock intensity used. In the two studies which have followed the avoidance paradigm, however, this was found not to be the case. It was suggested that this finding might be due to the use, in both cases, of a re-sponse-terminated CS. We would therefore expect that if a trace-conditioning procedure, where the CS is not response-terminated, were used, shock intensity would have a significant effect on avoidance learning; this ex-periment is currently in progress in Solomon's labora-tory.

(c) <u>Intensity of the CS</u>. The experimental vari-ation of CS intensity was first stimulated by Pavlov's assertion in his discussion of generalization that ". . . the magnitude of the conditioned reflex is rigidly determined by the intensity of excitation" (114, p. 186).

There have been seven studies of this parameter published in which classical aversive or non-aversive conditioning procedures were used (24, 49, 50, 60, 76, 77, 111). Of these seven, <u>not</u> <u>one</u> found a <u>significant</u> relationship between intensity of the conditioned stimu-lus and strength of conditioning. This is interesting, in view of the contrary predictions stemming from Hull's stimulus intensity dynamism postulate.

The only experiment designed to test the effect of CS intensity on avoidance learning was performed by Kessen (73), using rats. Kessen attempted to demon-strate that stimulus intensity affects performance and not, as Hull had proposed, habit strength. He felt that he had demonstrated his point because there were no differences between groups during extinction; the sig-nificant differences between groups in acquisition, how-ever, pointed to an effect on s$\underline{H}$r as well as on perform-ance and were puzzling to Kessen. However, Kessen's experiment provided evidence for a positive relation-ship between CS intensity and avoidance behavior.

In 1954, Miller and Greene (94) used an avoidance situation to test the generalization of a response to different intensities of sound. Their rationale was that avoidance responses might be more sensitive to changes in the CS, since they are more resistant to extinction than are approach responses. Although they were testing generalization, we may compare a group of rats which received both acquisition and extinction with a CS of 108 decibels with a group trained and extinguished at 93 db. The group trained with the more intense CS took fewer trials to reach the acquisition criterion and was more resistant to extinction. These differences, however, were not significant.

Our brief survey of classical conditioning studies led us to the conclusion that CS intensity has no _signif-icant_ effect on the rate of _respondent_ conditioning. But both experiments which varied this parameter in an _avoidance_ training situation found that CS intensity _did_ have an effect, although only in Kessen's experiment was it a significant one. We may tentatively conclude that while the intensity of the conditioned stimulus may have some influence on the learning and/or performance of an avoidance response, this influence is probably not a particularly important one.

The data on non-temporal parameters in the avoidance situation are thus neither extensive nor very conclusive. Their bearing on existing theories is neither clear nor critical at present.

(2) _Temporal Parameters_. Of the many temporal variables in the avoidance learning situation, the best known is the interval between the onset of conditioned and unconditioned stimuli. The other, less well studied parameters include the response-shock interval (a temporal conditioning situation, in which a response will delay the onset of shock by some specified length of time), the duration of the US, the duration of the CS (although, as we shall see, this never has been varied independently of certain other parameters), temporal

contiguity of the CS with shock onset or shock termination, and temporal contiguity of CS termination with the occurrence of the avoidance response.

(a) CS-US Interval. Before going into a review of the studies of CS-US interval stimulated by the work of Pavlov, two earlier studies must be mentioned, the origin of which was in the work on association going on at the University of Chicago. Both of these were actually avoidance studies, although they antedated the "invention" of the avoidance paradigm by over a decade.

The first of these was a 1919 experiment by Carr and Freeman (23) entitled "Time relationships in the formation of associations." In this study, a rat chose one of two paths to a goal box. If the door at the end of the path it chose was locked, it had to return to the choice point and go the other way. In one of the three groups in the experiment, the rat could avoid going into the locked door if it turned around in response to a buzzer which was presented one second before it arrived at the door; in the other two groups, the buzzer was presented, respectively, with the turn, and one second after it. There were thus two problems under investigation: the relative efficacy, first, of "simultaneous" and "successive" association, and, secondly, of backward vs. forward association within the "successive" paradigm. The results showed forward association to be most effective and backward least so.

An experiment by Yarbrough (171) in 1921 used much the same design, but added, among other complications, electric shock. The rats were first trained to avoid a locked door by receiving shock (of 0.5-sec. duration) somewhere in the alley leading to that door. When this had been learned to a criterion, a buzzer, also of 0.5-sec. duration, was introduced at definite intervals before the shock; the intervals, measured from CS termination to shock onset, were 0, 1, 2, 4, or 6 secs. If the rat turned in response to the buzzer, it avoided the shock. The number of responses to criterion (the criterion, as in the first phase, was 90% correct responses in the last 100 trials) increased, although not in a linear fashion, as a function of the CS-US interval.

Pavlov investigated several temporal parameters of classical conditioning. It is to him that we owe the terms "delayed conditioning" and "trace conditioning," as well as the procedures to which these terms apply. He meant by a trace procedure one in which there is a lapse of time between the termination of the CS and the onset of the US; thus, the animal, when it makes a conditioned response, is responding not to the stimulus itself but to some "cerebral trace" of it. In delayed conditioning, on the other hand, the CS remains present until either the onset or the termination of the US. Pavlov reported that in this type of procedure, the occurrence of the CR was subject to a <u>delay</u> proportional to the length of the CS; he termed this phenomenon "inhibition of delay."

Two points should be noted here. First, the only difference between trace and delayed conditioning procedures lies in the proportion of the CS-US interval which is filled by the CS. Secondly, in the delayed procedure, duration of the CS and length of the CS-US interval are confounded. Pavlov, and later investigators, frequently spoke of the effects of CS duration when, in fact, they were varying the CS-US interval as well.

(i.) <u>The problem of the "optimal interval.</u>" Many of the early CS-US interval studies had as their chief purpose the determination of the "optimal interval" for conditioning. These experiments were all intended to be classical conditioning studies, but in only three of the eight to be mentioned is the Pavlovian nature of the procedure unambiguous. Wolfle published two studies of finger withdrawal (167, 168) in 1930 and 1932, in which she described the procedure in Pavlovian terms (e.g., she used test trials), but Hilgard and Marquis (59, p. 164) have pointed out that avoidance was possible with the circuit used in both experiments. Studies of human eyelid conditioning by Bernstein in 1934 (5), Reynolds in 1945 (118), and Kimble in 1947 (74) are all open to interpretation in terms of the avoidance paradigm, since, as was pointed out above, closing the lid before the air-puff is delivered may be considered to be an avoidance response.

All of these studies, whether they are classical or instrumental, studied skeletal responses, and all of them found the optimal CS-US interval for conditioning to be around half a second. Other experimenters have attempted to study the effects of CS-US interval on conditioned autonomic responses, with the aim of determining whether the optimal interval for conditioning was dependent on the latency of the response being conditioned. (Since autonomic responses have longer latencies than skeletal ones, the optimal conditioning interval might be expected to be greater in the former case.) These experiments used an unambiguously Pavlovian procedure. Hilgard, Dutton, and Helmick (57) unsuccessfully attempted to study human pupillary conditioning at four CS-US intervals; the failure of their attempt is probably due to the particular response chosen rather than to the fact that it was an involuntary response, since pupillary conditioning is generally quite difficult to establish. In 1952, White and Schlosberg (163) varied the CS-US interval in conditioning the galvanic skin response (GSR) in human subjects, with a delayed-conditioning procedure. They found the optimal interval to be the same as for skeletal responses. Moeller (96) repeated their experiment in 1954 with a trace procedure and obtained the same result (i. e., an optimal interval of about half a second).

Let us turn now to experiments intentionally designed to study the effects of CS-US interval on avoidance behavior. The earliest of these was published by Warner (157) in 1932. He first trained rats to escape shock by crossing a barrier and then later introduced a buzzer 1, 10, 20, or 30 secs. before shock onset. The duration of the buzzer was 1 sec., so this was a trace procedure for the longer CS-US intervals. Warner found that the number of trials required for his rats to achieve an avoidance criterion increased as the CS-US interval increased from 1 to 20 secs.; none of the rats in the 30-sec. group met criterion, leading Warner to conclude that "the association span of the white rat," which he was studying, was at least 20 secs., but less than 30.

Kappauf and Schlosberg (72) conditioned leg flexion in rats but found no influence of CS-US interval; yet the incidence of breathing changes in response to the CS was influenced by the interval, with conditioning being better at the shorter intervals. Another finding of this experiment was that although a delayed procedure was used, there were no delayed CRs.

The first extensive test of the effects of CS-US interval in avoidance learning was conducted by Kamin (69) in 1954. He used the dog shuttle-box apparatus, with these conditions: first, the gate between the two halves of the box remained up all the time, allowing the dog to jump the barrier at any time; secondly, the CS was a buzzer lasting a maximum of 2 secs. (If a CR occurred with a latency shorter than 2 secs., the buzzer terminated with the response.) The CS-US intervals used were 5, 10, 20, and 40 secs. Learning rate and resistance to extinction, as measured by a number of indices, were both inverse functions of CS-US interval. Most of these differences were highly significant.

A very recent experiment by Brush, Brush, and Solomon (22) reported on the effects of CS-US interval with a delayed-conditioning procedure, as compared with the trace procedure used by Kamin. Unfortunately, the delay-trace difference was not the only one between the two studies, since Brush, Brush, and Solomon used gate-up-and-light-out as the CS and did not allow spontaneous (intertrial) responses. The CS-US intervals used were 2.5, 5, 10, 20, 40, and 80 secs. Although some indices of acquisition appeared to be an inverse function of the interval used, these trends were not large and were further obscured by reversals in the 2.5- and 80-sec. groups. Asymptotic avoidance latency

-258-

was a monotonic increasing function of CS-US interval; although adjacent group differences were not significant, the trend was. Resistance to extinction was not a function of the training interval: not one dog of the 38 run for 200 trials of extinction met the extinction criterion. Although preventing the occurrence of the response or punishing it when it occurred did produce extinction in some of the animals, the efficacy of these procedures was not an orderly function of CS-US interval.

Brush, Brush, and Solomon compared their results with those obtained by Kamin, using a two-way analysis of variance in which the main effects were _interval_ and _procedure_. The interval effect was significant in all the indices of acquisition tested (largely because of the magnitude of Kamin's differences, but also because the extreme groups from the Brush _et al_. experiment could not be included in the comparison), and on some indices there was significant _interaction._ The authors said:

> These significant interactions arose because the CS-US interval, as it increased in magnitude, caused a relatively greater hindrance to learning in the trace-conditioning procedure. In using the delayed-conditioning procedure, the effects of lengthening the CS-US interval were "flattened out" and mitigated (22, p. 290).

One of the most striking features of the comparison was the difference in resistance to extinction produced by the two procedures. In the Brush _et al_. study, there were no signs of extinction during 200 trials, whereas Kamin obtained extinction within 100 trials and found highly significant trends, resistance to extinction being inversely related to CS-US interval.

Since the trace-delayed difference was not the only procedural dissimilarity between the Kamin and the Brush, Brush, and Solomon experiments, Church, Brush, and Solomon (26) ran an experiment in which they duplicated Kamin's experiment in every respect except the duration of the CS: they used a delayed procedure, in which, as in the Brush et al. experiment, the CS terminated with the occurrence of the response. Their results were the same as those of Brush, Brush, and Solomon: the use of a delayed CS served to minimize the differences between CS-US interval groups observed with a trace procedure.

There are two possible explanations for the superiority of the delayed-type CS-US relationship. One is that a longer CS, given the CS-US interval, results in faster conditioning and greater resistance to extinction. The other possibility is that this effect is not due to the duration of the CS per se but to the fact that in the experiments reported, the delayed CS always terminated with the occurrence of the instrumental response. Although the accumulated data, as well as the results of some experiments to be reported later in this section, would seem to indicate that response termination of the CS is the more reasonable explanation, a further experiment must be done before the point can be regarded as settled. The necessary experiment is one in which the duration of the CS is varied independently of CS-US interval and of response termination of the CS. Such an experiment will be described later.

One final comment about the optimal interval for avoidance learning is in order. In the studies reported by Kamin and by Solomon and his associates, the interval producing the fastest learning, and, in the Kamin experiment, greatest resistance to extinction was 5 secs.; learning seemed to be more difficult at a 2.5 sec. CS-US interval (Brush, Brush, and Solomon). This is in marked contrast to the 0.5-sec. optimum reported by the classical conditioning studies. The most apparent explanation for this discrepancy is that the execution of a rather effortful jump requires a larger stimulus interval than does the withdrawal of a finger or paw or the blinking of an eye. The dogs in the 2.5-sec. group might well have been pushed to their physiological limit in

maintaining short enough latencies to meet the avoidance criterion and might therefore have had greater
difficulty in learning to avoid consistently. Maintaining an avoidance training paradigm but varying the type
of avoidance response trained across groups would get
at this problem.

(ii.) Backward conditioning. Another problem
which received considerable attention in early CS-US
interval studies was that of negative CS-US intervals--
that is, backward conditioning, in which the US, and
sometimes the response, precedes the onset of the CS.
No attempt will be made here to present an exhaustive
review of experiments on backward conditioning; we
will mention, in addition to US-CS groups in some of
the studies already presented, only a few well known
experiments on this problem. A bibliography of studies
of backward conditioning may be obtained in an article
by Nagaty (110).

In the 1919 Carr and Freeman experiment, as was
mentioned earlier, a backward-association group was
run. No conditioning can actually be said to have occurred, since the curve representing per cent correct responses in each block of 100 trials was a fairly stable
horizontal line running along at the chance level. Yarbrough
"ran two back-ward-conditioning groups," one with the CS
presented immediately after the shock and one with a gap
of 1 sec. Learning was only slightly more difficult for
the backward 0" group than for the forward 0" rats, but
learning with a 1-sec. backward interval was much more
difficult.

Later studies of backward conditioning seem to have
been stimulated largely by Pavlov's statement that "If
(the) order is reversed, the unconditioned stimulus being
applied first and the neutral stimulus second, the conditioned reflex cannot be established at all" (114, p. 27).
He modified this statement the following year in the
light of further evidence, saying:

... if the stimulus is introduced _after_ the beginning of the activity, then, although, as our present
experiments seem to show, a conditioned reflex
may also develop, it is insignificant and evanescent;
on continuing the procedure the stimulus, which in
this connection we term the _neutral agent_, becomes
inhibitory (115, p. 381, author's italics).

Of the studies discussed previously, those by Wolfle
(167, 168) on finger withdrawal and Bernstein (5) on
eyelid conditioning included groups run with backward
intervals. A study by Switzer in 1930 (147) used a conditioned eyelid response in humans, with a tap from a
padded hammer just below the eye as the US. Spooner
and Kellogg (145) established backward conditioning of
human finger withdrawal in a 1947 experiment which was
a considerable improvement over those by Wolfle in that
it really _did_ employ the classical procedure. The same
general results were obtained in all of these studies and
will therefore be presented only once. First, all of the
studies found _some_ evidence of backward conditioning.
Secondly, conditioning was distinctly inferior to that
obtained with forward intervals of the same magnitude.
Thirdly, there was a gradient, with conditioning being
better at shorter backward intervals; but the generally
poor level of backward conditioning did not leave much
room for a gradient to evince itself. Finally, the number of CRs on a test trial _decreased_ as training with
backward intervals was continued.

This final observation provides indirect evidence
for Pavlov's assertion that a backward CS becomes inhibitory with continued training. This statement was
tested in the only study of backward conditioning explicitly designed as an avoidance experiment. Nagaty
(110), in 1951, established an avoidance response of
wheel-turning in rats with a 2-sec. _forward_ interval,
his idea being that to test the inhibitory effect of a
stimulus there must be an on-going response to inhibit.
When the rats had met the acquisition criterion, he divided them into three groups of 12 rats each, and a

-262-

group of four as a control for fatigue. Of the three
experimental groups, one received 50 trials in which
the CS came on 1 sec. after shock termination, a second group received 50 trials with a 20-sec. interval
between shock termination and CS onset, and the third
group received ordinary experimental extinction. The
frequency and amplitude of response decreased under
all three conditions, but both measures were greatest
in the 1-sec. group and least in the extinction group.
The 1- and 20-sec. groups were significantly different
from the extinction group but not from each other.
Nagaty concluded that a backward association does not
strengthen the connection between the conditioned and
unconditioned stimuli and, in fact, as Pavlov reported,
weakens it.

(iii.) <u>Inhibition of delay</u>. One final effect of CS-
US interval remains to be considered: that on <u>latency</u>
of response. Once again, this effect was brought to
our attention by Pavlov:

> . . . in reflexes which have been established with
> a longer interval between the two stimuli the onset
> of the salivary response is delayed, and this delay
> is proportional to the length of the interval between
> the two stimuli and may even extend to several
> minutes (114, p. 88).

Pavlov apparently observed this phenomenon only
with a delayed-conditioning procedure, so he named it
"inhibition of delay." There are very few experimental
data pertinent to this question, but what there are seem
largely to confirm Pavlov's observations. The 1937
experiment by Kappauf and Schlosberg constitutes the
only exception to this statement: they failed to find that
latency of response was a function of CS-US interval.
However, the level of conditioning obtained in this experiment was poor enough so that a positive finding would
have been more surprising than the negative one reported.

The only other studies of the effect of CS-US interval

on avoidance learning which reported latency data are
those published by Solomon and his associates. Kamin
found the latency of the first avoidance response, and
of the responses on the criterion trials, to be a positive function of CS-US interval, although he used a trace
procedure. This would suggest that the Pavlovian inhibition of delay factor is more general than Pavlov
thought it to be. Brush, Brush, and Solomon obtained
the same results using a delayed procedure, and in addition they found the same relationship between CS-US
interval and asymptotic latency. Church, Brush, and
Solomon, again using delayed conditioning, found a
positive relationship between CS-US interval and criterial and asymptotic avoidance response latencies.

There are two alternative interpretations which may
be derived from these data. One is that some factor like
Pavlovian inhibition of delay operates in the instrumental
avoidance learning process as well as in respondent
conditioning. The other possible conclusion, and the
one to which the present authors are inclined, is that
the finding of this inhibition in avoidance learning data
constitutes support for the theory that there are two
processes involved in avoidance learning, one of which
obeys the Pavlovian laws of associative conditioning.

Our survey of experiments varying the CS-US interval has raised a number of questions, particularly
about temporal properties of the CS, but there is at
least one question it has settled. The interval between
the onset of a conditioned stimulus and the onset of an
unconditioned stimulus is definitely of major importance
in the learning and performance of an avoidance response.
The degree of relationship between CS-US interval and
rate of learning may vary as a function of the length of
the CS or the conditions of CS termination, but the fact
that an inverse relationship between interval and learning rate exists seems to us now to be well established.

(b) Response-shock Interval. In 1953, Sidman
(129, 130) introduced a new temporal parameter into

the techniques of avoidance training: the interval between a response and a response-delayed shock. After
establishing that a rat could learn a bar-pressing response which delayed the occurrence of a brief shock
by a certain number of seconds (129), Sidman moved
on to a study of the effects of varying the length of time
by which the response delayed shock (the R-S interval)
and the length of time which would elapse between two
shocks if no response occurred (the S-S interval) (130).
The subjects used were three rats, each of which was
tested with various combinations of S-S and R-S intervals. This procedure means, of course, that Sidman's
conclusions are applicable only to the effects of these
parameters on asymptotic performance and not on the
acquisition process. Sidman found that as the R-S interval decreased, the response rate increased to a
maximum and then fell off sharply, presumably because
a very short R-S interval meant, in effect, that the rat
was being punished for making the response. He obtained
the same general result with the variation of S-S intervals, with the limitation that very long S-S intervals
seemed to have little or no influence on the response
rate, which was then controlled entirely by the R-S interval. With S-S intervals at or longer than the one
producing the maximum rate of response, the S-S interval used did not affect the shape of the function relating response rate to response-shock interval, al-·
though the R-S interval at which the maximum response
rate occurred decreased as the S-S interval decreased.
These rather complex relationships were discussed by
Sidman in terms of two gradients, one of "distribution
of punishment" and one of "delay of punishment." Of
the two, the latter is easier to understand: it refers
to the brief R-S intervals at which the rate of the avoidance response is depressed. The distribution of punishment, according to Sidman, depressed non-avoidance
behavior; its shape was independent of the S-S interval.
This gradient must therefore be related to the finding
that the S-S interval did not affect the shape of the function relating response rate to the R-S interval.

Milner (95) has also obtained data on response-shock intervals. The response which would delay the onset of shock was climbing over a barrier which divided the two halves of his apparatus. Once the shock had come on, it remained on until the subject escaped by crossing the barrier. Milner's work is different from Sidman's in that the former ran two different rats at each of the R-S intervals used. With intervals ranging from 10 to 60 secs., learning and performance were non-significant U-shaped function of the interval, with optima around 20 to 25 secs. Milner also found that the first avoidance response occurred with a latency only slightly shorter than the R-S interval; the CRs then backed up gradually toward the beginning of the interval.

Three general observations should be made about this conditioning technique. First, it established that a rat can be temporally conditioned in an avoidance-learning situation. Secondly, "spontaneous" (inter-trial) instrumental responses cannot occur, since every response results in a new delay of shock. In most avoidance experiments each presentation of the CS by the experimenter defines the beginning of a new trial; here each response made by the subject defines the start of a trial. And, thirdly, S learns to avoid without there being an escape response which will terminate the US.

Sidman's work is of theoretical importance because it points up the existence of temporal pacing factors in avoidance behavior. The proprioceptive theory of Schoenfeld might be most applicable at this point if we assume that the animal is punishing himself by not responding, and all responses but the avoidance response will acquire secondary negative reinforcing properties. Each avoidance response would be the only thing left to do in the situation which is reinforcing. This might account for the persistence of avoidance in Sidman's experiments. The temporal pacing is harder to analyze in purely proprioceptive terms. Postulation of a build-

up of conditioned fear during the R-S interval, as a
consequence of trace or delay conditioning, with proprioceptive stimuli as the CS and shock as US, might
account for Sidman's results. Here one might apply
the results showing Pavlovian inhibition of delay in
CS-US interval experiments mentioned above. Physiological measures might be required, however, in order
to show that the intensity of conditioned anxiety is greater toward the end of the R-S interval than at the beginning.

(c) Duration of the US. The next temporal parameter to be considered is the duration of the aversive
unconditioned stimulus. Since the duration of the US
is not usually under the experimenter's control in avoidance learning, our consideration of this variable will
be very brief. True, Traum and Horton (154, p. 289)
reported a greater number of avoidance responses in
rats when the shock was response-terminated than when
its length was constant (p = .01), but they did not vary
the duration of the shock.

The four studies available on the effects of US
length were all motivated by the deduction from Hull's
and Miller's reasoning that a stronger fear reaction will
be conditioned when a CS is followed by a brief shock
than when the shock is of longer duration. This follows
from the idea that drive reduction usually occurs in
closer temporal contiguity with the onset of the fear reaction when the shock is of short duration.

Sullivan (146), Chambers and Coppock (25), and
Bitterman, Reed, and Krauskopf (6) all varied US
length in conditioning the human GSR. Sullivan was the
only one to obtain results in the direction predicted by
Hullian theory, but even they were confounded by the
fact that the short US group had a higher response level
from the start. All others could detect no effect of US
duration on the conditioned GSR. The conclusion drawn
by Chambers and Coppock and by Bitterman et al. was
that the important determinant of GSR conditioning was

-267-

shock <u>onset</u> rather than shock termination.

   In a recent study, Mowrer and Solomon (106) measured the strength of fear conditioned with short and long
shock, by observing the depression in the rate of rewarded bar-pressing produced by the introduction of a CS
which had previously been paired with shock in a different apparatus.   Two groups of rats were run with a
short shock and two groups with a longer one.   The
CS-US interval was constant at 3 secs.   In one of the
groups at each duration, shock termination was abrupt,
while in the other it was gradual.   (Hullian theory would
predict better learning with abrupt drive reduction.)
The four shock patterns were:

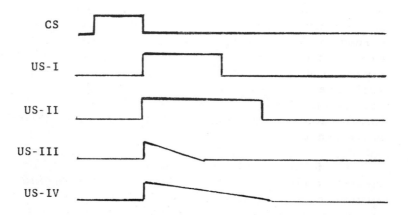

The finding that there were no significant differences
(in fact, there were hardly any differences at all) between groups supported Mowrer's contention that fear
is conditioned by the <u>onset</u> of shock and not by its termination, since the CS onset-US onset interval was constant across US duration groups.

   The finding that a reaction such as fear is controlled
by onset of shock rather than its termination lends
further support to the proposition that avoidance learning involves two processes.   The fear response is conditioned to the CS by a process of simple sensory as-

sociating, through the close CS contiguity with shock onset; the instrumental avoidance response is acquired to the CS (and possibly to the stimuli produced by the fear reaction) through a process of Hullian reinforcement because of its temporal association with shock termination, or drive reduction. Schoenfeld's analysis seems to us equally applicable to the data on US duration.

(d) Duration of the CS. The literature on CS length in conditioning is even more sparse than that on US length; in fact, it is nonexistent. Various experiments by Pavlov and later investigators were supposed to be studies of this parameter, but they were actually studies of CS-US interval with a delayed-conditioning procedure. A study by Mowrer and Lamoreaux (103) entitled "Avoidance conditioning and signal duration" was actually concerned with the temporal relationship between CS termination and the occurrence of the response. Traum and Horton (154, p. 288) reported that the mean number of avoidance responses was greater (though not significantly so) when the CS terminated with the response than when its duration was constant, but they did not vary the length of the constant CS.

The following statement, taken from a recent review of animal studies of learning (16), is typical of the difficulties surrounding this point. (The statement is quoted in its entirety -- no experimental references have been omitted.)

The factor of duration of CS is relative to the duration of the US and to the latency and duration of the UR and the expected CR. The duration of the CS is customarily greater than the latency of the CR. It may be greater or less than the duration of the US. Duration of the CS does affect acquisition, but it is not independent of the interval of time between termination of the CS and onset of the US. In general, a CS of relatively long duration results in slow acquisition (16, p. 575).

The last sentence of this quotation undoubtedly refers to Pavlovian inhibition of delay, but we have found
that to be a function of CS-US interval rather than of CS
length. The author of the above statement must have
been aware of this too, since he later said: "Certainly
there is no evidence that the duration of the CS affects
either the acquisition or the characteristics of CRs
independently of the interval between onset of CR and
onset of CS" (16, p. 579).

The problem is complex because of the natural
confounding of three variables. If the time interval between CS onset and US onset (CS-US interval) is held
constant, then it follows that CS duration cannot be
varied without varying the trace period (the time interval from the moment of CS termination to the moment
of US onset). If CS duration is held constant, one cannot vary the trace period without varying the CS-US
interval. If the trace period is held constant, one cannot vary CS-US interval without varying CS duration.
Not only that, but any variation of CS duration with
CS-US interval held constant automatically varies the
percentage of CS-US time filled by the CS, or the ratio
of filled to unfilled time prior to US onset. Despite
such difficulties of interpretation, CS duration can be
varied with the CS-US interval held constant. This has
been done recently by Brush[2] in an avoidance training
experiment which attempted to determine the extent to
which CS duration per se could account for the superiority of delayed conditioning over the trace procedure.
Three groups of dogs were run in the shuttle-box situation, each with a different CS length, but all with a
CS-US interval of 25 secs. The lengths of CS used in
the different groups were 0.25, 10, and 20 secs. The
duration of the CS was constant; if a dog jumped with a
latency shorter than the length of the CS, it was not rewarded by immediate termination of the CS. Her general

---

[2]Brush, E. S. Duration of the conditioned stimulus as
a factor in traumatic avoidance learning. Unpublished
Ph. D. thesis, Harvard University, 1956.

finding was that duration of the CS has little, if any, effect on the acquisition of an avoidance response, but does have a direct relationship with resistance to extinction. She concluded from this that CS length is not one of the important parameters of the avoidance learning situation and cannot, therefore, be called upon to explain the superiority of delayed-conditioning procedures over trace procedures. Rather, it seems more likely than ever that the superiority of the delayed procedure is due to the fact that in all avoidance learning experiments using delayed conditioning, termination of the CS occurred at the moment the response took place.

(e) Contiguity of the CS with shock onset or shock termination. In the experiments on US duration, the S-R reinforcement assumption that anxiety is strengthened by shock termination rather than by shock onset was tested by varying the duration of shock while maintaining a constant temporal relationship between the CS and shock onset. The result obtained was that there were no differences between groups, a finding which favored two-process theory by suggesting that the important interval was the one between onset of the CS and onset of the US. We turn now to another way of testing this same Hullian reinforcement assumption, this time by holding the duration of the shock constant and varying the time of occurrence of the CS relative to shock onset and termination. In this case, for the results to support two-process theory, we would have to find that conditioning of an anxiety reaction is better when the CS is associated more closely with shock onset than when the close temporal association is with shock termination. A finding that a stronger fear reaction to the CS is learned in a group having the CS associated with shock termination would support the monistic drive reduction position.

Coppock (29) found superior conditioning when the CS was associated with shock onset in an experiment conditioning the human GSR to stimuli contiguous with the beginning or end of shock. GSR conditioning apparently did not develop in the group trained with a CS presented just before shock termination.

In 1952, Barlow (2) reported a rather complicated study of this parameter in which there were three experimental groups of rats and two control groups. Group I received a 5-sec. CS, immediately followed by 10 secs. of shock. Group II received 10 secs. of shock, with the CS present during the last 5 secs. Group III received 10 secs. of shock, immediately followed by a 5-sec. shock. The relationship between the US and the CS in each group may be presented thus:

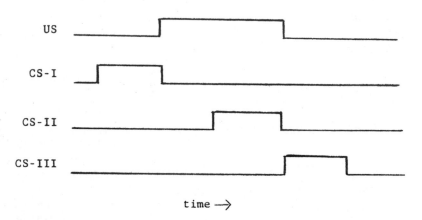

time →

Group IV received shock only, and Group V received CS only, and so served as controls. There was only one conditioning trial. The next day, all groups were tested in a bar-pressing situation. For half the rats in each group, the CS stayed on as long as the animal was in contact with the bar; for the other ten rats in each group, contact with the bar terminated the CS, which was otherwise present all the time. Barlow found that in Group I, the total duration of response was greater when the response terminated the CS ($p = .01$), whereas in Groups II and III, the total duration was greater when the response resulted in the occurrence of the CS (significant in Group III only, at .01 level). The performance of Groups IV and V indicated that no pseudo-

conditioning occurred. These results suggest not only
that a CS associated with shock onset is feared but also
that a CS associated with shock termination actually has
secondary <u>reward</u> value. This is the first clear experimental demonstration of Schoenfeld's hypothesis.

In a 1954 experiment of similar design, Mowrer
and Aiken (102) tested the depressant effect of a CS,
previously paired with shock, on the rate of bar-pressing for food. Ss were rats. Shock was of 10 secs.
duration in all five groups, and the CS lasted for 3 secs.
In Group I, the CS terminated at shock onset; in Group
II it began at shock onset; in Group III it terminated at
the end of shock; and in Group IV it began at shock termination. The design is demonstrated in the following
diagram:

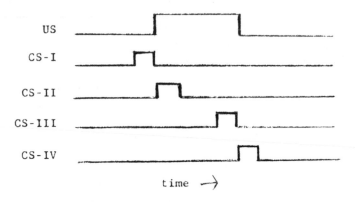

time ⟶

Group V was a control group, in which the onset of the
CS came 2 minutes after shock termination. All groups
were later presented with the CS in another situation,
while they were bar-pressing to obtain food. The depressant effect of the CS on rate of bar-pressing was
greatest in Group I and decreased monotonically from
I to V. All differences were significant except the
adjacent ones between Groups II and III, and III and IV.

Mowrer and Suter (107) performed an experiment
on rats in which, once again, Hullian theory would pre-

dict that one group would be superior to the other, while
two-process theory would predict that they would be the
same. The CS came on 5 secs. before the US in both
groups; in Group I, however, it terminated with shock
onset, while in Group II it terminated at the same time
the shock did. The rats could not escape the shock once

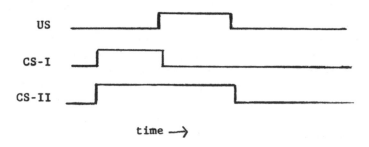

time ⟶

it had come on, but they could avoid it. No differences
were found between groups in mean number of avoidance
responses. Traum and Horton (154) included this parameter in a factorially designed avoidance experiment, again
on rats, and obtained the same results as Mowrer and
Suter had.

Miller (91, p. 446) has suggested two ways in which
a monistic S-R drive-reduction theory could account for
the general finding that fear is conditioned by shock onset
rather than by shock termination. The first possible
explanation is based on Adrian's finding that the onset
of a stimulus at first produces a strong burst of impulses, followed by a rapid reduction in the rate of firing.
Miller proposed that this reduction in the rate of neural
transmission constitutes partial drive reduction. The
other mechanism he suggested (and the two are not mutually exclusive) was that temporary drive reduction occurs when an animal leaps into the air from a charged
grid.

Two experiments have been reported in which these
objections were overcome by (a) preventing the rat from
leaping off the grid and (b) increasing the intensity of shock

-274-

from the moment of onset to the moment of termination.

In an experiment by Davitz (33), two groups of rats were run, one with a 2-sec. CS which started one sec. before shock onset, and the other with the CS starting one sec. before shock termination. Davitz then recorded the decrease in activity produced by presentation of the CS alone; fear was assumed to lead to a reduction in activity. The results confirmed those of earlier studies which had found that fear was conditioned by shock onset. And more recently, Montgomery and Galton (97) associated a black compartment with the shock onset and a white compartment with shock termination; this was done by transporting a rat through the compartments in a little trolley car while it was receiving the shock. They then placed the rat in the apparatus and recorded the time spent in the black and white compartments. In comparing these data with the time spent in each compartment before shock, they found a significant ($p < 0001$) decrease in the time spent in the black (onset) compartment. Montgomery and Galton took this to indicate that the rat had learned to fear stimuli associated in time with shock onset. However, there is also a distinct possibility, in view of Barlow's results, that the white compartment had acquired secondary reward value by its association with shock termination. This possibility can be tested by adding a third, neutral compartment. If the valence of the white compartment were positive, the rat should go there rather than to the neutral compartment. However, if the valence of the white compartment were negative, but less strongly so than the valence of the black compartment, the rat should go to the neutral compartment. A two-process theory such as Mowrer's would predict that the rat should go to the white compartment, whereas Miller, to maintain his position that a fear reaction is conditioned by shock termination, would have to predict that the rat should go to the neutral compartment.

An approach to such an experiment has very recently been reported by Goodson and Brownstein (48). They shocked rats in a black compartment and allowed them to escape to a white compartment. They then paired each compartment with a neutral compartment in place-preference tests. The results were in the direction predicted by Mowrer: there was a <u>decrease</u> in the preference for the black chamber as compared with the neutral chamber, and an <u>increase</u> in the preference for the white compartment; but this experiment does not meet the requirement of showing an increase in the preference for a place where <u>shock is first on and then goes off.</u> The necessary change in the procedure used by Goodson and Brownstein would be for the shock to be on in both black and white compartments and go off in the white compartment <u>after</u> the rat has entered it.

When we consider the evidence on the contiguity of the CS with either US onset or termination, the inadequacy of Hull's and Miller's interpretation of fear conditioning suggests itself. The two-process formulations of Mowrer, Schoenfeld, and Solomon and Wynne appear to organize the findings with greater ease and plausibility.

(f) <u>Contiguity of CS termination with the instrumental avoidance response.</u> The last temporal parameter to be considered here is the relationship between occurrence of the instrumental response and termination of the CS. The best-known investigation of this relationship was published in 1942 by Mowrer and Lamoreaux (103). They trained three groups of rats to avoid shock by crossing from one half of a Mowrer-Miller shuttle-box to the other in response to a buzzer. In Group I, the buzzer remained on for one second; in Group II, it was always response-terminated; and in Group III, the termination of the buzzer was delayed until 5 sec. after the occurrence of the response. The mean number of CRs made over the ten days of training was found to be significantly greater in Group II than in Groups I and III, but the latter two groups did not differ significantly from each other. What little difference there was between Groups I and III favored the brief stimulus (Group I). Mowrer and ·Lamoreaux also recorded spontaneous crossings and found that the average number of these was greatest in Group I and least in Group III; this difference was significant (p = .02). They concluded from this that the higher level of conditioning in Group II was not due to a higher level of general activity. Later they suggested an explanation for the high rate of spontaneous responding found in Group I:

> There were, in a manner of speaking, two stimuli which preceded the shock--buzzer and silence. Both, therefore, became dangerous and tended to elicit running (as well as other) responses. Since a running response was counted as conditioned only if it occurred within five seconds after the onset of the buzzer and since silence persisted indefinitely, one can see why the animals in this group, being more or less "left up in the air," made many responses which would necessarily be counted as "spontaneous" (101, p. 117).

The Traum and Horton study mentioned previously found that the number of avoidance responses was greater, though not significantly so, with a response-terminated CS than with a CS of fixed duration.

In 1951, Mowrer and Lamoreaux (105) published an experiment which was very similar to their 1942 study, except that only Groups I and II were run, and the CS in Group I was "instantaneous" instead of lasting for a second. The results were the same, too: the Group II rats produced more aversive responses and fewer spontaneous ones. The chief difference from the earlier experiment ·was the increased emphasis placed on the point quoted above, namely, that the danger situation (i. e., the CS-US interval) could be discriminated from the safe situation more clearly in the group having a response-terminated CS. They reasoned that fear was at first conditioned not only to the buzzer but also to the experimental situation as a whole, so that some operant responses would occur between trials. However, these responses would not be reinforced by fear reduction and would therefore tend to extinguish. This extinction effect would generalize to the situation with the buzzer, in which case the rat would be shocked again. In this way, a discrimination would be built up between the danger situation (buzzer present) and the safe situation (buzzer absent), and responses would occur only when the CS was present. They then pointed out that this discrimination was easier with a response-terminated CS than with a very brief one and predicted that instrumental learning would be faster in the former case. This reasoning also led to the prediction that the rate of spontaneous responding should decrease as learning progresses; this was the result obtained. We would like to modify this guess that a spontaneous response does not reduce fear. We would say, rather, that a spontaneous response probably does not reduce fear as much as does a response which terminates the CS. But it might also be that situational cues do not arouse as much anxiety as do those cues plus the CS, so there might not be as much anxiety to be reduced between trials.

A recent study by Wickens and Platt (165), mentioned above in another connection, compared the effects of a response-terminated CS with those of a CS whose termination was delayed for 450 msecs. after shock termination (or after the response). The CS-US interval was also 450 msecs. The subjects were students in an elementary psychology course. One pair of groups was run under classical aversive conditioning conditions, the other pair under instrumental avoidance training ones. They compared the mean number of CRs made during successive thirds of the conditioning process. All of the differences between the response-terminated-CS and delay-of-CS-termination groups were in favor of response-termination, but the only difference reaching statistical significance was that for trials 2-9 in the instrumental group. The fact that the Guthrian prediction of better classical aversive conditioning with a response-terminated CS was not upheld seems to be mitigated by the failure to obtain this result reliably in the instrumental training situations. Wickens' and Platt's conclusion that their results could be predicted better by Mowrer's theory than by Guthrie's would therefore appear to be unwarranted at present.

With the exception of the Wickens and Platt effort, studies of the temporal contiguity between the instrumental response and termination of the CS have all found that avoidance learning is significantly better when the CS ends at the moment the response occurs, rather than terminating either earlier or later. This is presumably because a CS-terminating response is immediately reinforced by the reduction of fear or anxiety when a danger signal terminates; or, put in contrasting light by Schoenfeld, delay of secondary reinforcement is minimized by such a condition. This has been suggested as an explanation of the faster learning and greater resistance to extinction found by Solomon and his associates for delayed- as compared with trace-conditioning procedures. Although our review of the experimental literature on this parameter makes it all the more reasonable to assume that this explanation is the most nearly correct, a final conclusion must be deferred until the temporal delay gradient for secondary reinforcement has been systematically explored for aversive learning.

Discussion

We have reviewed nine techniques often used to produce aversion experimentally. We have discussed at length the contrasting characteristics of classical aversive conditioning and avoidance training and have shown how competing theories of aversion have struggled with the logical ordering of these contrasting characteristics. Finally, we have described some important parameters of avoidance training and their effects on anxiety and avoidance learning, relating the results to various competing theories.

To the reader it must be clear that we have favored heavily the alternative varieties of two-process "anxiety theory" in organizing the results of aversion experiments. Such theories offer an interesting and provocative framework for our thinking. It seems to us that they describe, more adequately than do the various single-process theories, the development of acquired fear reactions and the selection of acts which the organism will perform in adapting to aversive stimuli, both innate and acquired. The general properties of the two-process anxiety theories that at the present moment seem to order the existing data in a fairly satisfactory manner have certain distinctive features in common. First, they assume that the conditioning of fear or anxiety is a Pavlovian process. The temporal relationship between the onset of the CS and the onset of the aversive US is the most important parameter controlling the development of an acquired anxiety reaction. Other variables, like the perceptual salience of the CS and the intensity of the US, are, of course, important. It is assumed that the development of anxiety reactions do not depend in any way upon drive reduction or hedonic reinforcement. In contrast, such theories assume that the development of an instrumental escape response depends heavily on the time relationships between the occurrence of an instrumental act and the termination of a noxious US. The development and maintenance of an instrumental avoidance response is assumed to depend heavily on the development of conditioned anxiety reactions which serve a motivating function. In addition, the occurrence of instrumental avoidance responses, if they are successful in removing the CS, are assumed to be followed closely in time by anxiety reduction, which is considered to be a reinforcing event. It should be pointed out that it isn't too clear at this time whether it is the CS termination which does the reinforcing (Schoenfeld), or whether it is the decrease in intensity of anxiety level (Mowrer).

However, the value of any theory of aversive motivation and aversive behavior must also lie in its future products, its general fruitfulness. Therefore it seems necessary to indicate the various directions for future research implied in the current use of two-process "anxiety theories" as working models.

Existing two-process "anxiety theories" leave many questions open for investigation; indeed, their inadequacies are partly their strength.

(1) The indices of anxiety development are handled in a vague way. Schoenfeld's criticism of the use of the anxiety concept applies here. What objective evidence for the existence of anxiety are we to accept? How are we to define the concept objectively? Mowrer would employ ANS reactions exclusively. Schlosberg, and Solomon and Wynne would look at both ANS and skeletal NS reactions. But which responses, of all the variegated and correlated responses occurring to aversive stimuli, are to be designated as anxiety indices? The answer to this question seems to us to lie in the future discovery of strong functional laws relating the occurrence of conditioned aversive respondents to the occurrence of changing aversive operants. If Miller is correct, the occurrence of certain conditioned respondents might serve functionally as _drive_ or _motivator_. Which respondents?

(2) The specification of anxiety reduction is vague. It is not clear at the moment what types of indices are to decrease in value in order for the observer to believe that anxiety reduction has taken place. For example, with a well learned and stably performed avoidance response, we rarely see signs (either ANS or skeletal) which indicate intuitively to the observer that S is anxious at all. Therefore, how can the avoidance response and termination of the CS result in anxiety reduction? In order to get at this problem theoretically, Solomon and Wynne postulated the operation of the principle of anxiety conservation (138, p. 359 ff.). But the invocation of this principle did not solve the basic problem. It merely added new dimensions to it, dimensions which

are, fortunately enough, open to empirical investigation.

(3)   The specification of the classes "operant" and
"respondent" is vague. Do these classifications coincide
perfectly with the ANS-skeletal NS distinction? Do they
correspond perfectly with reflexive, "involuntary" acts
compared with "voluntary" ones? Are they merely a
reflection of a statistical distinction, with respondents
having high p-values in the presence of a specified
stimulus and operants having low p-values? Or is the
definition purely circular within two-process theory?
Are respondents conditionable successfully using Pavlov's
methods, while operants are successfully trained using
Thorndike's methods? It seems to us that this classification problem will take care of itself with adequate
empirical research. Probably there are many reactions,
classifiable as respondents under all criteria above,
which, with adequate ingenuity on the part of E, can be
made into operants and vice versa.

(4)   Developments in cognitive or perceptual learning theories are not being taken advantage of. Perhaps
both the anxiety reactions and the instrumental avoidance
responses are produced by some central cognitive event.
How the S emotes and behaves may be a function of what
he knows, and existing two-process anxiety theories do
not take this possibility into account.

It seems to us that these four problems lead us into
some very interesting experimental programs employing
both psychophysiological and purely behavioral techniques.
While the experiments cannot be spelled out in detail here,
the general strategy seems to have been comprehended
in many laboratories, and we look forward to much progress in this area in the next few years.

Let us first look at the specification of anxiety and
anxiety reduction in the instrumental learning process.
A very recent experiment of Black (7) will be illustrative. Black studied the simultaneous development of
conditioned cardiac acceleratory reactions in dogs who

were in the process of avoidance training in the same
experimental situation we described earlier (the head-
turning situation), in order to illustrate the avoidance
phenomenon. (See p. 5 ff.) At the outset, Black was
willing to accept the heart rate as an anxiety index.
Using the method of gradual emergence, he found that
the cardiac acceleratory reaction conditioned rapidly,
so that the previously neutral CS could reliably elicit
an increase in heart rate after very few CS-US pairings. The first successful avoidance response in
Black's head-turning situation came after 5 to 10 trials,
a few trials after the appearance of the first conditioned
cardiac reaction. However, avoidance behavior was
not stable in this particular training situation, and after
the first avoidance response had occurred, there usually
ensued a long sequence of trials during which S shifted
from escapes to avoidances and back in an erratic manner. During these trials there was a correlation between the presence of a high-magnitude cardiac CR and
the occurrence of a successful avoidance response. If
the CS did not elicit a vigorous cardiac rate elevation,
the S usually failed to avoid and received a shock at the
end of the 5-sec. CS-US interval. However, Black
found that about two-thirds of the total magnitude of the
cardiac elevation could be attributed to the muscular
occurrence of the head-turning response itself.

Black further found that cardiac conditioning was
obtainable in only 80% of his dogs. The slowest avoidance learners were those dogs who showed no cardiac
conditioning. In those dogs who did show good cardiac
CRs, the CRs were of greater amplitude after the S was
removed from the training situation and then later put
back into it.

In extinction, the relationship between conditioned
cardiac reactions and the occurrence of avoidance responses disappeared. The heart-rate reaction gradually declined, along with the resting, pre-CS-presentation
levels. Spontaneous recovery was great during extinction.

Typifying data from all the dogs who met the learning criterion of 10/10 successful avoidances, Black
found the conditioned cardiac reaction on the criterion
trials to look like this:

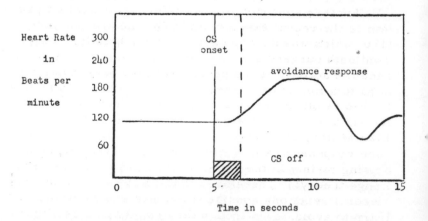

Time in seconds

The graph shows a quick avoidance response, with
a latency of slightly less than 1 sec. The cardiac rate
has begun to rise from its pre-CS level before the avoidance occurs, and the rise continues for several seconds
after the avoidance response has occurred and the CS
has been removed. Then the rate subsides slowly,
sometimes going below the resting level before it returns
to a stable level. If cardiac rate itself is to be taken
as the anxiety index, the peak of anxiety follows the occurrence of the learned avoidance response, and then
the reduction of anxiety requires several seconds following the attainment of the peak anxiety level. Naturally,
this poses a serious problem for any anxiety theory of
avoidance. All one can say at the moment is that CS
onset seems to be able to initiate the cardiac acceleration with an extremely short latency; whether the termination of the CS by the avoidance response truncates the
acceleration reaction remains to be seen and is a critical
observation for a theory involving the concept of anxiety
conservation. It seems clear that simple explanations
for Black's findings will be difficult to generate. Certainly the concept of anxiety conservation, as used by Solomor

-284-

and Wynne (138), will need an overhauling, because Black's data show that a well learned **avoidance response** does not succeed in <u>preventing</u> the occurrence of the conditioned cardiac rate elevation.

Another approach to the anxiety specification problem is the recent experiment by Wynne and Solomon (170) which was described above very briefly. They used both surgery and autonomic blocking agents to reduce the activity of the peripheral ANS responding members to a minimum. Their initial hypothesis was Mowrer's. He had assumed that the responses giving rise to anxiety as a drive state were those of the peripheral ANS. Like Miller, Mowrer felt that the motivation for avoidance responses came from patterns of drive stimulation arising mainly in the viscera. (Shades of the James-Lange theory!) Therefore, if one were to reduce such visceral reactions considerably, perhaps Ss would not learn to avoid, even though they could learn readily to escape under the motivation from the noxious US.

Wynne and Solomon trained one group of dogs in the shuttle-box situation <u>after</u> they had been prepared surgically and pharmacologically so that peripheral ANS responses were considerably decreased. In these Ss, escape learning, as well as avoidance learning, was retarded, but all Ss eventually met a stiff criterion for avoidance learning. They extinguished faster than did normal Ss. However, two Ss with ANS blockade introduced <u>after</u> avoidance learning had occurred did not show any effects of the procedure.

These results may be interpreted to mean that peripheral components of anxiety reactions are important during early phases of the avoidance learning process, but they are not important during later phases or during extinction. We might further point out the correspondence between these results and those of Black (see above). Black found the correlation between presence and absence of a high-magnitude conditioned cardiac elevation to the CS and the occurrence of an avoidance to be highest during the early training trials; but during extinction this correlation vanished. Perhaps Schoenfeld and Mowrer need to be amalgamated. Perhaps, early in training, <u>before</u> discriminative learning has proceeded far enough for the termination of the CS and the proprioceptive stimuli of the successful response to become secondary reinforcers, the stimulus pattern from the viscera serves as an important aversive stimulus pattern (drive) in its own right. Later on, when the avoidance response is quick, not as much goes on in the way of peripheral ANS responding (the anxiety conservation principle), but the reinforcing properties of proprioceptive stimuli and CS termination now are very important. This interpretation helps the very different experiments of Black and Wynne and Solomon to achieve some consistency. It has both behavioral and physiological implications.

That conditioned cardiac acceleration is not merely an artifact of skeletal responding, as Kendon Smith (134) once rashly postulated, has been clearly demonstrated by Black (7). Using dogs completely immobilized by large doses of d-Tubocurarine, he was able to show the development of cardiac acceleration reactions to the occurrence of a previously neutral CS. There is thus no reason to believe that anxiety reactions need to have peripheral skeletal components in order to occur, if we are willing to use heart rate as one indicator of anxiety. This observation is substantiated by the use of a human S in a state of complete flaccid paralysis under the influence of d-Tubocurarine. Smith <u>et al</u>. (133) reported that their S was made anxious by inability to cough up mucous during the curarization. Or so their S claimed; and we have no good reason to dispute this!

We have not progressed recently in the better designation of the classes operant and respondent. It would be helpful if some kind of technique could be developed to assign each different response a value on a continuum from operant to respondent. Then a program for testing the conditionability and trainability of such Rs could be developed. Can a well trained operant function subsequently as a respondent? Can a respondent be used functionally as an operant? The psychology of aversive motivation could profit greatly by research in this area. One can think of great chances for application to psychosomatic medicine; if the hypertensive could only be _taught_ to keep his blood pressure low-- but by what techniques?

An example of the recent use of cognitive theory _along with_ two-process theory in developing a very ingenious set of experiments is now available in a paper by Kamin (71). He argued that Hilgard's and Marquis's cognitive interpretation of the success of avoidance training methods has not been taken seriously. Hilgard and Marquis, in referring to the omission of the US, had said: "In instrumental avoidance training the new response is strengthened in 'the absence of any such stimulus; indeed it is strengthened because of the absence of such a stimulus. Absence of stimulation can obviously have an influence on behavior only if there exists some sort of preparation for or expectation of the stimulation" (59, p. 58 ff.). Kamin very cleverly teased out two possible reinforcing events, CS termination and US prevention, and varied them independently. CS termination is a reinforcer in S-R reinforcement theory. US prevention, the _absence_ of the otherwise _expected_, is a reinforcer in cognitive learning theory. Kamin compared the frequency of CRs in four experimental groups: the first group was the usual avoidance training group in which the R both terminated the CS _and_ prevented the onset of the US; Group Two could only terminate the CS with R, since the US occurred anyway; Group Three could not terminate the CS by R, but _could_ prevent the onset of the US; and Group Four was a Pavlovian aversive conditioning group which could _neither_ terminate the CS nor prevent the onset of the US. Groups Two and Three were very much alike in their performance; they were intermediate in number of CRs, with Group One best and Group Four by far the worst. Analysis of variance showed that CS termination and US prevention were <u>both</u> significant contributors to variance, and there was no appreciable interaction variance. Kamin asks how non-occurrence of the US could have had a reinforcing effect according to S-R reinforcement theory. He has some answers, but they all require more experimentation for their verification. It is clear that at present Kamin's data pose a serious threat to non-cognitive theories of aversive learning.

These are but a few examples of current experimental attacks on difficult questions raised by two-process anxiety theories of aversive learning. In each case, interesting and challenging data emerged which threatened the concepts which suggested the experiments. We can only conclude that the study of aversive behavior is progressing in a promising manner. Perhaps it soon will be empirically and theoretically mature enough to allow application to problems in human aversive motivation.

Selected Bibliography

1. Aldrich, C. A. A new test for hearing in the newborn. <u>Amer. J. Dis. Child.</u>, 1928, <u>35</u>, 36-37.

2. Barlow, J. A. Secondary motivation through classical conditioning: one trial nonmotor learning in the white rat. <u>Amer. Psychologist</u>, 1952, <u>7</u>, 273 (Abstract).

3. Bechterev, V. M. <u>La psychologie objective.</u> Paris: Alcan, 1913.

4. Bechterev, V. M. <u>Objektive Psychologie oder Psychoreflexologie. Die Lehre von den Assoziationreflexen</u>. Leipzig: Teubner, 1913.

5. ·Bernstein, A. L. Temporal factors in the formation of conditioned eyelid reactions in human subjects.
J. gen. Psychol., 1934, 10, 173-197.

6. Bitterman, M. E., Reed, P., and Krauskopf, J.
The effect of the duration of the unconditioned stimulus upon conditioning and extinction. Amer. J. Psychol.,
1952, 65, 256-262.

7. Black, A. H. The extinction of avoidance responses
under curare. Unpublished Ph.D. thesis, Harvard
Univ., 1956.

8. Brady, J. V. The effect of electroconvulsive shock
on a conditioned emotional response: the permanence
of the effect. J. comp. physiol. Psychol., 1951, 44,
507-511.

9. Brady, J. V. The effect of electroconvulsive shock
on a conditioned emotional response: the significance
of the interval between the emotional conditioning and
the electroconvulsive shock. J. comp. physiol. Psychol.,
1952, 45, 9-13.

10. Brady, J. V., and Hunt, H. F. A further demonstration of the effects of electroconvulsive shock on a
conditioned emotional response. J. comp. physiol.
Psychol., 1951, 44, 204-209.

11. Brady, J. V., Hunt, H. F., and Geller, I. The effect
of electroconvulsive shock on a conditioned emotional
response as a function of the temporal distribution of
treatments. J. comp. physiol. Psychol., 1954, 47,
454-457.

12. Brady, J. V., Stebbins, W. C., and Hunt, H. F. The
effect of electroconvulsive shock (ECS) on a conditioned
emotional response: the effect of additional ECS convulsions. J. comp. physiol. Psychol., 1953, 46,
368-372.

13. Brogden, W. J. The effect of frequency of reinforcement upon level of conditioning. J. exper.
Psychol., 1939, 24, 419-431.

14. Brogden, W. J. Unconditioned stimulus-substitution
in the conditioning process. Amer. J. Psychol.,
1939, 52, 46-55.

15. Brogden, W. J. Acquisition and extinction of a conditioned avoidance response in dogs. J. comp. physiol.
Psychol., 1949, 42, 296-302.

16. Brogden, W. J. Animal studies of learning. In Stevens
S. S., (Ed.), Handbook of Experimental Psychology.
New York: Wiley, 1951. Pp. 568-612.

17. Brogden, W. J., Lipman, E. A., and Culler, E. The
role of incentive in conditioning and extinction. Amer.
J. Psychol., 1938, 51, 109-117.

18. Brown, J. S. In Mowrer, O. H., Learning Theory
and Personality Dynamics. New York: Ronald, 1950.
Pp. 510-511.

19. Brown, J. S., and Jacobs, A. The role of fear in the
motivation and acquisition of responses. J. exper.
Psychol., 1949, 39, 747-759.

20. Brown, J. S., Kalish, H. I., and Farber, I. E. Conditioned fear as revealed by magnitude of startle response to an auditory stimulus. J. exper. Psychol.,
1951, 41, 317-328.

21. Brush, F. R. Acquisition and extinction of avoidance
learning as a function of shock intensity. Unpublished
Ph.D. thesis, Harvard Univ., 1956.

22. Brush, F. R., Brush, Elinor S., and Solomon, R. L.
Traumatic avoidance learning: the effects of CS-US
interval with a delayed-conditioning procedure. J.
comp. physiol. Psychol., 1955, 48, 285-293.

23. Carr, H. A., and Freeman, A. S. Time relationships in the formation of associations. Psychol.
Rev., 1919, 26, 465-473.

24. Carter, L. F. Intensity of the conditioned stimulus
and rate of conditioning. J. exper. Psychol., 1941,
28, 481-490.

25. Chambers, R. M., and Coppock, H. W. Effects of
prior, immediate and delayed reward in conditioning
of the galvanic skin response. Paper read at Midwest.
Psychol. Assoc., Chicago, 1951.

26. Church, R. M., Brush, F. R., and Solomon, R. L.
Traumatic avoidance learning: the effects of CS-US
interval with a delayed-conditioning procedure in a
free-responding situation. (In preparation)

27. Church, R. M., and Solomon, R. L. The effect of
delay of shock termination on traumatic avoidance
learning in dogs. Paper read at East. Psychol.
Assoc., Phila., April, 1955.

28. Church, R. M., and Solomon, R. L. Traumatic
avoidance learning: the effects of delay of shock
termination. J. comp. physiol. Psychol. (In press)

29. Coppock, H. W. In Mowrer, O. H., Learning Theory
and Personality Dynamics. New York: Ronald, 1950.
P. 25 (footnote) and pp. 304-305.

30. Coppock, H. W., and Mowrer, O. H. Intertrial
responses as "rehearsal": a study of "overt thinking" in animals. Amer. J. Psychol., 1947, 60, 608-
616.

31. Culler, E., Finch, G., Girden, E., and Brogden,
W. J. Measurements of acuity by the conditioned-
response technique. J. gen. Psychol., 1935, 12,
223-227.

32. Davitz, J. R. Decreased autonomic functioning and extinction of a conditioned emotional response. J. comp. physiol. Psychol., 1953, 46, 311-313.

33. Davitz, J. R. Reinforcement of fear at the beginning and end of shock. J. comp. physiol. Psychol., 1955, 48, 152-155.

34. Davitz, J. R., and Mason, D. J. Socially facilitated reduction of a fear response in rats. J. comp. physiol. Psychol., 1955, 48, 149-151.

35. Deese, J., Lazarus, R. S., and Keenan, J. Anxiety, anxiety reduction, and stress in learning. J. exper. Psychol., 1953, 46, 55-60.

36. Diethelm, O., and Jones, M. R. The influence of anxiety on attention, learning, retention and thinking. Arch. neurol. and Psychiat., 1947, 58, 325-336.

37. Dinsmoor, J. A. Punishment: I. The avoidance hypothesis. Psychol. Rev., 1954, 61, 34-46.

38. Dinsmoor, J. A. Punishment: II. An interpretation of empirical findings. Psychol. Rev., 1955, 62, 96-105.

39. Eglash, A. The dilemma of fear as a motivating force. Psychol. Rev., 1952, 59, 376-379.

40. Estes, W. K., and Skinner, B. F. Some quantitative properties of anxiety. J. exper. Psychol., 1941, 29, 390-400.

41. Estes, W. K. An experimental study of punishment. Psychol. Monogr., 1944, 57, No. 263.

42. Farber, I. E. Response fixation under anxiety and non-anxiety conditions. J. exper. Psychol., 1948, 38, 111-131.

43. Farber, I. E., and Spence, K. W. Complex learning and conditioning as a function of anxiety. J. exper. Psychol., 1953, 45, 120-125.

44. Finch, G., and Culler, E. Relation of forgetting to experimental extinction. Amer. J. Psychol., 1935, 47, 656-662.

45. Freud, S. The Problem of Anxiety. (Translated by H. A. Bunker) New York: Norton, 1936.

46. Geller, I., Sidman, M., and Brady, J. V. The effect of electroconvulsive shock on a conditioned emotional response: a control for acquistion recency. J. comp. physiol. Psychol., 1955, 48, 130-131.

47. Gibson, E. J. The role of shock in reinforcement J. comp. physiol. Psychol., 1952, 45, 18-30.

48. Goodson, F. E., and Brownstein, A. Secondary reinforcing and motivating properties of stimuli contiguous with shock onset and termination. J. comp. physiol. Psychol., 1955, 48, 381-386.

49. Grant, D. A., and Schneider, D. E. Intensity of the CS and strength of conditioning: I. The conditioned eyelid response to light. J. exper. Psychol., 1948, 38, 690-696.

50. Grant, D. A., and Schneider, D. E. Intensity of the CS and strength of conditioning: II. The conditioned galvanic skin response to an auditory stimulus. J. exper. Psychol., 1949, 39, 35-39.

51. Grice, G. R. The relation of secondary reinforcement to delayed reward in visual discrimination learning. J. exper. Psychol., 1948, 38, 1-16.

52. Guthrie, E. R. The Psychology of Learning. New York: Harper and Brothers, 1935.

53. Gwinn, G. T. The effects of punishment on acts motivated by fear. J. exper. Psychol., 1949, 39, 260-269.

54. Hamel, I. A. A study and analysis of the conditioned reflex. Psychol. Monogr., 1919, 27, No. 118, 65 pp.

55. Hebb, D. O. On the nature of fear. Psychol. Rev., 1946, 53, 259-276.

56. Hilden, A. H. An action current study of the conditioned hand withdrawal. Psychol. Monogr., 1937, 49, No. 217, 173-204.

57. Hilgard, E. R., Dutton, C. E., and Helmick, J. S. Attempted pupillary conditioning at four stimulus intervals. J. exper. Psychol., 1949, 39, 683-689.

58. Hilgard, E. R., Jones, L. V., and Kaplan, S. J. Conditioned discrimination as related to anxiety. J. exper. Psychol., 1951, 42, 94-99.

59. Hilgard, E. R., and Marquis, D. G. Conditioning and Learning. New York: Appleton-Century, 1940.

60. Hovland, C. I. The generalization of conditioned responses. IV. The effects of varying amounts of reinforcement upon the degree of generalization of conditioned responses. J. exper. Psychol., 1937, 21, 261-276.

61. Hull, C. L. A functional interpretation of the conditioned reflex. Psychol. Rev., 1929, 36, 498-511.

62. Humphreys, L. G. Extinction of conditioned psychogalvanic responses following two conditions of reinforcement. J. exper. Psychol., 1940, 27, 71-76.

63. Hunt, H. F., and Brady, J. V. Some effects of

electroconvulsive shock on a conditioned emotional response ("anxiety"). J. comp. physiol. Psychol., 1951, 44, 88-98.

64. Hunt, H. F., Jernberg, P., and Brady, J. V. The effects of electroconvulsive shock on a conditioned emotional response: the effect of post-ECS extinction on the reappearance of the response. J. comp. physiol. Psychol., 1952, 45, 589-599.

65. Hunt, H. F., Jernberg, P., and Lawlor, W. G. The effect of electroconvulsive shock on a conditioned emotional response: the effect of electroconvulsive shock under ether anesthesia. J. comp. physiol. Psychol., 1953, 46, 64-68.

66. Hunt, H. F., Jernberg, P., and Otis, L. S. The effect of carbon disulphide convulsions on a conditioned emotional response. J. comp. physiol. Psychol., 1953, 46, 465-469.

67. Hunter, W. S. Conditioning and extinction in the rat. Brit. J. Psychol., 1935, 26 (II), 135-148.

68. Kalish, H. I. Strength of fear as a function of the number of acquisition and extinction trials. J. exper. Psychol., 1954, 47, 1-9.

69. Kamin, L. J. Traumatic avoidance learning: the effects of CS-US interval with a trace conditioning procedure. J. comp. physiol. Psychol., 1954, 47, 65-72.

70. Kamin, L. J. Personal communication, 1954.

71. Kamin, L. J. The effects of termination of the CS and avoidance of the US on avoidance learning. J. comp. physiol. Psychol., in press.

72. Kappauf, W. E., and Schlosberg, H. Conditioned responses in the white rat: III. Conditioning as a

function of the period of delay. J. genet. Psychol.,
1937, 50, 27-45.

73. Kessen, W. Response strength and conditioned
stimulus intensity. J. exper. Psychol., 1953, 45,
82-86.

74. Kimble, G. A. Conditioning as a function of the
time between conditioned and unconditioned stimuli.
J. exper. Psychol., 1947, 37, 1-15.

75. Kimble, G. A. Shock intensity and avoidance learning. J. comp. physiol. Psychol., 1955, 48, 281-284.

76. Kupalov, P. S., and Gantt, W. H. The relationship
between the strength of the CS and the size of the resulting conditioned reflex. Brain, 1927, 50, 44-52.

77. Kupalov, P. S., Lyman, R. S., and Lukov, B. N.
The relationship between the intensity of tone-stimuli
and the size of the resulting conditioned reflexes.
Brain, 1931, 54, 85-98.

78. Lazarus, R. S., Deese, J., and Hamilton, R. Anxiety and stress in learning: the role of intraserial
duplication. J. exper. Psychol., 1954, 47, 111-114.

79. Lichtenstein, P. E. Studies of anxiety: I. The production of a feeding inhibition in dogs. J. comp.
physiol. Psychol., 1950, 43, 16-29.

80. Liddell, H. S. A laboratory for the study of conditioned motor reflexes. Amer. J. Psychol., 1926, 37,
418-419.

81. Liddell, H. S., James, W. T., and Anderson, O. D.
The comparative physiology of the conditioned motor
reflex based on experiments with the pig, dog, sheep,
goat, and rabbit. Comp. Psychol. Monogr., 1934,
11, No. 1.

82. Logan, F. A. A comparison of avoidance and non-avoidance eyelid conditioning. J. exper. Psychol., 1951, 42, 390-393.

83. Lucas, J. D. The interactive effects of anxiety failure, and intraserial duplication. Amer. J. Psychol., 1952, 65, 59-66.

84. Malmo, R. B., and Amsel, A. Anxiety-produced interference in serial rote learning with observations on rote learning after partial frontal lobectomy. J. exper. Psychol., 1948, 38, 440-454.

85. Maltzman, I., Fox, J., and Morrisett, L. Some effects of manifest anxiety on mental set. J. exper. Psychol., 1953, 46, 50-54.

86. Mandler, G., and Sarason, S. B. A study of anxiety and learning. J. abnorm. soc. Psychol., 1952, 47, 166-173.

87. Masserman, J. H. Behavior and Neurosis. Chicago: Univ. Chicago Press, 1943.

88. May, M. A. Experimentally acquired drives. J. exper. Psychol., 1948, 38, 66-77.

89. Miller, N. E. An experimental investigation of acquired drives. Psychol. Bull., 1941, 38, 534-535, (Abstract).

90. Miller, N. E. Studies of fear as an acquirable drive: I. Fear as motivation and fear-reduction as reinforcement in learning of new responses. J. exper. Psychol., 1948, 38, 99-101.

91. Miller, N. E. Learnable drives and rewards. In Stevens, S. S., (Ed.), Handbook of Experimental Psychology. New York: Wiley, 1951. Pp. 435-472.

92. Miller, N. E. Comments on multi-process conceptions

of learning. Psychol. Rev., 1951, 58, 375-381.

93. Miller, N. E., and Lawrence, D. H. Studies of fear as an acquirable drive. IV. Effect of strength of electric shock as a primary drive and of number of trials with the primary drive on the strength of fear. 1950 (In preparation).

94. Miller, W. C., and Greene, J. E. Generalization of an avoidance response to various intensities of sound. J. comp. physiol. Psychol., 1954, 47, 136-139.

95. Milner, P. M. Personal communication, 1955.

96. Moeller, G. The CS-US interval in GSR conditioning. J. exper. Psychol., 1954, 48, 162-166.

97. Montgomery, K. C., and Galton, B. B. A test of the drive-reduction explanation of learned fear. Paper read at East. Psychol. Assoc., Phila., April, 1955.

98. Mowrer, O. H. Preparatory set (expectancy): a determinant in motivation and learning. Psychol. Rev., 1938, 45, 62-91.

99. Mowrer, O. H. Anxiety-reduction and learning. J. exper. Psychol., 1940, 27, 497-516.

100. Mowrer, O. H. On the dual nature of learning: a reinterpretation of "conditioning" and "problem-solving." Harv. educ. Rev., 1947, 17, 102-148.

101. Mowrer, O. H. Learning Theory and Personality Dynamics, New York: Ronald, 1950.

102. Mowrer, O. H., and Aiken, E. G. Contiguity vs. drive-reduction in conditioned fear: variations in conditioned and unconditioned stimuli. Amer. J. Psychol., 1954, 67, 26-38.

103. Mowrer, O. H., and Lamoreaux, R. R. Avoidance conditioning and signal duration: a study of secondary motivation and reward. Psychol. Monogr., 1942, 54, No. 5, 33 pp.

104. Mowrer, O. H., and Lamoreaux, R. R. Fear as an intervening variable in avoidance conditioning. J. comp. Psychol., 1946, 39, 29-50.

105. Mowrer, O. H., and Lamoreaux, R. R. Conditioning and conditionality (discrimination). Psychol. Rev., 1951, 58, 196-212.

106. Mowrer, O. H., and Solomon, L. N. Contiguity vs. drive-reduction in conditioned fear: the proximity and abruptness of drive-reduction. Amer. J. Psychol., 1954, 67, 15-25.

107. Mowrer, O. H., and Suter, J. W. Further evidence for a two-factor theory of learning. In Mowrer, O. H., Learning Theory and Personality Dynamics. New York: Ronald, 1950. Pp. 279-283.

108. Mowrer, O. H., and Viek, P. An experimental analogue of fear from a sense of helplessness. J. abnorm. soc. Psychol., 1948, 43, 193-200.

109. Munn, N. L. The relative effectiveness of two conditioning procedures. J. gen. Psychol., 1939, 21, 119-136.

110. Nagaty, M. O. The effect of reinforcement on closely following S-R connections: I. The effect of a backward conditioning procedure on the extinction of conditioned avoidance. J. exper. Psychol., 1951, 42, 239-246.

111. Newhall, S. M., and Sears, R. R. Conditioned finger retraction to visual stimuli near the absolute threshold. Comp. Psychol. Monogr., 1953, 9, No. 43.

112. Osgood, C. E. Can Tolman's theory of learning handle avoidance training? Psychol. Rev., 1950, 57, 133-137.

113. Passey, G. E. The influence of intensity of unconditioned stimulus upon acquisition of a conditioned response. J. exper. Psychol., 1948, 38, 420-428.

114. Pavlov, I. P. Conditioned Reflexes. (Translated by G. V. Anrep) Oxford: Oxford Univ. Press, 1927.

115. Pavlov, I. P. Lectures on Conditioned Reflexes. (Translated by W. H. Gantt) New York: Liveright, 1928.

116. Perin, C. T. The effect of delayed reinforcement upon the differentiation of bar responses in white rats. J. exper. Psychol., 1943, 32, 95-109.

117. Ramond, C. K. Anxiety and task as determiners of verbal performance. J. exper. Psychol., 1953, 46, 120-124.

118. Reynolds, B. The acquisition of a trace conditioned response as a function of the magnitude of the stimulus trace. J. exper. Psychol., 1945, 35, 15-30.

119. Ritchie, B. F. Can reinforcement theory account for avoidance? Psychol. Rev., 1951, 58, 383-386.

120. Rosenbaum, G. Stimulus generalization as a function of level of experimentally induced anxiety. J. exper. Psychol., 1953, 45, 35-43.

121. Sarason, S. B., Mandler, G., and Craighill, P. G. The effect of differential instructions on anxiety and learning. J. abnorm. soc. Psychol., 1952, 47, 561-565.

122. Schlosberg, H. A study of the conditioned patellar

123. Schlosberg, H. Conditioned responses in the white
      rat. J. genet. Psychol., 1934, 45, 303-335.

124. Schlosberg, H. Conditioned response in the white
      rat: II. Conditioned responses based upon shock
      to the foreleg. J. genet. Psychol., 1936, 49,
      107-138.

125. Schlosberg, H. The relationship between success
      and the laws of conditioning. Psychol. Rev., 1937,
      44, 379-394.

126. Schoenfeld, W. N. An experimental approach to
      anxiety, escape and avoidance behavior. In Hoch,
      P. H., and Zubin, J., (Eds.), Anxiety. New York:
      Grune and Stratton, 1950.

127. Sheffield, F. D. Avoidance training and the con-
      tiguity principle. J. comp. physiol. Psychol.,
      1948, 41, 165-177.

128. Sheffield, F. D., and Temmer, H. W. Relative
      resistance to extinction of escape training and
      avoidance training. J. exper. Psychol., 1950, 40,
      287-297.

129. Sidman, M. Avoidance conditioning with brief
      shock and no exteroceptive warning signal. Science,
      1953, 118, 157-158.

130. Sidman, M. Two temporal parameters of the main-
      tenance of avoidance behavior by the white rat. J.
      comp. physiol. Psychol., 1953, 46, 253-261.

131. Skinner, B. F. Two types of conditioned reflex
      and a psuedo type. J. gen. Psychol., 1935, 12,
      66-77.

132. Skinner, B. F. The Behavior of Organisms. New

York: Appleton-Century, 1938.

133. Smith, S. M., Brown, H. D., Toman, J. E. P., and Goodman, L. S. The lack of cerebral effects of d-Tubocurarine. Anesthesiol., 1947, 8, 1-14.

134. Smith, K. Conditioning as an artifact. Psychol. Rev., 1954, 61, 217-225.

135. Solomon, R. L., Kamin, L. J., and Wynne, L. C. Traumatic avoidance learning: the outcomes of several extinction procedures with dogs. J. abnorm. soc. Psychol., 1953, 48, 291-302.

136. Solomon, R. L., Sidd, J. J., Watson, P. D., and Black, A. H. The use of d-Tubocurarine in the extinction of fear in dogs. Amer. Psychologist, 1955, 10, 395, (Abstract).

137. Solomon, R. L., and Wynne, L. C. Traumatic avoidance learning: acquisition in normal dogs. Psychol. Monogr., 1953, 67, No. 4 (whole No. 354).

138. Solomon, R. L., and Wynne, L. C. Traumatic avoidance learning: the principles of anxiety conservation and partial irreversibility. Psychol. Rev., 1954, 61, 353-385.

139. Spence, K. W., and Beecroft, R. S. Differential conditioning and level of anxiety. J. exper. Psychol. 1954, 48, 399-403.

140. Spence, K. W., and Farber, I. E. Conditioning and extinction as a function of anxiety. J. exper. Psychol., 1953, 45, 116-119.

141. Spence, K. W., and Farber, I. E. The relation of anxiety to differential eyelid conditioning. J. exper. Psychol., 1954, 47, 127-134.

142. Spence, K. W., Farber, I. E., and Taylor, Elaine.

The relation of electric shock and anxiety to level of performance in eyelid conditioning. *J. exper. Psychol.*, 1954, 48, 404-408.

143. Spence, K. W., and Taylor, Janet A. Anxiety and the strength of the unconditioned stimulus as determiners of the amount of eyelid conditioning. *J. exper. Psychol.*, 1951, 42, 183-188.

144. Spence, K. W., and Taylor, Janet A. The relation of conditioned response strength to anxiety in normal, neurotic, and psychotic subjects. *J. exper. Psychol.*, 1953, 45, 265-272.

145. Spooner, A., and Kellogg, W. N. The backward conditioning curve. *Amer. J. Psychol.*, 1947, 60, 321-334.

146. Sullivan, J. J. Some factors affecting the conditioning of the galvanic skin response. Unpublished Ph.D. thesis, State Univ. of Iowa, 1950.

147. Switzer, St. C. A. Backward conditioning of the lid reflex. *J. exper. Psychol.*, 1930, 13, 76-97.

148. Taylor, Janet A. The relationship of anxiety to the conditioned eyelid response. *J. exper. Psychol.*, 1951, 41, 81-92.

149. Taylor, Janet A., and Spence, K. W. The relationship of anxiety level to performance in serial learning. *J. exper. Psychol.*, 1952, 44, 61-64.

150. Thorndike, E. L. *Animal Intelligence: Experimental Studies.* New York: Macmillan, 1911.

151. Tolman, E. C. *Purposive Behavior in Animals and Men.* New York: Appleton-Century, 1932.

152. Tolman, E. C. Theories of learning. In Moss, F. A., (Ed.), *Comparative Psychology.* New York: Prentice-Hall Inc., 1934.

153. Tolman, E. C. Demands and conflicts. Psychol. Rev., 1937, 44, 158-169.

154. Traum, Alice, and Horton, S. H. In Mowrer, O. H. Learning Theory and Personality Dynamics. New York: Ronald, 1950.

155. Upton, M. The auditory sensitivity of guinea pigs. Amer. J. Psychol., 1929, 41, 412-421.

156. Warden, C. J., and Diamond, S. A preliminary study of the effect of delayed punishment on learning in the white rat. J. genet. Psychol., 1931, 39, 455-461.

157. Warner, L. H. The association span of the white rat. J. genet. Psychol., 1932, 41, 57-90.

158. Watson, J. B. The place of the conditioned reflex in psychology. Psychol. Rev., 1916, 23, 89-116.

159. Watson, J. B., and Rayner, R. Conditioned emotional reactions. J. exper. Psychol., 1920, 3, 1-14.

160. Welch, L., and Kubis, J. F. The effect of anxiety on the conditioning rate and stability of the psychogalvanic response. J. Psychol., 1947, 23, 83-91.

161. Wever, E. G. The upper limit of hearing in the cat. J. comp. Psychol., 1930, 10, 221-233.

162. Whatmore, G. B., Morgan, E. A., and Kleitman, N. The influence of avoidance conditioning on the course of non-avoidance conditioning in dogs. Amer. J. Physiol., 1946, 145, 432-435.

163. White, C. T., and Schlosberg, H. Degree of conditioning of the galvanic skin response as a function of the period of delay. J. exper. Psychol., 1952, 43, 357-362.

164. Whiteis, U. E. In Mowrer, O. H., Learning

Theory and Personality Dynamics. New York:
Ronald, 1950. P. 260 (footnote).

165. Wickens, D. D., and Platte, C. E. Response
termination of the cue stimulus in classical and
instrumental conditioning. J. exper. Psychol.,
1954, 47, 183-186.

166. Wolfe, J. B. The effect of delayed reward upon
learning in the white rat. J. comp. Psychol.,
1934, 17, 1-21.

167. Wolfle, Helen M. Time factors in conditioning
finger withdrawal. J. gen. Psychol., 1930, 4,
372-378.

168. Wolfle, Helen M. Conditioning as a function of the
interval between the conditioned and the original
stimulus. J. gen. Psychol., 1932, 7, 80-103.

169. Woodworth, R. S., and Schlosberg, H. Experimental Psychology. New York: Holt and Co., 1954.

170. Wynne, L. C., and Solomon, R. L. Traumatic
avoidance learning: Acquisition and extinction
in dogs deprived of normal peripheral autonomic
functioning. Genet. Psychol. Monogr., 1955,
52, 241-284.

171. Yarbrough, J. U. The influence of the time interval upon the rate of learning in the white rat.
Psychol. Monogr., 1921, 30, No. 135, 52 pp.

172. Yerkes, R. M., and Dodson, J. D. The relation
of strength of stimulus to rapidity of habit formation. J. comp. neurol. Psychol., 1908, 18, 459-482.

173. Zeaman, D. Proprioception as a conditioned reinforcement. M. A. thesis, Columbia Univ. Library,
1947.

COMMENTS ON PAPER
BY DRS. SOLOMON AND BRUSH

Sigmund Koch
Duke University

Solomon and Brush have done a most commendable
and solid job in running down and organizing the extensive experimental literature on anxiety and avoidance
phenomena, and in interlarding this account with an ex-
pert running commentary on the theoretical formulations
that have at once prompted and been instigated by this
research.

In many ways, their paper is a model of the handbook
writer's or overviewer's art: it addresses itself to a topic
which has been figural in "fundamental" research, particularly since the war, and yet one which has been handled
in terms of such diverse and subtly differentiated techniques and vocabularies as to leave the non-specialized
student more than ordinarily benumbed by confusion. The
authors show refreshing sensitivity to the relations, sometimes quite arbitrary or accidental, between scientific ideas
and their historical antecedents -- some of our more youth-
ful clinicians, for instance, will be quite astounded to dis-
cover that basic techniques and problems of current "anxiety" research derive largely from certain unintentional
divergencies in classical conditioning procedures which,
prior to about 1934, had not been clearly discriminated.
Further, the authors have struck an almost unique note in
the nontendentious way in which they represent all theoretical positions discussed, despite their own two-factor
bias, and in their willingness to admit (sometimes even
stress) the difficulties and lacunae in their own position.

One might, in short, say that the inadequacies of this
excellent paper are the inadequacies of the scientific orienting attitudes and research tradition, of which both the
paper and its subject matter are instances. I have tried
to spell out certain of the limitations of that tradition in
my own contribution to the present symposium, and will

-306-

therefore spare the reader repetition. The very excellence of the Solomon-Brush paper relative to its genre makes it the best possible illustration of certain of the trends in recent psychology which I regard as regrettable.

In my paper, though I was determined to be stingy in the extreme about introducing intervening variables, I did rather lose control in one instance: I posited the construct of the independent variability of the two sides of the mouth of certain of the theorists who dominated our recent age of autism. I essayed a few tentative linkages to independent variables in the original text, but I am now prepared to broaden that definition base.

At the beginning of their paper, the authors make an exceedingly sound point: they strongly lament the "virtual neglect" of "noxious stimuli" other than electric shock in the experimental study of aversion. They imply that we cannot, because of this limitation, prejudge the question as to whether "all aversive, anticipatory states" are "alike, " and they dourly suggest the possibility that "perhaps each aversive US breeds its own type of conditioned anticipatory reaction pattern, qualitatively and quantitatively different from any other. " Let us call this "Side 1 of the scientific mouth, " a sober, conservative side which is modestly hinting that in the experimentally based formulations of anxiety we read "shock-produced anticipatory reaction pattern" for "anxiety"; "shock-avoidance" for "avoidance"; "shock-escape" for "escape, " etc. In other words, Side 1 is hinting (among other things) that it would be very dangerous indeed to confuse the experimental "anxiety" discussed in the present paper with its human homonym in most of its specifiable (and all of its important) senses.

Eighty pages later, after their detailed review of the homogeneously shock-preoccupied, but methodologically and conceptually heterogeneous, literature we find the authors saying:

We can only conclude that the study of aversive behavior is progressing in a promising manner. Per-

haps it soon will be empirically and theoretically mature enough to allow application to problems in human
aversive motivation (ital. mine).

Clearly, these words are being formed with the smiling,
optimistic, reassuring side of the writers' mouth -- the
side that can issue a promissory note, despite eighty pages
which say that there is nothing in the bank.

One might feel reassured if one could dismiss such a
promissory note as a kind of idle public-speaking routine --
a standardized peroration designed to counteract the despair
of the innocent. But unfortunately there is nothing in the
paper which might indicate that its authors are disposed to
think seriously about problems of human anxiety, or even
the requirements for dealing with such problems. Thus,
in their useful reconstruction of the nine experimental methods which have emerged in the study of anxiety, escape,
and avoidance behavior (in most instances of which shock
is the "aversive stimulus"), the authors include as Method
9 the "method of contrasts." This is epitomized by Hebb's
observations on the reactions of chimpanzees to the de-
capitated head of another chimpanzee, to the sight of the
anaesthetized body of another chimpanzee, or to human
strangers. It is at least conceivable that such phenomena
are as relevant to "anxiety" in certain of its human (and,
indeed, subhuman) forms as are the phenomena generated
by the variations of the shock paradigm. Yet this single
instance of the "great need to broaden the base of the study
of aversive motivation" alluded to by the authors is dis-
missed as a "mysterious and relatively unexplored technique," along with the dutiful hope that "perhaps experimenters will someday use this technique in avoidance
experiments, with the purpose of discovering the laws
governing such dramatic instances of aversion for unfamiliar stimulus patterns."

Another token of the extent to which the authors are
serious in calling for a broadening of the base of anxiety
research may be found in the statements that "One need
not fear at present the 'stifling' effects of increased demands

for operational uniformity and standard measuring devices, "
and that "we probably could profit by some judicious standardization of procedures and measures." To be sure, the
very marked and as yet largely unanalyzed differences used
by experimenters in this field, even as within each of the
nine categories of method distinguished by the authors,
makes such statements seem eminently reasonable. But
Solomon and Brush must make up their minds: they must
decide whether they really want to broaden the empirical
base of anxiety research or whether they want standarization
within the problem context as defined by extant research.

The manful cry for standardization reflects one of the
fixed stereotypes of zealous fundamentalists in the recent
psychology of learning and motivation. It should be recognized that a research strategy, like any other human
gamble, must involve risk, no matter how attractive the
apparent advantages. Standardization can mean compar-
ability, replicability, the possibility of pooled, cumulative
advance; it can also mean constriction of effort to the pooled
delineation of the contours of artifact. The critical factor
in a strategy of standardization is that of timing. When
standardization may become fruitful in a given area of in-
quiry is not easy to judge. But it seems to me that Solomon
and Brush are making a very sound judgment indeed in their
initial call for a diversification of the "unconditioned stimuli"
used to produce aversive behavior.

Disregarding the short-range, if significant, orally
bilateral fluctuations, the major interpretive trend in the
paper is to regard the anxiety and avoidance research primarily as an arena for theoretical conflict and discovery in
the recent psychology of learning, rather than for the systematic analysis of "anxiety" phenomena in the senses which
users of human language must perforce ascribe to such a
term. This is doubtless the most sober way to represent.
the historical function of the present research area. It is
useful to note, however, that even if the material on aversion is regarded as a limited-scope context for testing and
perfecting competing formulations of the learning and performance phenomena local to this research, the current

prospects for a coherent account of extant findings seem very dim indeed. The authors do not conceal this. Quite the contrary; on the assumption that the "inadequacies" of "existing two-process . . . 'anxiety theories' . . . are partly their strength," they fairly revel in the weaknesses of their own formulation. The subsequent enumeration of these weaknesses leaves the authors holding a theory no basic concept of which ("indices of anxiety development," "specification of anxiety reduction," "specification of the classes 'operant' and 'respondent'") escapes their own characterization as "vague." Perhaps their buoyant belief that future research will somehow straighten such matters out will prove justified, though I, for one, do not think so.

Let me terminate this discussion by stating a few prejudices about the bearing of the "anxiety" research on problems of motivation -- prejudices which are suggested by the line of thinking developed in my paper. In my pretheoretical language, the central initial problem of "anxiety" becomes that of isolating the negative value-determining properties governing specifiable sub-classes of abient behavior. Negative value properties intrinsic to physical pain and to the effects of various irritant or discomforting conditions are no doubt potent determiners of abience, and no doubt may become elaborated by learning and possibly other mechanisms into more differentiated conditions of directed behavior. But, as everyone agrees, it is absurd to assume that other negative value properties do not govern abience (either of similar, overlapping, or different forms), and, as everyone does not agree, it is equally a pre-judgment to assume that such diverse value properties are functionally effective in behavior according to the same laws that specify pain-produced abience. Nevertheless, I hold it as more than an article of faith that negative value properties necessary for the analysis of abience, though plural, need not be very great in number.

More importantly, I strongly doubt that aversive conditions have the almost ubiquitous importance in human and higher mammalian motivation attributed to such "drives" by much current theory. Though such a position can be made

-310-

to appear plausible by easy plays on words which, in an extrinsic grammar, can be used to render all "drives" as essentially "irritants" or to translate all "acquired motivations" into primary-drive-frustration "anxiety," one cannot fail to see filmy Hobbsian images through this verbal smoke screen. A survey of human evidence plainly available to all makes the assumption inescapable that positive and negative value properties are implicated in behavior in qualitatively and functionally different ways. As I tried to show in my descriptive analysis of creative behavior and in other examples, there are certain types of performance, very important in the organismic economy, which are rendered impossible or vitiated by negative value properties of the sort believed associated with anxiety. The fact that recent motivational theory has all but legislated such performances out of existence makes their range difficult as yet to assess, but none the narrower.